# AT HOME IN COSTA RICA

# AT HOME IN COSTA RICA

*Adventures in Living
the Good Life*

Martin P. Rice

To order additional copies of this book, contact:
Xlibris Corporation
1-888-795-4274
www.Xlibris.com
Orders@Xlibris.com
25807

# CONTENTS

For Robin,
my dear wife and
partner in adventure.

# CHAPTER ONE

## By Way of Introduction

On October 20, 2000, my wife Robin and I departed San Francisco with our dog, Jessie, to move permanently to Costa Rica. All our possessions were already on their way by boat.

To our family and friends it must have seemed a rather foolish thing to do, given that we had only visited Costa Rica once before in March 2000 and on the basis of that two-week trip decided to become expatriates. I had actually been there once before, about six years earlier, for a week's vacation with my ex-wife, Baker Moorefield. We loved the little we saw and I was determined to go back sometime.

There were two reasons Baker and I went there originally. First, we both very much liked Spanish, specifically Latin American, culture. I had been to Mexico several times and loved it. Baker and I had even bought a time-share there. So the idea of visiting another Latin American country was quite appealing.

The second reason has to do with a family story, which I heard a few times when I was growing up. Supposedly, a second cousin of mine, much older than I, had been a physician during the Second World War. For some reason or another, he went to Costa Rica. The story goes that he fell so in love with the country that he never lived in the United States again.

I was just a kid and didn't ask any questions, of course. Now that I'd like to know more about the story, everyone of that generation in my family is dead and there's no one to ask. But that story was what brought Costa Rica to mind when Baker and I were looking for a place to visit. Now, thinking more about it, the story might not even have been about Costa Rica. It easily could have been Puerto Rico, a place-name that many people tend to confuse with Costa Rica.

I suggested to Robin that we go there on our honeymoon because I had enjoyed my first trip there so much. About then I was also thinking about a place to retire. I was just a few months away from retirement at the time. I had always had a theory that retiring to a foreign country would be a good thing to do. One would not easily and quickly fall into a rut the way so many retired people do. There would simply be too many challenges and things to do: learning a new language; learning how to fit into a foreign culture; learning about common things which would be quite different, such as traveling, gardening, building, dealing with municipal services, shopping, cooking, making new friends. Almost everything that makes up our quotidian life would be different and would have to be learned.

Now after more than three and a half years of living here, I truly think I was right about not easily falling into a rut and becoming bored in retirement.

As part of the preparation for the honeymoon trip, we contacted a few real estate agents, whom we had encountered on the Internet and who agreed to take us around and show us various properties in the areas we would visit. Our first stop was the city of San José, the country's largest city and its capital. It didn't take us more than about two hours to know that this was the last place in the world we'd ever want to live.

The next stop on our trip was Dominical, a very small town, no more than a village, on the Central Pacific Coast, which is a popular surfers' destination. Dominical is located about forty-five kilometers south of Quepos, a well-known resort area where Baker and I had spent our vacation.

Although Robin and I had three more areas of the country to visit, we never left Dominical until it was time to return to California. We felt we had truly found paradise. The area is just what many of us city dwellers imagine when we think about a tropical jungle on the Pacific: endless stretches of beach with almost no one to be seen; the densest, most exotic vegetation everywhere; magnificent palms of all kinds; strange, brightly colored flowers; wildlife at every turn in the road; perfect weather. What more could anyone possibly want?

We stayed at the guesthouse of the realtors, Dave and Liz Stephenson. Every day Dave would take us out to look at properties they had listed for sale. Each one seemed more beautiful than the next. Finally, he took us to one property that seemed absolutely perfect to us. It was about twelve acres with the most exquisite view of the Pacific. A large area had been cleared for building and the rest of the property was jungle. We were enchanted. The price was a little more than we wanted to pay— though not outrageous. Dave and Liz told us this was only the asking price and that the owner would certainly entertain offers.

Clearly this was going to be a hard decision to make in that everything we read and heard, not to mention knew intuitively, said not to buy on a whim. Spend more time looking, go to the country, rent a place and actually live there a while; in fact, live in different areas of the country so you can get a good feel for what living there would be like in general and where you'd be most comfortable.

One day Dave, clever salesman that he is, told us to drive up to the property about 5:30 in the evening with a couple of chairs and a bottle of wine and watch the sunset. So we bought a bottle of wine and took a couple of plastic chairs Dave loaned us and went up to the property. As it happened, it was the very end of March, just when the sun sets directly in the middle of the ocean view from the property. As it also happened, it was the most beautiful sunset we had ever seen. Robin took a picture of it that I then used as the wallpaper on my computer while I finished my time with the company to remind me of what was waiting for me at retirement.

Well, that sunset was the final push. The next day we made an offer, and the day after that it was accepted. We now owned property in Costa Rica, and we decided that we would move there seven months later.

The next seven months were frantic. Finding a place to rent in Costa Rica. Designing a house to build. Learning all about how to move a household a few thousand miles away to a foreign country. Getting legal advice about residency in Costa Rica. Finding out how to transport our dog. Figuring out how and where to forward our mail. Advising everyone we knew about the impending changes. Dealing with our families. Just an endless series of tasks. But all very exciting because we were preparing to embark on a grand adventure.

We decided early on that we would keep a detailed record of our experiences as we learned to live in our new country. That record took the form of twenty-nine letters, most rather long, which we sent by e-mail to a list of about eighty relatives and friends at irregular intervals. I decided to gather these letters into a book so that people contemplating moving to Costa Rica, or to almost any other emerging Latin American country, could read about one couple's rather typical experiences in becoming established in a foreign country.

And now, a couple of words about the people you'll be spending so much time with as you read this book. I'm sixty-six years old. I was born and grew up in Philadelphia, Pennsylvania. I'm a retired university professor of Russian language and literature. I taught for twenty-five years at the University of Tennessee, Knoxville. I'm also a retired executive of a California educational software company I helped found. Robin is considerably younger—and more mature—than I, thirty-nine years old. She was born and raised in Battle Creek, Michigan. She has worked in human resources, was a veterinarian technician, and an interpreter for the deaf. Here in Costa Rica she spends much of her time rehabilitating wildlife.

Finally, you can see many pictures of our life in Costa Rica by visiting our Web site at http://www.homeincostarica.net

# Chapter Two

## November 5, 2000

### Our First Day in Costa Rica

Hello, friends and family:

Thought you might get a kick out of reading a bit about the day of our arrival in Costa Rica, Friday, October 20, 2000. Were this a book rather than a letter, this chapter would probably be entitled: And This Is Just the Beginning!

We left San Francisco on a red-eye in order to make sure that our dog Jessie would not get too hot and that we'd arrive in the morning. The trip to Costa Rica was fortunately uneventful, except for an unplanned plane change in El Salvador and Robin's worry for Jessie's safety.

But upon arrival, our luggage was first off the plane, a very good sign. Jessie came off almost immediately after, and getting her and us through customs went without a hitch, largely due to Robin's having ensured that all the paperwork was in order before we left.

The car rental people were there waiting for us at San José's modern airport, and they took us straight to the car rental office, though we had to do it in two trips because we had so much luggage with Jessie's huge cage.

An hour later we were making our way through the insane San José traffic trying to find our hotel, the Dunn Inn. This is a hotel that allows dogs, which, of course, was a requirement. Our room was not yet ready, and it was going to be two hours until we could have access. They did, however, allow us to put our luggage into a small room furnished with two chairs to wait.

By this time we had been up for more than thirty hours and were hot, dirty, and tired. However, we hadn't planned to sleep yet anyway because we had a lot of things to take care of.

I went to call the attorney who was going to help us with these things, Ulises Obregón. As I was asking the receptionist if I could make a call, Ulises called me. We met at the hotel a half hour later and began our odyssey around San José. There were three main objectives: (1) to open two bank accounts at the Banco Nacional, a dollar account and a *colones* account; (2) to open an Internet account with RACSA (*Radiográfica Costarricense SA*), the state-owned ISP monopoly; (3) to get photocopies made of the documents we had brought with us in order to apply for residents' status so that we could stay in the country legally for more than three months.

I had brought a cashier's check with me to open the bank accounts, for I had been told that a normal check required thirty to forty days to clear. This way the cash would be immediately available. There would be enough to buy a car and then we would transfer money from the dollar account to the *colones* account as needed. We'd be able to withdraw money from the *colones* account through an ATM machine in San Isidro de El General, a large provincial town about an hour from where we'd be living in Dominical. San Isidro is also where we do most of our shopping and pick up our mail. Living where we do means at least one trip a week there. Though we've been there probably six times in the two weeks we've been here. It's hard to anticipate at this early stage everything we need.

It seems as though Banco Nacional, one of Costa Rica's national banks, treats a foreign cashier's check the same way it does a foreign personal check. It was still going to be at least thirty days before the money would be available. So, after long deliberations with the woman at the bank and with Ulises as translator, we decided that I'd just send the check back to the States to be re-deposited. Then I'd open the accounts at the San

Isidro branch and have the money wired to the dollar account, thereby not having to wait thirty days.

As it ultimately turned out, although the bank received the money the day it was wired, because of the paperwork involved it was still going to be an additional three to five working days before the money was available.

To tide us over, I eventually made two ATM withdrawals from my account in North America, got two cash advances on my credit card, and exchanged a couple of hundred dollars I had into *colones*. I even borrowed a few thousand *colones* from one of our friends.

Because we had Jessie with us in San José that first day and because she was so insecure after her life had been turned upside down, we couldn't possibly have left her in the hotel while we went on our rounds in San José.

We had decided to walk everywhere with Ulises because parking is just impossible in San José—as is driving, too, as far as I'm concerned. The traffic is horrendous; except for several major boulevards, most streets are very narrow. The Costa Ricans, who are by and large non-confrontational, are often aggressive drivers. And there are hundreds of buses everywhere, all belching black smoke. All in all quite anxiety provoking until you get used to it—which probably only takes a couple of years. Fortunately we'll be living far, far away from San José.

Our dog, Jessie, for those of you who don't know her, is a very large ninety-pound Great Dane—Greyhound mix, jet black. Walking her through the crowded streets of San José on a leash attracted an enormous amount of attention—stares, smiles, fear-stricken faces, and even a woman's loud, shrill scream—of joy or terror we'll never know because she ran around the corner.

It seems that not many people walk their dogs on leashes in downtown San José. What walking her also meant was that poor Robin spent a lot of time standing outside of various buildings waiting for extended periods while Ulises and I were doing battle with the long lines and complex problems of trying to get a lot of things done in one afternoon within a system that usually requires as long as thirty minutes to sixty minutes in line just to make a deposit in a bank. The reason Robin stayed with her instead of me is that Jessie was still so nervous that she panicked when Robin was out of sight.

Almost everywhere you go to do some kind of transaction in Costa Rica requires you first to take a number from a machine and wait until you're called. And that was the case at RACSA when we went in to set up an Internet account. All in all we waited about thirty minutes until our turn came. During this time Robin, who was not allowed in the building with the dog, had to stand outside and deal with dozens of people who wanted to know everything about Jessie. Every ten minutes or so, Ulises or I would go outside for a few minutes to check to see how Robin was doing.

Finally it was our turn. Fortunately, the young woman who served us spoke excellent English. That made things go much more smoothly because it meant that Ulises didn't have to translate. After about forty minutes, she had all the forms filled out on her computer and clicked the button to submit our application to the system.

At that point, the system, as she explained, "fell," the Spanish equivalent of "crashed." It was clear that we were going to be there for quite a while yet, so Ulises was kind enough to walk Robin back to the hotel, which was about fifteen minutes away, while I stayed to deal with the fallen system. The young woman checked with someone and was told to resubmit. However, some of the information had to be reentered. Once again, a click on the button to submit. But we were still submitting to the fallen system.

At this point we found out that the system would be down until about 9 PM. The alternative turned out to be that all the forms would be filled out by hand and signed. Then, the evening shift would resubmit everything electronically after the system came up again. I would be called eventually to be told when my account was effective. Although I was convinced that years would pass before I ever heard from RACSA by phone, I was amazed when they did, in fact, call me two days later to tell me my account was open and working.

After RACSA, it was time to get photocopies made. According to Ulises, in all of Costa Rica there are no copy shops where one can go to a machine, put in a few coins, and make one's own copies. Rather, you go to a copy shop—and there are many of them—take a number, wait your turn, and then have the work done by someone behind the counter. In most cases— for we went to three copy shops before we got anything done— there would be about ten people waiting and perhaps two or three machine operators. But many people had complex jobs such as two-sided printing, collated books, blueprint reproduction, paper trimming, and virtually anything else that could be done with copy machines in a print-shop environment.

This meant that the waits could be interminable. We left the first two shops we went to after waiting fifteen to twenty minutes because it was clear that there might still be an hour to wait. Finally we went to a third shop where our number was only three behind the current number. Our turn came in just a few minutes. Ulises explained what we needed to be done. As the operator started to do our job, Ulises suddenly realized that he was still missing some papers and that it would make no sense to finish the job now and he told the operator to stop. What he was missing I never did find out, but I took his word for it.

At this point we were finished. Four hours spent, the only result of which was the completion of a form by hand that might or might not result in the opening of an Internet account.

What I didn't know at this point was that back at the hotel, there was a sign on the desk that said: "Copies, fifteen cents each." There was, of course, no line to wait in.

While saying goodbye to Ulises before walking back to the hotel, I remarked that we really had accomplished very little. He gave me his big, charming, very boyish, and sweet smile and said, "And this is only the beginning!" How right he seems to be from the vantage point of sixteen days later!

But these are just part of the challenges we anticipated during the process of acculturation. This is no place for A-type personalities, which is why I am working on my transformation into Marty Mañana. The upsides of being here, which I'll write about later, are truly many.

Best regards to all of you,
Martin and Robin

# CHAPTER THREE

## November 19, 2000

Hi, friends and family:

Today marks a month since we arrived in Costa Rica. It's hard to believe. You've all received our first letter about our first day. Quite a bit has happened since then, and we thought we'd send you another update about our life here. Some of you have already read some of what follows in individual letters we've written. We're going to avoid doing that again so as not to waste your time having to read some things twice.

### Robin's Message to Her Mother

We'll start with something Robin thoughtfully wrote and sent to some of her friends and—if you can believe it—her family, including her mother!

"Everything is going as smoothly as could be expected considering the civil war that broke out the morning we arrived. Martin is in prison, and I haven't been able to see him—but I hear it's one of the better ones as they only have ten people per cell. I am in hiding, living in a lean-to in the jungle. I haven't had anything to eat for a few days. But Jessie made a meal of a brightly colored snake she found last night. Unfortunately, it bit her before she ate it, but she seems OK so far, just a little foaming at the mouth, and a few tremors. You may have heard about that little earthquake; don't worry much about that. It's the hurricane brewing that I'm more concerned about."

We've concluded that because her mother survived reading that paragraph, she is most likely immortal! In fact, however, we did have a small earthquake yesterday—I was sitting on the couch reading, and the couch began to shake. It was over in about five seconds. Robin was at the other end of the house and didn't feel it. Small quakes are very common in this area, and no one pays any attention to them.

## Back in the '40s Again

Our initial days here were indeed complicated as you could tell from our last letter, and in fact, many of the following days were complicated as well. But it's all part of becoming acculturated to our new home. Clearly life in an emerging country is radically different from what we knew in the United States. Once in a while there's something that is a true throwback to the 1940s for me. For example, although the place we're renting has a new washing machine, there is no dryer, but there is a line to hang our clothes. And yesterday when I was doing that, I remembered clearly how, when I was little, my mother had neither washer nor dryer and how I used to help her hang out the clothes and take them in. And it's not bad at all; in fact, it's fun (now it's fun— ten weeks from now—probably not). Because it's still the rainy season here, however, you have to get the clothes out in the morning when the sun shines and then in before the rain starts in the afternoon. But the sun is so warm that the clothes dry very quickly. And yes, it's true, clothes do smell better for drying in the sun—though they're not as soft as they are when they come from the dryer.

## Life in the Big City

We've been back to San José twice since our last letter, and we're getting to like it a bit more. The idea of living there is still appalling—the air is like that of Mexico City, about 90 percent carbon monoxide at times—or at least that's the way it seems. But it's very colorful with an intense street life.

Now that we know our way around a little better, we're quite a bit more relaxed there and can devote more of our attention to the surroundings. San José is not an attractive city, by any stretch of the imagination. But it's vibrant, loud, and dynamic, and has its own exciting rhythm. It also has a couple of great malls where local yokels such as we can get neat stuff when we venture in from the provinces.

## The Pan-American Highway

The best thing about San José, however, is probably the four-hour car ride from Dominical to get there. The road is the Pan-American Highway, a grandiose appellation for a moderately well-paved, two-lane road. But it goes high over the mountains that separate the Central Valley (where San José is) from the Pacific Coast reaching a height of about nine thousand feet before you start heading down. The entire route is hilly and extremely winding, but it goes through the most magnificent rain forest and there are stunning vistas everywhere. Frequently you're in patches of cloud and fog and then break out into glittering sunlight with a view of the valleys and peaks that is simply breathtakingly beautiful. With the road's being so narrow, you do feel the presence of the jungle strongly, and you are easily able to see the huge variety of plants and trees quite close up. There are ferns as big as houses, and huge splashes of color from flowering bushes, which we have not yet identified. There are many different types of palms, mango trees, and "toucan" trees. (We don't know the name of these yet, but they're trees that toucans frequently perch on because of their attraction to the fruit growing on them.)

## Buying a Car

Our last three-day trip was mainly to buy a car. We had been renting one thus far. We bought a great Jeep Cherokee—not the Grand Cherokee Laredo, but the smaller model called the Cherokee Classic which is a gussied-up Sport. I don't even know if they sell them in the States. But it's rugged and powerful which is what we must have here given that probably 85 percent of our driving is off-road. Actually, it'd be off-road in America, but here, most of our roads are off-road so I guess in a sense it's on rough-road driving.

The agency where we bought the car is located on a street with perhaps the worst traffic I've ever been in. Robin and I just couldn't imagine driving a brand-new car through that traffic, especially being so new to the area. So when we decided to buy it and agreed on a price, I told the salesman that we'd buy it only if he delivered it to our hotel. He agreed, naturally.

## The Rental House and Its Surroundings

As far as the rental house is concerned, it turned out to be a bit of a disappointment. Robin put it well. At first blush it's quite charming until you start noticing bare wires, holes in the walls and screens, the temperamental plumbing, and the like. But the grounds are simply beautiful with huge crotons and begonias, ginger and palms, banana trees, heliconias, and hibiscus.

The roads around our house are lined with bird-of-paradise plants as big as palm trees, and the branches of the huge trees in our backyard are just covered with epiphyte bromeliads, many a good three feet in diameter. Sometimes they get too heavy for the branches and just fall out of the tree. Our yard backs up to the Barú river, which runs quite swiftly behind our house on its way to the ocean, just a couple of kilometers away. There are, in fact, three rivers very close to us, and when we go to the beach, we see them meeting the ocean. We'll talk more about the rivers, the beach, and the ocean in another letter.

And there are many things we have simply never seen before. The garden is full of so many different types of birds that it's a joy to wake up in the morning to their songs. And I have twice seen a most amazing butterfly. It's about six inches from wingtip to wingtip. It flies slowly for a butterfly. The top of its wings is the most intense powder blue we've ever seen, and the bottom of the wings is a dark orange. It's spellbinding to watch. We found out that it is called a Blue Morpho.

The wildlife here is incredible. Just taking out the garbage, we've seen swallows, a scarlet-rumped tanager, a flock of cattle egrets, and a little blue heron flying up the river. And there were many more; those I mentioned were only the ones we could identify. We have two basilisk lizards that play on the roof in the mornings. Many times while traveling to the house of our friends, Liz and Dave, we've seen troops of capuchin monkeys crossing the road through the treetops. At our property, for several days, there were two sloths living in one of the trees in plain view. In another tree, we spotted two different types of toucans at the same time. Dave told us recently that he had seen a jaguarondi that day. (It's a wild cat, smaller than but similar to a jaguar.) Dave and Liz are two wonderful people. They've been an endless source of help and marvelously friendly—we try to spend as much time with them as we can. We'll tell you more about them in a future letter about the people here.

## The *Cabina*

The upside of our dissatisfaction with the rental house, however, is that we decided that since we didn't want to live in it for a year (that's how long it will probably take to build our house rather than the six months we originally thought), we would first build what is called a *cabina* in Costa Rica. A *cabina* is a small house, usually one or two rooms plus bath which, in our case, will be about six hundred square feet. We've cleared a place on our land for it, and it will only take about two months to build. It will be quite attractive in the Spanish style with a beautiful bath and kitchenette, large arched windows, lots of tile surfaces, and modern appliances. At the same time, on another spot on our site, we are building what first will be a secure storage facility for all of our things—eighteen feet by twenty-one feet—and then, after the main house is built, we will convert it into a stable for the horses we hope to have.

After our house is built, we will probably use the *cabina* as a home for a Costa Rican couple who will work for us. This is a fairly common arrangement here. It could be a guesthouse, but because we'll have two very nice guest rooms in the main house, we don't expect to need a guesthouse.

We're very excited about living in the *cabina* for a variety of reasons. The two foremost are just being able to live on our beautiful property that much sooner, and, second, being right there during the construction of the house so that we can keep a close eye on things.

## Medical Care

Here is something interesting about medical care and costs in Costa Rica. Some of you remember that Robin had hurt her hip a couple of months before we left and had been in physical therapy. Well, it never really got completely better, and about two weeks ago, she woke up in the morning and virtually couldn't move. So we drove to San José to go to a private hospital.

The bottom line is that she is totally pain free now. The doctor confirmed that nothing was broken or fractured, and all he did was to prescribe, in addition to the pain medicine that she had, some muscle relaxants. That did the trick overnight. But here's the interesting thing. The visit there consisted of a consultation with the doctor, a leading orthopedist here, then x-rays, then back to the doctor, then the prescriptions filled. Everything was in one building; the entire time spent there, including having the x-rays developed, was less than an hour and a half, and the entire cost, including the prescriptions, was about ninety dollars. And it was "that much" because we didn't yet have national health insurance. With the insurance it would have been about twenty dollars.

## Some Prices

And speaking of prices: a pair of extremely heavy vinyl, calf-high boots, Wellingtons for walking through the jungle, costs $6.25; chicken breasts—freshly killed the day of purchase—at the most expensive butcher's in San Isidro—for $1.00 per pound; dinner for two with wine in an Italian restaurant in Dominical, which, if not quite as good as Il Fornaio or Piatti's in Palo Alto, is very, very close, for $15.00—not per person, but for two; a two-pound loaf of fantastic, whole-wheat bread, baked the day before we bought it, for about a dollar; at a stop at a roadside fruit stand on the way to San Isidro we bought three tomatoes (vine ripened, of course), a watermelon, four papayas, a bunch of cilantro, about three pounds of bananas (cut from the stalk for us), and a fresh pineapple for under $5.00!

There is so much more to tell, but this is probably more than enough for one sitting. We'll send another installment next month, by which time we should be in our *cabina*.

Our warmest and best personal regards,
Martin and Robin

# CHAPTER FOUR

## December 22, 2000

Hello, friends and family!

It's December 22, two months and two days since our arrival in San José. The country is about to close down tomorrow until January 2. Virtually every store and all sectors of the government stay closed for the holidays. Sounds like a good idea as long as one is stocked up with food, which we are.

### Beginning to Build

November 7, 2000, was the day things began to happen. From the seventh to the tenth we had bulldozers on the site. They enlarged the original building site for the main house—a building site here is called a *plantel*. Then they created the *plantel* for our *cabina* and, finally, cleared a *plantel* where our storage building (called a *bodega*)—later to be the stable—will be. The *bodega* will be located on the other side of the road which runs past our property. We have land on both sides of the road. The reason we're building there is because there's a nice flat area that will serve well as a pasture.

On November 20, the electric transformer was installed on the pole so that we could start having service on the sites. This was also a very big day for the project because the builders brought up a cement mixer, the first piece of equipment to arrive for the construction.

On this day the workers began building their own *bodega* as well. Building here is like nothing we've ever seen before. First of all, the workers, almost none of whom have cars as far as we can tell, live on the site Monday through midday Saturday. Their *bodega* is a building that is a combination of kitchen, laundry, dining room, and dormitory. There are also bathrooms—chemical toilets. The workday is a long one. It's always light here by about 5:15 AM—there is not much change in the times of the sun's rising and setting here because we're so close to the equator—and the men are up and about at that time. They seem to work from about 6:00 AM until sunset at 5:30 PM. Of course there's electricity so there are radios and plenty of lights. Sometimes they'll knock off a little early and have a game of soccer on the *plantel*.

A couple of days later, work began on the first structure, the *cabina*. Everything here is essentially done by hand. The foundations are dug by hand; the rebar forms are shaped and wired together by hand; the concrete is mixed in a small electric-powered cement mixer. There's no backing up of a huge cement-mixer truck to the foundation ditches and pouring the whole thing at once. It would be almost impossible for a cement mixer with a full load to get up the roads to the sites. But the workers have the timing down so well that there is essentially no pause in pouring the foundations. The mixer contents are dumped into a wheelbarrow, and while the men pour and spread one batch, the next batch is mixed up. By the time the men need another load, the cement is ready for them.

## The Workers

So by December 4, everything was ready to begin pouring, just awaiting the architect's inspection on that morning. By the end of the week of the fourth of December, all the walls were up! It's astounding. The crew consists of seven men: two men named Marvin (Marvin?), one of them is the foreman and the other the cook; two men named Alejandro; one Ángel; one Juan; and one Tigre—a nickname because he wears a necklace of something that looks like tiger's teeth around his neck.

Marvin, the foreman, goes out of his way to explain to Robin and me, in simplified, slowly spoken Spanish, full of circumlocutions, what has been accomplished during the course of the day and what's coming next.

Marvin the cook keeps two roosters on the site, which he calls his pets. He says he has had them on almost all of his construction jobs. But, in addition, he also keeps two hens near the kitchen as well. The hens provide fresh eggs every day. One day Marvin told us that he had the hens sitting on fifteen eggs. Robin and I assumed that these were to provide chicken dishes for the men. But, a couple of days later, when Robin was talking to him and asked him how long it would take until the chicks— which she fell in love with—would be "ready," Marvin was appalled. According to him, these fifteen chicks are also to be pets. Why do I have a hard time believing this? But time will tell. He also offered Robin one of the chicks for a pet! I'm trying to get him fired.

## Permits and the *Bodega*

Also during the week of the fourth, a second crew was supposed to be brought up to start building the *bodega* or stable building. As it turns out, we had a delay getting our building permit for the *bodega*. It seems as though the corruption in the municipality bureaucracy just got to be too much, and there was a big shakeup which slowed things down. We do now, however, have the permit, and construction of the *bodega* will start on January 2. This building should go extremely quickly as we're building a prefabricated structure. Of course foundations will have to be dug and laid, and the floor will have to be poured, but the whole job is not expected to take more than about three weeks.

We're particularly excited about this because when the storage *bodega* is finished, it will be extremely secure with steel doors and walls that have been strongly reinforced, and it will be dehumidified—dampness and mildew are a story all by themselves. We'll then be able to have our container brought here from San José, and we will finally have our things. We've missed them sorely. It's a long story, but we only packed for three weeks when we left for Costa Rica because, according to the plans we'd made, we assumed that we'd have a place to store our things here in Dominical immediately. As it turned out, it's more like two months. Needless to say, we wash a lot of clothes.

By December 6, the shape of the *cabina* was totally visible. You could see the layout of all the rooms and the beginnings of the walls. Places are marked for the conduit for all the switches and lights. We spent some time that day going over the placement of all the outlets, switches, and fans with Kiki.

## Kiki the Builder

Kiki, also known as José Enrique Gómez Alvarado, is our contractor. He's a young man of about thirty-five and has been building quality houses in our area for some time. Before we decided on contracting with him, we visited at least half a dozen houses in the area with our realtor friend Dave. After a time, it was easy to know if one we were looking was built by Kiki—the difference in quality was so apparent.

Kiki was born right where we're building and has lived there all his life. In fact, the whole community was once his father's farm. Until quite recently, the area was a challenge to get to during the rainy season—the roads were impassable. It is only in the last few years or so, due to the initial efforts of a local realtor, Kent Brown, and then to the work of the local residents' road committee, that the roads have become some of the best unpaved roads in the entire Dominical area.

I should clarify that the community we're building in is referred to as Lagunas and sometimes as Lagunas de Barú. Barú is the tiny village at the foot of the mountain upon which Lagunas is located. However, most people here, when talking about where they live, simply say Dominical, because no one outside of the area has ever heard of Lagunas. Dominical is about a five-minute drive from Barú.

## More about Building the *Cabina*

As of today, the walls are all up, the arches on the windows are finished, and the conduit is all in. The *cabina* is ready for the beginnings of the roof. The ceilings will be beautiful wood that will peak at about seventeen feet from the floor. The roof will be red tile.

The way the walls are finished is quite unusual. The walls are cement block. Then they are covered with cement—the workers literally splash the cement over the block. When the splash has dried a bit, it's wet down and then trawled smooth—not totally smooth, but partially. Then another coat is done, then a third, and finally a fourth. It's a slow process, but by the time they're done, the walls are so smooth that you'd think they're made of wall board. Two splash coats are done so far. We think that we'll have the fourth and final coat done in a method called *repello con color* (we've only heard this word and haven't seen it spelled so the Spanish might be wrong). This means that the final splashed cement has color mixed in it. Consequently the walls don't have to be painted, and the finish lasts much longer than paint.

## Garden Work and Landscaping

I mentioned earlier that part of our land is on the other side of the road. This week we had Róger, the man who is doing some gardening for us, cut narrow *caminitos* (little paths) through the jungle on that side of the road, so that we can wander through it and see what's there. He did it Tuesday, but we've been in San José on a shopping trip since Sunday so we haven't yet wandered on our *caminitos*. We're going to do so first thing tomorrow, early in the morning.

There is a lovely ground cover here called *maní*. It grows to a height of about six to eight inches, has a beautiful shade of medium dark green, and has beautiful little yellow flowers all year round. One of its primary uses is to stop erosion on the banks of hills, which have been cleared to make *plantels*. It spreads extremely quickly and has very deep roots. Our friends, Warwick and Barbara, through whom we met Róger the gardener, allowed him to take hundreds of cuttings from the acres of *maní* they've planted to begin seeding our hills. *Maní* belongs to the peanut family.

So one day a couple of weeks ago, Róger almost covered two of our hillsides with *maní* cuttings. The very next morning, when Robin and I drove up to the site to see the work, there was not a single leaf on a single cutting! It seems that at the top of one hill and at the bottom of the other were nests of cutter ants. These little things are simply amazing. You see columns of them all over. The columns can extend for a mile. And these little ants heading to the nest all have huge pieces of leaves on their backs. In the nest, the leaves produce some kind of fungus that they eat. We have read that in the course of a year, the cutter ants cut 25 percent of the jungle canopy! But this is part of the ecological chain, and they are not a threat to the environment.

Well, they are a threat to the man-made, home-garden environment. So the way you get rid of them is by pouring a substance called mirex along their trails and in their nests. The mirex does not harm the ants. It does, however, kill the fungus that they're farming and does away with their food supply. When that happens, they simply abandon their nest and move on to start over.

We applied the mirex immediately, and now, two weeks later, all the *maní* cuttings are in full leaf again. Ain't nature grand?

I have so many notes about things which have happened in the month since we last wrote you that, were I to write about everything in this letter, it would probably take a month to read. So I'll just mention three more things briefly.

## The Festival at Platanillo

A couple of miles down the road toward San Isidro is the village of Platanillo. As do most towns and villages in Costa Rica, Platanillo has a small annual festival. This year the one at Platanillo was two Sundays ago. Robin and I, along with several of our North American friends from the area, went there to see the sights.

Basically, the festival consists of several stalls set up around the church, selling food. The main event is a small parade of ox carts and a few horses. But the atmosphere is so friendly, and the people seem to be having so much fun, watching the parade and one another, drinking beer at a couple of small outdoor restaurants, and eating food from the stalls—that it is all truly festive. Ox carts in Costa Rica are both a mainstay of small landholders and a national arts and crafts treasure. They're all painted in complex patterns in bright colors. Robin and I will eventually buy one when our house is finished.

Anyway, when the parade started, some friends and I were standing right where the carts come off a small road on to the main paved road. As the second cart went by, one of the oxen let fly with a mighty *poop!* I don't know a lot about ox poop, so I can't say with certainty whether they're always so soft and splatter so far, but what I can say is that if ox poop is as lucky as bird poop, I will spend the rest of my days a very lucky man—but not nearly as lucky as our friend Liz, who was almost covered! Lucky girl.

## Getting a Driver's License

The second thing I wanted to mention is that Robin and I took a step toward becoming real *Ticos* a couple of days ago in San José. (I want to explain *Tico* and *Tica*. The Costa Ricans refer to themselves as Ticos. The explanation that we've heard says that the name is the result of a Costa Rican linguistic regionalism in Spanish. Evidently, instead of using—*tito* as a diminutive ending, they say—*tico*. For example, *momentico* instead of *momentito*. The appellation seems to be a source of pride for them, for it is used everywhere—newspapers, magazines, television, books, conversation, etc.—to refer to themselves.)

Anyway, Robin and I got Costa Rican driver's licenses. Believe it or not, in all of Costa Rica you can only get your first driver's license in one place, San José. There are other places in the country to get them renewed. The lines are so long that people spend up to five hours in them. If you have a valid license from the United

States, you can get a Tico license without taking a test. You do, however, have to go through the paper process which means going to San José and becoming part of the huge crowd. Well, we got the license, and that was the step toward becoming good citizens of our new country. But we also engaged in a process called *chorizo*, literally "sausage," but actually slang for bribery and corruption. For ten thousand *colones* (five thousand *colones* each) total of $31.75, paid to the right person by a fellow who drives a taxi in San José, we were able to reduce our wait from five or more hours to a mere one and a half. We were very proud of ourselves.

## Clean Living

And finally, the wages of good living. When we arrived in Costa Rica, my waist was a comfortable (and very overweight) size 40. As of Wednesday, exactly two months later, I bought pants size 36 that fit perfectly! Four inches off my waist. I've lost twenty pounds as well. My high blood pressure and high blood sugar are both down, a result of both having lost all that weight and, I assume, of being so happy here. But what's really interesting is that I've lost this weight without any conscious effort. It has happened because of the way Robin and I have been eating. We never eat between meals nor before bed, as we used to. And what we eat consists mainly of fruit—loads of it: watermelon, bananas, the best pineapple I've ever tasted, papaya, mango, etc., vegetables and lots of rice, chicken, and seafood. We have a freezer full of meat and never cook it. For breakfast we eat fruit and very often whole-wheat oatmeal (*avena integral*)—which evidently is different from most processed oatmeal—anyway it's delicious.

So, that's certainly more than enough for this time around. There's so much more to tell that I'm thinking of writing more often.

## Miss Bug Joins the Family

But wait!! There is one more thing that has to be added. The Rice family has a new member, Miss Bug, Bug for short. She is a new puppy who has joined the family. She's a little mutt that some friends found on the streets of San Isidro and brought home with them. But they already have four dogs and couldn't keep her so they brought her to a gathering, and Robin, of course, went totally gaga and I couldn't refuse her. The puppy is very cute, white and brown, and seems to be smart—got housebroken very quickly. I originally named her Miss, short for mistake, which I was sure we were making. But now she's Miss Bug because she's a mistake that really knows how to bug you.

It was a bit traumatic for Jessie at first, she having been an only child for so long. She sulked for a few days, tried to ignore the puppy who wouldn't leave her alone, knocked her around three times, and growled at her a lot. But the vet said it was normal and evidently it is. Now they play together constantly, and it seems that all sibling rivalry has been overcome, or at least repressed.

We wish all of you a happy holiday season and hope that the coming year brings you everything you wish for.

Martin and Robin

# CHAPTER FIVE

## December 30, 2000

Hi, family and friends!

It hasn't been very long since we sent our last letter from Costa Rica. The impetus for writing so soon was Robin's remarks today as we were driving to San Isidro about how very happy she is here and how glad she is that we've made the move. And it's true, we are extremely happy here. What is interesting, I think, is that our happiness seems to grow in direct proportion to the increasing degree of comfort we feel as we get more used to our new environment.

### Feeling at Home

When we first arrived, both of us experienced a relatively high degree of anxiety and tension. Everything was so unknown, strange, and foreign. We barely spoke the language—in fact, we didn't speak the language at all—we merely knew a couple of hundred words between us.

We certainly didn't know whom to trust and of whom to be wary. Because we had joined some expat online groups and read the *Tico Times* and *La Nación* (Costa Rica's leading English—and Spanish-language newspapers respectively) for a few months before we left the United States, we had heard a myriad of stories about scams perpetrated on tourists and new arrivals; crimes—sometimes violent such as car jackings and muggings—dishonest taxi drivers, rampant petty thievery, and so on. Everything you would expect in any country where you were foreigners, especially in a big city such as San José, or even in many places in your own country, too.

But somehow you feel much more vulnerable in a foreign country where you know hardly anyone and where you know neither the language nor have much knowledge of the society and cultural mores that surround you. You tend to be always on guard and suspicious. And this prevents you from starting to join fully in the new society you are living in.

But in two months here we've become much more acclimated to our surroundings. We've learned much more Spanish; we've met dozens of people, Ticos as well as expats. We know and are known by shopkeepers and workers, restaurant owners and waiters, taxi drivers, and our Tico neighbors. We know our way around San Isidro well and greet and are greeted by the people in the supermarket, the hardware store, the bank, our favorite Mexican restaurant, our favorite small department store, and our favorite coffee and bakery shop. We are even starting to feel as though we have a much better knowledge and understanding of San José. We're beginning truly to feel at home here in our neighborhood of Barú, Dominical, San Isidro, and Lagunas.

We're finding that we're getting better and better at fitting ourselves into the rhythms and routines of life here. For example, we spend a lot of time at the bank for various reasons, mostly paying bills and transferring money. The lines are almost invariably long. We knew early on that this was the case, and we told ourselves that we'd be patient—remember "Marty Mañana."

But the fact was that we'd stand in line, shifting from foot to foot, counting the people ahead of us in line, looking at the clock continually, and although not growing angry and being able begrudgingly to accept that this is just the way it is, we nevertheless would feel stress and discomfort—I much more so than Robin.

But now, we've reached the point where it really isn't any big deal to stand in line at the bank anywhere from fifteen to forty-five minutes. Rather than fidget, fuss, and fume, we mostly watch the people. Frequently we'll bring something with us to read while in line. And eventually, we get our business taken care of, and we go on to our next errand. Though in honesty, I'm very much looking forward to January 15, when our bank is supposed to go online in a big way. We're hoping that this will result in fewer trips and more rapid transactions.

And being more relaxed and much less tense and stressed allows us to be that much more aware of our beautiful surroundings. Every trip to San Isidro (we're down to about twice a week now instead of three or four times) is something we look forward to because of the ever-changing beauty of the mountains and valleys through which the road slowly winds. We often stop at one of the many fruit and vegetable stands along the forty-five-minute drive and choose from a huge variety of foods, all freshly picked that day or just a couple of days before. From time to time we'll stop the car on the side of the road to get out and gaze at a panoramic view of San Isidro far off in the El General valley, flanked by the mountains with their compelling display of cloud, shade, and sun. We take the time to look at the way the rivers below us flow down from their sources in the mountains and then meander through the valleys.

Often on the way back, we'll stop for *bocas* (snacks) or a full lunch at *La Chosa de Alejo* (Alejo's Hut), a wonderful small restaurant on the road between Dominical and San Isidro. And there we feel especially comfortable because Alejo is the husband of Julia, who does the cooking, and Julia is the aunt of Gerardo, about whom we'll tell you below.

And we are constantly waving and honking in greeting or returning greetings to the taxis, trucks, and cars we pass on the road going in the opposite direction. Because the community here is so small, you get to recognize people and their vehicles even if you don't know them personally. And they recognize you, too. And because Ticos are generally very friendly, there's a lot of greeting of strangers always going on. All of this, too, helps contribute to our growing sense of well-being and the beginnings of feeling at home.

We're getting more into the pace of life of the expats and retirees as well. Eventually you realize that since you're not working regular hours and don't have to be at an office on a regular schedule, you can make plans for almost anytime rather than focusing on weekends, holidays, and vacations. In fact, for the first couple of weeks in Dominical, both Robin and I had the strange, recurring experience of wondering for an instant how many more days we had left on our vacation.

A good example of how this realization that your life is structured so differently now begins to dawn on you comes from our trying to make a date to meet some people in Quepos, the lovely resort town about forty-five kilometers north of Dominical, the place where years ago Baker and I spent our vacation the first time I came to Costa Rica.

These people, Scott and Diana, are the son and daughter-in-law of a colleague in the United States. They left California and moved here relatively recently. They've been having a very busy holiday schedule, and we were trading e-mails trying to find a weekend that would work for all of us to meet. Then I suddenly realized that the meeting didn't have to be on a weekend at all. We could hop in the car and drive to Quepos any day that they had time to meet us! A liberating realization.

Or take yesterday, Thursday, when I suggested to Robin that we hop in the car and drive to Quepos and have lunch at an especially nice place that a friend had recommended. As so we did. An hour's drive there, a leisurely two-hour lunch—the best food we've had in Costa Rica so far, but unfortunately at California prices—and an hour's drive back. A lovely afternoon—all on the spur of the moment.

## A Giant Step for Tropical Indolence

It's that spur-of-the-moment lifestyle that helps to make our life here so attractive. And this week we have taken a giant step for tropical indolence. We hung our hammocks! To paraphrase Karl Zuckmeyer, "Oh, how beautiful, how wonderful will it be / when we move into our hammocks!" (Zuckmeyer wrote "heaven" rather than "our hammocks"—*Ach, wie schön, wie herrlich wird es sein, wenn wir in den Himmel ziehen ein!*)

The nicest feature of the house we're renting is the wonderful large backyard. It measures about 300 feet from front to back and about 150 feet across. It backs right up to the Barú river. It's totally fenced so that the dogs have complete freedom to play there, and we don't have to worry about them. It's full of very large old trees; including beautiful coconut palms and other trees we haven't identified yet, but whose branches are covered with literally hundreds and hundreds of bromeliads; and there are well-established, very exotic-looking bushes, plants, and flowers. There are always beautiful birds and butterflies to be seen. In addition, there is a constant, gentle breeze there because of the swiftly running Barú river. Due to all the trees, much of the area is heavily shaded, much has lovely, dappled light, and there are still plenty of sunny spots as well, so that whatever your mood, there's a place for you in some spot of the garden.

So we hung our hammocks between some palms. There are almost no words to describe the feeling of peace, comfort, and well-being that you get resting in the hammocks in dappled light, with a book and a *refresco natural*, while the breeze blows softly over you. Those of you concerned with sin, forget about fornication and worshiping Mammon! The truly dangerous temptation is life in the hammock! Rarely have we felt so sinful, most likely because we still haven't overcome our middle-class belief about something this good being either immoral, illegal, or fattening.

And speaking of fattening, for those of you who don't know, *refrescos naturales* are the most wonderful drinks imaginable. You take any of the fresh fruits that we get so readily here: pineapples, mangos, papayas, bananas, etc.; cut them up; put them in a blender with ice and milk, or perhaps yogurt; and blend until frozen, frothy, and creamy. In five minutes—ambrosia! So combine your *refresco* with the hammock and something delicious to read— and there you have it, instant sin! The first time I did this, I read three pages, finished the drink, and was suddenly asleep for an hour and a half!

## Thanksgiving and the Expat Community

Several of you have asked how we spent our first Thanksgiving here. Our friends, Liz and Dave, whom we've mentioned before, have a huge traditional Thanksgiving dinner at their house every year for the whole local expat community—between thirty and forty people, depending on how many are in town. This year there were about thirty. Liz—who has owned a restaurant with Dave back in Kentucky, and is a marvelous cook—provides the two turkeys, which are readily available here; a large spiral-cut ham; and the rolls. All the other folks bring their favorite Thanksgiving dishes. There were all sorts of appetizers and dips, potatoes, vegetable casseroles, two types of stuffing, giblet gravy, pumpkin pie with whipped cream, and lots of drinks.

The community here is rather close, and most people seem to like one another and enjoy each other's company. There are, of course, enmities that you pick up on, and from time to time you hear a little gossip, rarely malicious, but at times not very flattering either.

When the expats get together for a festive occasion such as Thanksgiving, or a week later at the local Christmas crafts sale, and the various holiday open houses, everyone seems to have a wonderful time. Robin and I certainly enjoyed these days. We knew most of the people there already, but there were several whom we hadn't met yet, and the overall festive mood was a perfect one in which to get acquainted.

The expat community is diverse. It's probably least diverse in terms of age. I think the youngest are probably in their early forties, and they range from there until—well, I thought that at sixty-two I was the oldest, but I've met another neighbor who is sixty-four. The majority ranges from early to late fifties. But as a group, this conglomeration of middle-, late-middle-, and early-old-age people are among the liveliest and most adventurous imaginable. Of course I'm speaking of the permanent community. There's a large transient and tourist community of surfers, birders, ecology students, students of Spanish, hikers, and outdoor adventurers, too, in Dominical. All these people—with the exception of the birders—are generally quite young.

The diversity I spoke of comes from the people's varied backgrounds. There is also a strong economic diversity as well. Some people come here because they do not have much money with which to retire, and they can live a very good life quite inexpensively. Others come here for a variety of reasons that have little or nothing to do with money.

## Gerardo and Ana and Bob and Carla

Sometimes you're amazed at the stories you hear about how people wind up in Costa Rica. For example, the first time Robin and I went back from Dominical to San José, we stopped at an interesting little place about fifty kilometers this side of San José called (both) Charlie's Coffee Shop and Jack's Souvenirs.

The place has been owned and run for the last ten years by a very sweet Tico couple, Gerardo and Ana. Most of the time their two little girls, Theresa (known as Tracy) and Carla, are there playing with several puppies. The place is a small restaurant with a very limited menu with items cooked to order by Ana. The last time we were there we had wonderful tamales, a traditional Christmas meal here. They also sell comfortable large locally made hammocks (about nine dollars) and ceramics and crafts from different parts of Costa Rica.

Their store and house is located in the middle of the jungle on the Pan-American Highway, about five kilometers from the nearest small town. Every time we stop there, they always give Robin fresh flowers to take with her on the road. On one of our recent trips to San José, the girls and Ana weren't there. They were in Cartago, the old Spanish provincial capital of Costa Rica, just a short ride from downtown San José. Teresa was having her first communion. So when we were in San José, Robin bought a little present for her and we dropped it off on the way back.

The first time we stopped there, we met a couple from Miami named Bob and Carla. They had only been in Costa Rica for a couple of months when we met them and were renting a little shack from Gerardo and Ana, to live in while they built a house on some land they had bought in the neighborhood.

Bob and Carla are in their forties and are professional dog trainers, specializing in attack dogs. When we asked them how they happened to wind up where they were, they told us that they had been training dogs in Miami for twenty years. Most of their customers were Cuban. Eventually, Cubans also got into the dog training business. Bob maintained that as the number of their Cuban competitors grew, their customers tended to prefer the Cuban trainers for cultural and historical reasons. Eventually they were having a hard time making ends meet. So they decided to chuck it all and move to Costa Rica.

When I asked them how many times they had previously visited Costa Rica before deciding to settle there, Carla said they had never visited the country but liked what they had heard and read about it. So they threw everything they owned into their big Chevy pickup with a camper shell on back and just took off for Costa Rica to find a place to live and to set up in business again. Just like that!

The last time we were there, we found them erecting jumps and walls and steps, encircled by a fence, where they're going to do their training, all visible from the road. I asked them if they had any business yet, and they told us that they had run one small ad in the *Tico Times* and had had a great response. They were expecting the arrival of their first two dogs to train in the next few days. (As it turns out, about two years later Bob and Carla moved back to Miami. They just couldn't make a go of it here. Their house is only half-built, and Ana and Gerardo are trying to sell the building and the land for them.)

## More about the Expats

In our area, the expats' backgrounds and stories are equally as interesting. One of the most interesting is that of Kent Brown. Kent is a partner with Jack Ewing in South Coast Realty, the company for which Dave and Liz work and from which we bought our land here. Jack started the company over twenty years ago when there was virtually nothing here. He is not active in the day-to-day running of the company—he devotes all his time and effort to *Hacienda* Barú, a private ecological reserve. Kent would be called, I imagine, the managing partner. Kent came here about ten years ago, and there still wasn't much here then at all. Kent lived in extremely rough conditions for a long time: no electricity, a kerosene-powered refrigerator, a small house with no screening or glass in the windows, roads that were impassable for months at a time, and in general, no supporting infrastructure. But he worked very hard and seems to have prospered mightily. I believe he's in his fifties. He's married to a lovely young woman named Laura, who is our Spanish teacher. Laura is a local woman whose father, Don Lulo, runs a business that takes tourists on horseback into the jungle to a beautiful waterfall.

Kent is a very well-known person here as well as in San Isidro. His biggest and most successful project, so far as we can tell, was the creation of Lagunas, the community where our land is. He's a supporter of the local soccer team in San Isidro and, as such, is recognized by many of the citizens there as a supporter of the area as well. His support consists of paying for a billboard advertising his business at the soccer stadium. But he also told me that he pays the salary of one of the local team's best players, otherwise the team wouldn't be able to afford to have him. Evidently, that is not unusual here, and a number of local business people support the team, Pérez Zeledón, and individual players in the same way. The name Pérez Zeledón is the name of the *canton* (county) in which San Isidro is located.

The respect Kent enjoys comes not only from the fact that his successful development efforts in the Dominical area have also resulted in a great deal of business for the San Isidro merchants. Kent also puts much back into the community. Last Christmas, for example, he and Laura invited all the children from the San Isidro orphanage, about forty, to their house where they provided a huge meal, lots of games and fun, and multiple presents for every child.

Kent and Laura have a lovely spread in the mountains above us—in fact, from their place you can look down and see our building site across the valley. He and Laura also have a place in

San José where they are spending more and more time. Kent plays golf there at the country club. They are traveling more and more around the world, and I get the impression he'll be drawing back from business a great deal more as time passes. He's ready to enjoy the results of his labors before he's too old, though you would never guess his age from looking at him. He's a handsome, vibrant guy who seems to radiate health and strength along with enthusiasm and good humor. (Eventually a couple of years later, Kent and Laura sold their place and moved to San José where they now live full time. I don't know what his relationship with South Coast Realty currently is.)

Then you meet people and you just can't imagine what goes on in their minds. At the Thanksgiving dinner we ran into a man named Dan. It seems that Dan is looking for property to buy in the area and wants to settle here. The story is that he was a police officer in New York City. Eventually he just became so fed up with crime and corruption that he decided New York City was a place he just couldn't live in any longer. So where did he go to get away from it? To Colombia! There was a reason: he's married to a Colombian woman. But on what planet has he been living? I don't know how long it took him to realize that Colombia made New York City look like *Mayberry RFD*, but eventually he did and now he's ready to come here.

Then there are Barbara and Warwick Lowe. Barbara is from the United States and Warwick is from Australia originally. Warwick is about sixty, I believe, but looks very much younger. He's quite handsome and very fit, as is Barbara. I don't know much at all about their backgrounds yet or how they happened to have settled here, though I do know that for some years they ran a diving operation in Belize and managed an inn or diving resort there.

Currently, I think they have the loveliest house in Lagunas. Much as ours is going to be, their house is in a Spanish-Southwestern style. It's laid out interestingly and furnished beautifully. They are now in the process of creating a lovely garden and grounds. Their swimming pool overlooks a beautiful view of the ocean, and they have other views of the surrounding valleys that are mesmerizingly lovely.

They've also been extremely generous with their advice. From what we're learning from them about building and living here, I'm sure we're going to avoid making some very common mistakes. We were invited to dinner at their place a couple of weeks ago and discovered that Barbara is an extraordinary chef. They're delightful conversationalists and have a wonderful sense of humor. They also arranged for us to obtain the services of Róger, a gardener, who is doing wonderful things for us one day a week on our property.

## A Silly Problem

But living closely in a small tightly knit community, where everyone knows all about everyone else, has its silly little problems as well. Take the coming New Year's Eve, for example.

A while ago, Barbara and Warwick invited us to a party at their place for New Year's Eve. We accepted gladly, of course. Then about a week or so later, we heard about and were invited to a party at the house of Denny and Gail, one of the most delightful, friendliest, good-natured, and helpful couples here. It turns out that Denny and Gail, who have been here much longer than Barbara and Warwick, have a big, fun New Year's Eve party every year. Virtually everyone in the area—Ticos as well as expats— is invited and goes.

Our friends Liz and Dave go to the party every year. But this year, they too received and accepted an invitation to Barbara and Warwick's. What to do? Well, the first idea was to make an appearance at one for a while, then go to the other and finish the night there. Since Barbara and Warwick's party is going to be much smaller than Denny and Gail's, we thought we'd go to Denny's first, stay a while, and then go to Warwick's.

Ah! But then we discover that Barbara and Warwick's party begins at seven and Denny and Gail's begins at eight. So to go to Denny's first means making an initial appearance at Warwick's late. But since Warwick's is going to be so small, it probably would not be good if four (Robin and I, Liz and Dave) of about eight guests didn't arrive until two or three hours after it was scheduled to begin. What to do?

Good grief. We finally realized how ridiculous the whole thing was becoming. Why should we be spending time plotting strategy between ourselves and then with Dave and Liz for something so relatively petty in the scheme of things? Well, there is one reason—and that's the nature of the community. Living so closely together socially, and depending on one another so often for help and advice, one certainly doesn't want to offend anyone. But today we realized the easy and right solution. Tomorrow we'll go to Denny and Gail's, explain the situation honestly, tell them why we feel we have to go to Barbara and Warwick's, and then tell them how much we'll be looking forward to spending New Year's Eve with them next year.

## Darrylle and Ulises

Finally, we want to tell you about Darrylle Stafford and Ulises Obregón. From our first letter you might remember Ulises, the local lawyer with whom we spent our first day in Costa Rica. Darrylle is Ulises' partner.

We originally came into contact with Darrylle when he answered a question I had sent to the Yahoo! group, CostaRicaLiving, before coming here. Eventually after exchanging several letters, we decided that we wanted Darrylle to represent us in our application for Costa Rican residency. He and Ulises have been doing a great job for us, and we feel very comfortable working with them.

Until two weeks ago, we had only exchanged letters and several phone calls with Darrylle. But on our last trip to San José, we were finally able to meet him in person. He invited us to his apartment for lunch before beginning to do the work we had planned. His apartment is just lovely. It's located in a nice section of San José, is large (living room—dining room combination, nice-sized kitchen, two bedrooms, two baths, and a balcony), tastefully furnished, bright, and airy. And—for our friends in California—the rent is $450 per month!

Anyway, both of them are kind, very hospitable, extremely gracious, and have a wonderful sense of humor—not to mention that Darrylle is a very accomplished cook. In addition to the afternoon we spent with them at the apartment, we also went to dinner with them the next night at a very enjoyable Asian restaurant. What a menu: outstanding Chinese, Japanese, Indian, Burmese, Thai, and Vietnamese dishes in a very attractive setting.

We also received loads of tips from both of them: where to find very good-tasting, inexpensive wine in San José (from Chile); where to get outstanding cheese, made in Costa Rica—something not easily found here; a tip about an excellent furniture store specializing in things from Guatemala where Darrylle bought much of his furniture, which Robin and I so admired; the location of the only place to buy the best coffee we've had here so far— it's called El *Trébol*—virtually all of *Trébol*'s coffee is exported, so if you see it anywhere, be sure to snap it up. I don't know what it will cost, but here we paid about $1.50 a pound. We took ten pounds back to Dominical. And there was much, much more. Robin and I are looking forward to getting to know these delightful people better. We're expecting them to come to visit us in the not-too-distant future, and we've been talking about going together to Nicaragua, where Ulises was born and raised.

There is still so much more about which to tell: our trip to the duty-free city of Golfito, our acquisition of quads (all-terrain vehicles) and some of the rides we've taken on them, what's going on with our landscaping of the area surrounding our building site, the opportunities for high-yield investments here, our efforts to learn Spanish, what we're learning about the preservation of the Costa Rican environment, more about what the Ticos seem to be like, and much else. But this will come later.

Our love and best wishes to all for a happy, prosperous, and healthy New Year.

Martin and Robin

# Chapter Six

## January 12, 2001

Hi, family and friends:

### The Horse

First, Robin's been out all day, and I expect her to come home the proud owner of a horse! Most of you who've been reading these letters know that we're constructing a *bodega* and that after we move our things out of storage in the *bodega*, we'll convert it into a stable. But we won't be able to do that until the big house is built, and that will be close to a year.

But recently, Angelo and Maryanne (more about them later on) were talking to another couple who lives in Lagunas, Bob and Bea. Bea said she had a horse she has to find a home for and thus far she hasn't found anyone to whom she wanted to give the horse. Angelo told Bea about Robin and her wanting a horse. Then he told us. A couple of weeks later, Robin and I drove up to their house to meet Bea. We had met Bob already a few times, but never when Bea was with him.

They're an attractive young couple who has been here awhile and who has a wonderful spread of over one hundred acres with a fantastic view of the ocean, the mountains, and the valleys. They also have a very large *rancho*. A *rancho* is the same thing in Costa Rica as a *palapa* is in Mexico—that is, a cone-shaped roof, either thatched or made of palm fronds supported by logs and beams. Some of them are very small and others are so large and elaborate that they've been featured in *Architectural Digest*. Bob and Bea's *rancho*, however, has a tin roof with which they replaced the original thatch. They've built a lovely house, a beautiful stable, and have six horses on the property and one elsewhere, five or six dogs (I lost count), a pet kinkajou, and an aviary.

Bea is, as Robin, a lover of all animals, and although I'm writing this story as it's unfolding, I would be extremely surprised if she didn't feel that Robin was someone to whom she could safely give the horse, assuming, of course, that Robin likes the horse and that he and she hit it off well.

The horse, however, is not at Bea's place. She's keeping it with a Tico family on their farm way, way out in the boondocks. He's the youngest of the seven horses, and the other six seem to have picked on him, so Bea worked out an arrangement whereby this family would keep it. But now she feels she wants to move the horse out of there because the pastureland is too limited, and it's difficult for the family to provide enough supplements for the horse's diet.

So we all decided that Robin and Bea would go out to the *finca* (farm) today for Robin to meet the horse. Of course, we would have no place to put it for a year, but Bea is willing to keep him at her place, separated from the other horses, and Robin can care for him there and ride him until we can move him to our place. Once we're living in the *cabina*, Bea's place will be less than a ten-minute drive from ours.

In the meantime, because even if you drive to the *finca*, you still have to walk a couple of kilometers to get the rest of the way there, they decided that they'd make a real outing of it and go there by horseback. What an adventure. It's at least a two-hour ride from Bea's to the *finca*. Robin hasn't spent more than an hour on a horse in the last year. She will be one sore young woman tomorrow morning! So I'm waiting for them to return and find out how everything went.

So now it's a couple of days later and I can tell you the rest of the story. They didn't get back until 6 PM. So that means that they were at it from 7 AM until 6 PM! The family they were going to see lives at the very, very top of an extremely high mountain.

Robin and Bea probably walked the horses as much as they rode them, most of the time almost straight up the mountain. But they had an absolutely wonderful day. They really took their time, stopping to let the horses graze, looking at the amazing views, chatting a lot, and getting to know one another.

Unfortunately, as it turned out, when they finally arrived, the family wasn't there. So they went searching the pastures to try to find the horse but never did find him. When they were riding back down, they met the family who was walking up the mountain. They said that the horse was well, but it was too late for Robin and Bea to go back up with them to see him.

They'll go back again and Robin will meet him. Needless to say, Robin was sore for a couple of days, but she got over it a lot more quickly than I had expected. What a trooper!

## The *Cabina*

The second big deal of the day is that this morning, before they quit work for the weekend, the guys building the *cabina* put up the ridgepole and the first beam! I believe that the roof will be done by the end of next week. Another big milestone.

It's now Friday, January 12, 2001, and we just came back from the site. Big things are happening. The roof of the *cabina* isn't finished yet, but all the *vigas* (beams) are in place. This evidently was a very complex job requiring lots of work because not only does our roof have many, many angles, but also the beams have to be tied into the walls and then cemented into place. All of this requires lots of careful, painstaking work.

Now, however, Marvin, the foreman, told us that things would start moving very quickly. Next week he expects to have the ceiling finished (it's all made of beautiful wooden planks), then the roof over the ceiling. Then he also thinks that they'll have the floors poured. Then the week after, they'll put the final finishing *repello* (stucco) on the walls and start laying the tiles. Kiki says that we will be able to move in on February 15!

At the same time, another crew is working on the *bodega*, and it will be finished in order for us to have our things brought down from San José on February 1. We're getting there, little by little.

## Angelo and Maryanne

Past our property, at the end of the road, is Angelo and Maryanne's place. This road is considered a private one rather than public and had, until yesterday, no name. But we've decided to name it, and Robin, Maryanne, Angelo, and I decided to call it *Avenida Miramar*. Not all that original, perhaps, but extremely descriptive because there are such wonderful views of the sea from all the house sites there. Today we ordered a sign in Platanillo. It'll be ready in about two weeks. (Life moves slowly in the tropics.)

Angelo and Maryanne are real Philadelphians, as am I. The first time we visited them, Angelo asked, "Youse want a beer?" Talk about a blast from the past! "Youse" is to Philadelphia as "y'all" is to the American South. It turns out that they're both from South Philly, just about a ten-minute drive from where I grew up in Southwest Philly. Angelo is a master electrician, a millwright, and a contractor—or was before they came down here. He and Maryanne had their own business for many years in Philadelphia.

Angelo will be supervising the electric work for Kiki on our house, and that gives Robin and me a great deal of confidence. He's also giving us lots of ideas for saving money on the construction of the house without compromising the quality.

During our first visit with them, I think they both thought I was a psycho. Maryanne said that she attended high school at Little Flower, at which point I, in a rather loud voice, said "Little Flower! School of the day! *Ding, ding, ding, ding!*" They just looked at me with what seemed to be a rather fearful expression in their eyes, as though thinking, "This guy is going to be our next-door neighbor?" So I thought I'd better explain.

In the earliest days of *Bandstand*, when it was just a local Philadelphia show and wasn't *American Bandstand*, and even before Dick Clark had anything to do with it, I used to go there several days a week after school. The studios were only a fifteen-minute walk from my high school. At any rate, every day they had a "school of the day." I can't remember anymore how they selected it, probably based on how many kids from a given school were in the studio each day.

When they announced the school of the day, Bob Horne, the guy who was the original host of *Bandstand*, would shout "School of the day!" and then would ring a bell several times (hence the *ding, ding, ding, ding*). Seems as though Angelo and Maryanne are a lot younger than I and didn't remember those days. That's why they looked at me as though I were nuts.

The reason you've never heard of Bob Horne on any of the endless *American Bandstand* retrospectives is because he was convicted of running a call-girl ring, recruiting the girls from *Bandstand*; this was in the late 1950s.

## Buying Plants and Planning the Garden

As you all know, in the jungle, life is cheap—sorry, I meant plants are cheap. But still, what a surprise I got last week when Robin and I went to a nursery in San Isidro called *La Bonita*. It's owned by a fellow named Edgar and his family. His father started it many years ago. They have several farms all over Costa Rica where they raise the things they sell in the nursery. In addition, they have a thriving landscaping business. Edgar has landscaped most of the places in Lagunas, that is, our neighbors' places. He'll most likely do ours, as well.

At any rate, we bought huge hanging, moss-lined pots of impatiens, ferns, and other trailing plants. We also bought a beautiful phalenopsis orchid, in bloom, a begonia, two African violets (which a little old guy who was watching said were Russian violets), and two large hanging baskets without any plants in them. The cost: less than $25. At the nursery I regularly shopped in Menlo Park, this purchase would have been about $200! The orchid alone would have been at least $45.

There are other delights: how about ten-foot-tall palm trees, balled and ready to plant for $18 each? And here's one of my favorites: a huge extremely well-made, high-quality teak rocking chair for $100! At Smith and Hawkins it would cost a minimum of $600-$800.

We just can't wait to begin landscaping. As it turns out, we don't have to wait until the big house is finished at all. Above our building site there's a beautiful high hill that is part of our property. From almost the first day, Robin and I have been planning to turn the hill into a tropical garden. It's so high above the site that we can start on it immediately and not have to worry about the construction interfering with the garden.

We've already taken the first step. Róger, the man who chops our roadsides back and who has planted our ground cover for us (remember the cutter ants?), has cleared all the underbrush from the hill. Now there are just the trees. Many of them, because of the density of the jungle, are just straggly little things, and we'll now begin to clear these, leaving all the trees that are desirable. They'll also be able to grow better after the thinning.

This area is where, in March, at the very beginning of the rainy season, we'll begin planting our fruit trees. We'll be planting mango, papaya, banana, orange, and avocado. We'll also plant some coconut palms. According to Róger, all the trees, other than the coconut palms, will begin bearing fruit within two years! I told him that this was excellent, because at my age, I wasn't prepared to wait fifteen years for these things to start bearing!

Speaking of cutter ants, you probably remember my telling you about getting rid of them with mirex. Robin now tells me she heard that another way to save plants and trees from the cutter ants is to spread ashes around their bases. For some reason, the ants won't go through the ashes, perhaps because they're so caustic (the ashes, not the ants).

We'll be terracing the hillside, which is very steep, and we'll have a switchback path leading up. This will make access easy. We're also talking about building a small *rancho* up there where it's even cooler, a perfect place to hang our hammocks and relax with a wonderful view on all sides.

Two of the site's other sides have steep hills leading down as well. Here, too, we'll terrace the terrain and build other gardens. There's much planning to do and many decisions to make. But this is the kind of planning and the type of decisions that make our life here a joy.

## Army Ants

We almost had our first run-in with army ants. Fortunately they decided not to visit our house, but everyone tells us that if you live here long enough (and that's not very long), you'll have an encounter with them.

Unlike the African army ants, which will eat chickens and small mammals, the army ants here only eat bugs. Eventually, they'll invade your house sometime, and the only thing you can do is leave the house for a couple of days until they're finished. The upside of this is that there will not be a single bug or insect left in your house when they've gone.

A few days ago we saw a column of them in our yard at the rental house. They're very big and black in color. One bit me, and it really smarted! So there was nothing to do but wait to see if they were going to eventually come into the house—there's no way to keep them out if they want in. But the next morning they were gone. Whew! I hope it's a long time yet before we have what seems to be an inevitable encounter with them.

## Bad News About Telephones

Thus far Lagunas doesn't have telephones. Kent Brown has been working for two years petitioning ICE (*Instituto Costarricense de Electricidad*), the state-owned electric and communications monopoly, to bring phones into Lagunas. He finally got their agreement to bring ten lines up the Main Road. We were expecting that to happen within a few weeks to a couple of months. (In the meantime, we do have phone service in our rental house in Barú.)

The plan at that point was that about six months after that, they would begin to bring lines onto the Ridge Road and the private roads that run off of it. Our property is off the Ridge Road on a private road. So, Robin and I felt that in about eight months we'd have telephone service at our home. We're having the *cabina* and house wired for phones, of course.

Then, last week, Kent gave us some horrible news. It seems that, supposedly, one of the residents from the Ridge Road went to ICE and complained bitterly that it wasn't fair that the Main

Road would get phones right away and the other residents of Lagunas wouldn't. Well, evidently, this person (or persons) carried on terribly and the power company told them that ICE just wouldn't run any lines up there at present but would put in two phone booths!

Kent, who has lots of connections and not a little pull, will keep working to try to remedy the situation. He's also working to find out who it was who so messed up the deal. I for one hope that he doesn't find out. The community is so small, that this person will be immediately ostracized and essentially sent to Coventry. There are many, many bitterly disappointed people here. But with the community so small, Robin and I would hate to see that kind of bitterness become focused on one person or a family. What's done is done, and eventually there will be telephones—maybe even in our lifetime.

Of course there are cell phones here. The problem is that the wait is about a year now! Because I expected to have a phone at the house in a few months, I didn't bother to put in an application for a cell phone. I guess it's time to do it. But it might also be possible to buy a cell phone line or number from someone who doesn't want it anymore. We've seen lines for sale in San José. So we'll look into that on our next trip there.

## Quepos

Next week Robin and I will be spending a couple of days in Quepos. We've made a reservation at a hotel called ¿Sí, Como No?, which is one of the most highly praised hotels in an area, which has scores of outstanding places to stay. We'll tell you about it in our next letter.

Our warmest personal regards,
Martin and Robin

# CHAPTER SEVEN

## January 15, 2001

Hi, family and friends:

I thought I'd try in this letter to tell you a bit more about what daily life in Costa Rica is like for the Costa Ricans themselves.

### Inflation and Economics

The year 2000 saw an inflation rate of 10.25 percent. What's interesting about this is that it's considered stable—that is, it didn't seem something to be greatly alarmed about in the report issued by the chairman of the central bank, who, by the way, was voted by reporters as the best public official of 2000. The rate is stable because the rate has been approximately 10 percent over the last couple of years.

But the editorials and op-ed columns in *La Nación,* the nation's leading newspaper, are screaming for measures to control inflation in 2001. What seems to be of greatest economic concern here, however, is the rate of growth in the GDP. In 2000 it was just a little bit higher than an anemic 2 percent. The director of the central bank maintains that until and unless the country can attain a sustainable annual growth rate of 6 percent, there is no chance of reducing the country's level of poverty. Although Costa Rica has the lowest poverty level in Central America, it is still over 24 percent.

For people living here with an income in dollars, however, the inflation rate is not nearly as serious as for those whose income is in the local currency. This is because there is a daily planned deflation of the *colón's* exchange rate against the dollar. This is a far-sighted policy meant to avert a sudden collapse of the country's economy as has happened in other Latin American countries. What it means for us is that the annual rate of currency deflation is a bit greater than the annual rate of inflation. Thus, at the end of the year we're still ahead of the inflation rate.

The country has been hit hard by extremely soft prices in bananas and coffee, its two biggest agricultural exports. In addition, the outlook for '01 is not particularly good due to a recent ruling by the European Union that its member countries are not going to set quotas for the banana-exporting countries. That is, there is no longer going to be a guaranteed minimum purchase from these countries. The Costa Rican government has expressed worry that this new policy will result in reduced sales in the coming year.

On the other hand, the production of oranges for export has been growing steadily the last few years, and some forecasters predict that with the increasing number of hectares devoted to orange production, the bulk of which goes to concentrate, some of the slack in the weak banana and coffee markets might be taken up in the near future.

This is a positive development. But the agricultural sector will have to be careful to avoid in orange production the same problems that developed with the initial success of pineapple production. In that case, because pineapple production and sales were so successful, more and more people began growing them. Eventually, there was a glut of the fruit and prices began to fall quickly.

Finally, there is a disease attacking coffee beans on the bush in Central America. A little insect that bores a hole into the beans causes it. If this condition is not contained, it could result in severely reduced crops. This, of course, would result in higher prices, but much less coffee for export.

## Politics

This is the year when would-be presidential candidates begin to throw their hats into the ring in preparation for next year's presidential election. Those who declare are called pre-candidates. This is the last year of President Miguel Ángel Rodríguez's tenure. The president serves for a four-year term and is never eligible for reelection again. In fact this year, former president Oscar Arias, the Nobel Peace Prize laureate, tried to get a constitutional amendment passed that would have allowed him to seek election next year. His effort was rejected. The Ticos feel very strongly that their "one time and you're out" system has been a big plus in their history of sustaining democratic rule. (As it turns out, two years later the Supreme Court did, in fact, hold that ex-presidents could seek reelection. Thus, Arias will most likely do so.)

Another plus for stability and democracy, of course, has been the abolition of the armed forces on December 2, 1948. This obviously precludes a military strongman from taking power. The Ticos feel so strongly about this that they recently passed a law that requires the police force to change the names of their ranks from military ranks to civil service ranks.

There are two major parties in Costa Rica, the United Social Christian Party (PUSC) and the National Liberation Party (PLN). Thus far I have not been able to discern what the major differences between the parties are. I assume as the new candidates begin making speeches, I'll eventually get a better idea of their respective platforms. Currently, however, I suspect that there is not a great deal of difference between the parties. An interesting feature of the presidential elections is that the parties seem to alternate wins regularly.

This leads me to believe that either, as I mentioned, there is not a great deal of difference between the parties or that the people change parties the way they change presidents to ensure that a single party does not stay in power very long and thus does not get its partisan bureaucracy too entrenched through patronage. Resisting an entrenched bureaucracy and extensive patronage would be yet another way to try to ensure the continuation of democracy.

## An Ecological Paradox

Many of you have heard wonderful things about Costa Rica in relation to its efforts to preserve its ecology. And there are, indeed, many wonderful things going on here. For example, 25 percent of the country's land is held in ecological reserves. Also, the amount of rain forest actually increased here last year by 4 percent. To some degree this is due to foreigners buying land here and not developing it. Robin and I, for example, have our eye on about eighty acres of land across the valley from our home site, which we would love to purchase. This way our view would never be despoiled and the land, mostly rain forest, would be preserved. Furthermore, the lovely three-tier waterfall contained on this property would not become a tourist attraction.

Nevertheless, there are severe problems, too. There is a great deal of tree poaching going on in the Osa Peninsula, the country's biggest remaining stand of rain forest. There are other things going on that I still don't understand completely. It seems that the government has not yet paid for much of the land that is in reserve. I believe that if the payments are not made within some period of time, the land will most likely revert to its original owners. This could result in its future development.

On the other hand, the government seems not only to be cracking down on poachers but also issuing far fewer licenses to commercial loggers. And recently Costa Rica received a large loan, over fifty million dollars, if I remember correctly, for the preservation and management of its forests.

(I wrote the above in January 2001. It is now June 2004. A couple of days ago in *La Nación* I read something that truly shocked me. Here is an excerpt from that article:

"We Will All Come Out Losing
"A decree against tourism and the environment
"Ana I. Piza, journalist
"The Presidency of the Republic, by Executive Decree No. 31.750-MINAE-TUR, authorizes the

felling of 15 percent of first-growth forest and 25 percent of secondary forest for the purpose of tourist development.

"Costa Ricans have been able to prove that the country's greatest attraction is nature. Tourism is a productive and growing industry, and the foreigners, in their majority, come to see that which is not found in other countries: the forests with all the richness of their flora and fauna. To do away with these resources in order to promote tourism is the most insane thing that can be done. And this does not even consider the environmental consequences, which can be vouched for in Haiti with the human and material resources which so suffered in the recent tragedy."

Since then there are already many court challenges to the decree and its execution has been delayed. Let's hope that this insanity can be stopped dead in its tracks.)

A really paradoxical situation exists in the area of automobile emissions. Costa Rica, which has no domestic automobile production, imports all its vehicles. The import duty, however, is absolutely huge, putting the price of new cars well beyond the means of most of the country's citizens.

What this means is that cars are kept forever. And what this, in turn, means is that the roads are filled with cars emitting the most noxious fumes. Horrible blue and black smoke is constantly belching out of these cars, pouring tons of pollutants into the air. I've mentioned in an earlier letter how horrible the streets of cities such as San José and San Isidro smell because of these emissions. Unlike Mexico, where there has been a campaign under way for years now to switch as many cars as possible, especially taxis, to unleaded gas, there does not seem to be any such effort going on here.

And it's not just a problem in the cities. Even in the heart of the country, on the Pan-American Highway, deep in the rain forest, one is frequently behind ancient cars and trucks that are endlessly pouring noxious fumes into the atmosphere.

I've read many editorials and columns calling for a reduction in the import duty on cars and trucks in order to alleviate this problem. Thus far I haven't seen articles concerning the government's addressing the problem.

Vehicles do have to be inspected every year. Part of the inspection concerns emissions and theoretically, if they are bad, they have to be corrected before the car will be passed. Our friends, Dave and Liz, for example, had to replace their catalytic converter this year during the inspection process. But the fact remains that there are thousands of vehicles on the road that are polluting the atmosphere. There was a letter in today's paper that referred to the sight of hundreds of public transportation vehicles, that is, buses, which are continually "emitting great quantities of smoke." The writer points out that individuals' cars are subject to inspection and must be repaired at substantial cost and then asks, "Why are the laws in our country not applied equally? Could it be due to the existence of other interests [that allow the laws to be circumvented]?"

## Education

Costa Rica is rightly proud of its educational system. Virtually every little village has its own school. The school year runs from the first week in February to the end of November. I still have a lot to learn about the school system here. Thus far it seems to me that high school is not mandatory and that it can be expensive to send kids to high schools. Even elementary school is tough on poor parents. The kids here all wear uniforms, and although they look extremely neat and clean, the necessity of buying these uniforms is often a huge burden on the poorest families. One hears stories of families that cannot afford shoes for their kids. Since shoes are required, these children aren't allowed to attend classes. However, there are many schools that relax the rules a bit in order to help these poor families.

One also hears stories about kids who ride horses or walk miles every day to and from school, in all weather. These are kids who live on isolated farms, deep in the country, far from the nearest town or village. For example, in our last letter I mentioned the people Robin and Bea went to see about Bea's horse and how far it was up the mountain to their house. The school their young son attends is in Barú. In order to go to school he rides his horse every day. Robin and I figure that he must spend a minimum of two to three hours a day commuting.

But the children do it, and as a consequence, Costa Rica has an extremely high literacy rate, somewhere around 94 or 96 percent.

Of interest to the people who read this and who work for GlobalEnglish, my former company, is the fact that English is considered an area in which the professional working class is sorely lacking. In a recent survey published in *La Nación*, it seems that, in general, Costa Rica turns out a very highly educated, capable, extremely hard-working, and creative workforce, especially in high technology. Indeed, that's the main reason that Intel has such a large presence in the country. But the article goes on to say that poor English-language skills are keeping large numbers in the workforce from realizing their true potential.

As a result of this need, the newspapers here are filled almost daily with ads for large English-language schools and English study programs.

## The Costa Rican People

Before Robin and I arrived here, we read extensively about Costa Rica: travel books, informative Web sites, books and articles on the history of Costa Rica, sociological studies, etc. What you get from this reading is a great number of repeated clichés about the people here.

Among these ideas are the following: The Costa Rican people are adverse to confrontation. They tend to avoid any situation that would result in angering the people they're involved with. As a consequence, their attitude is always *quedar bien*—that is, "to be nice." To achieve this, they'll generally tell you what you want to hear, regardless of whether or not what you want is possible. They don't want to argue with you, and telling you what you want to hear is the easiest way to do this. As a result, deadlines for delivery of goods are almost always missed, and you hear very creative explanations for why this happens.

Family relationships seem to be the foundation of Costa Rican society. The extended family is a large part of a native's experience. Children stay close to their parents, siblings, and relatives throughout their lives. Family members are very loyal to one another. They try to throw business as much as possible to members of their family and expect the same treatment in return. In Costa Rica, nepotism is not a dirty word.

Just the other day, we were giving Minor, a young man who does odd jobs for the owner of the place we're renting and for us as well, a ride to San Isidro. On the way, he asked us if we'd like to stop at his aunt's farm. Of course we agreed. The farm is in Platanillo, right on our way to San Isidro. So we met his aunt, a friendly, elderly woman, got a tour of the house, and walked about the farm for a bit. If I remember correctly it's about fifteen hectares. Well, it turned out that the farm is for sale, and Minor took us there because he thought we might be interested in buying it.

When we left the farm and were continuing on our ride, Robin mentioned a fruit stand that she and I stopped at frequently on the road to San Isidro. Well, it turns out that the stand a couple of kilometers before the one we usually stop at is owned by another aunt. So we stopped there, too. He introduced us to her and we bought a couple of things (and were given a couple of slices of ice-cold, delicious watermelon for the road).

This networking extends to friends as well as relatives. When we bought our Honda ATVs in San Isidro, we were not going to drive them back to Dominical. They're not the thing for riding on the road. Needless to say, Minor had a close friend who had a cargo taxi. These are small trucks that people hire to haul things for relatively short distances. So we had his friend haul our ATVs from San Isidro to Dominical.

Then there is Rudy. The last time Robin and I were in San José, we were on a big shopping trip for furniture and many other things for the *cabina*. We were going to have to drive all over San José for days to go to all the places we needed to visit and to find stores that had the things we wanted. I certainly was not looking forward to that, so I suggested that we hire a driver to take us around. I checked with the desk clerk at the hotel we were staying, and he made arrangements for a driver. We agreed on the price and then met the driver, Rudy, at the hotel to begin our shopping tour.

Rudy seemed to know hundreds of people. At almost every stoplight he'd talk to other drivers he knew. His cell phone would ring constantly. Rudy is a real hustler, wheeler-dealer, and at first, Robin was apprehensive about him, worrying whether or not we could trust him to wait for us at stores with his car full of things we had already purchased. I felt relatively secure because the hotel clerk who knew him recommended him, and the hotel was one of the better, more expensive ones in the city. As it turned out, he was quite trustworthy and extremely helpful.

Not only did he drive us everywhere, he insisted in coming in the stores with us to help us find things and to carry packages. He also wanted to act as translator for us, which was a bit awkward. His English was not too much better than our Spanish. Although he was able to have long conversations with the people waiting on us, he was not able to transmit to us the substance of the conversations very well.

But back to his contacts. I mentioned in an earlier letter that Robin and I got Costa Rican driver's licenses and for a little *chorizo* (literally "sausage," figuratively "bribe") we were able to save a few hours in the transaction. It was Rudy, of course, who had a "friend" who was able to make this happen.

I also mentioned to Rudy that I needed to make an application for a cell phone, and that I was frustrated that the wait to get the line would be so many months. Well, it turns out that Rudy has an uncle who can't afford to keep his line and would be more than glad to sell it to us. As it happened, however, his uncle was very ill in the hospital. Nevertheless, Rudy would be glad to take us there to speak with him. We declined this kind offer.

On this trip we bought far more than we were able to carry in our Jeep, so we had to arrange for transportation for the furniture we had bought. And surprise! Rudy has an uncle who has a sixteen-foot van and who was just delighted to load it up with our things and follow us from San José back to Dominical for a not-outrageous price, but not super cheap, either. It all worked out quite well.

This networking among family and friends is not by any means altruistic. A long-time resident here explained to us that there's always a "finder's fee" involved, usually 10 percent. This even extends to hotel clerks who recommend restaurants to guests. When the clerk calls up to make a reservation for you, his name and yours are duly noted, and usually the next day he or she appears at the restaurant to collect the finder's fee.

So the clerk at our hotel probably collected a fee from Rudy, and Rudy probably collected from both the fellow who helped us get our driver's licenses and his uncle who hauled our stuff for us. I assume that Minor collected his fee as well from the cargo taxi driver who hauled our ATVs for us.

All in all, it's not a bad system, especially for people such as us who do not yet have many contacts.

I should mention, however, that a long-time resident recently said that in her experience in Costa Rica the 10 percent commission story is nonsense. The only regular commission of this type, which she knows of, is a finder's fee for real estate transactions.

## What Costa Ricans Look Like

To make a sweeping generalization, the Costa Ricans are extraordinarily clean and neat. Being clean and dressing nicely is a strongly embedded aspect of the culture here. Naturally you see people who look messy and dirty, but you're much more aware of how nicely dressed most of the people you see are, especially in the cities. Women here still wear dresses and high heels much more than they do pants. The men are usually dressed in nice slacks and shirts or suits. Many men wear ties to their office jobs, in spite of the heat (though most big businesses, such as banks, are air conditioned and that helps greatly).

The children not only wear uniforms to school, as mentioned, but their pants and dresses are always neatly pressed and the white shirts spotlessly clean and ironed. The kids' hair, at least at the beginning of the day, is always neatly combed.

The Costa Rican people are to a noticeable degree quite physically attractive. One thing that contributes to this impression is the fact that there is relatively little obesity here. The people are, as a rule, slender and well formed. To me it's astounding how many of them, men and women alike, are simply handsome and beautiful. I think I can say that, as a people, the Costa Ricans are the most attractive people of any country I've been in.

Also contributing to the overall impression of attractiveness, I believe, is the general pleasantness, helpfulness, and good humor that you encounter in your daily interactions. Of course you encounter surly clerks, bureaucrats, and functionaries, but they are much more the exception than the rule. In general you can count on being greeted courteously, listened to attentively, and served well.

## Political Correctness

PC has not had a profound impact on Costa Rica yet. Neither has gender equality. The wage gap for equal or similar work between men and women is more than a stunning 35 percent at this writing. There have been several laws passed recently to help women in the workplace and in the area of domestic violence, and there are many active and vocal groups engaged in working for gender equality. So the country is not only aware of the problems of inequality but is attempting to do something about it.

Coming from the United States, Robin and I were simply astounded when we began to read the help wanted display ads in the newspaper and the help wanted notices posted in stores.

Most ads are quite specific about the ages of applicants for positions. For example, I have here before me last Monday's newspaper—Monday is the big day for employment ads here. The first display ad I looked at was for a company's marketing department. In large type it says that applicants should be between the ages of eighteen and twenty-seven.

The next ad is for a company called La Artística, a large furniture and accessories store in San José that Robin and I have visited. It's for saleswomen, yep, women. The ad reads: "Age: between 25 and 40; Sex: female." The ad also calls for "advanced English," as do so many others—see my comments above about the problem of English proficiency. As an example of how often ads stipulate the sex of the applicant, sometimes you come across ads such as one I'm looking at for a tourism business that specifically states applicants can be of either gender—evidently something necessary to point out. Another ad calls for a bilingual, female secretary between the ages of twenty to thirty.

In general, age is almost always specified, sex to a lesser degree. You often, however, see the requirement that the person has to be "attractive" as well. You never see these kinds of stipulations in the ads run by large international companies with branches in Costa Rica.

The country has a long way to go in the areas of sexism and ageism.

## The Church's Influence

Of course Costa Rica is a predominately Catholic country. There are few if any laws, as far as I have been able to determine thus far, directed toward the separation of church and state. Indeed, the Costa Rican constitution explicitly states that Catholicism is the country's official religion. On the other hand, the country seems quite tolerant of other religions. The Baptists have a strong presence here as do the Seventh Day Adventists. There is a large and long-established Jewish community in San José.

But the religious influence on the country is felt in many ways. The most startling I've come across so far is a newly passed law, the only one of its kind in the entire world, that prohibits in vitro fertilization! This happened a month or so ago. I read in yesterday's newspaper that some people are challenging the law on the basis of a violation of human rights.

When the news hit the papers here that Holland had legalized same-sex marriages and the adoption of children by married same-sex partners, the outcry in the letters-to-the-editor sections of the newspapers was outraged and shrill. In general, there is little tolerance here for homosexuality, and one hears jokes and nasty comments in public and at social gatherings all the time. There have been stories in the papers about gay clubs being harassed and closed. Robin and I are friendly with two homosexual couples here, but we have not yet talked to them about difficulties they may have encountered in what seems to be a very hostile environment.

## International Relations

It seems that the country that most often appears in the newspapers in articles concerning Costa Rica's foreign relations is Nicaragua. There are two consistent areas of contention: navigation rights on the river San Juan, which forms part of the border between the two countries, and the question of illegal Nicaraguan immigration. Nicaragua is an extremely poor country.

The controversy over the San Juan extends back to October 1977 when Nicaraguan forces fired on some Costa Rican boats in the river. This was during the regime of then Nicaraguan dictator Samoza. The Organization of American States ruled in Costa Rica's favor that year, and Costa Rica decided not to ask for sanctions in order not to make the situation even more tense than it was. Although I haven't been following the story closely, there are frequently articles in the papers about ongoing talks over navigation rights in the river.

Compared to Nicaragua, Costa Rica is an economic paradise. Consequently, thousands of Nicaraguans seek to enter Costa Rica every year. Mostly the immigrants are laborers who take some of the hardest jobs. For example, they work in the sugarcane fields, a job that is extremely difficult, dirty, and exhausting. The Nicas, as they are called, are the scapegoats for much that is wrong here. For example, most people here will tell you that the recent elevated crime rate is due almost exclusively to the influx of Nicas. There seems to be little evidence to support this claim. Indeed, Nicas are involved in crime, but, according to all the accounts I read in the papers, not nearly to the extent that would justify this claim of rampant Nica lawbreaking and criminality.

The situation is reminiscent of the sad state of affairs in the United States' relations with Mexico. The Ticos have a prejudice that is mostly economically based (unlike the strong racial bias in the States, which accompanies the economic fears of our citizens). Also, the Nicas are often subject to rip-offs by those who "help" them enter the country. The Ticos and Nicas who take advantage of those trying to enter Costa Rica are called "coyotes," the same term, I believe, for those who take advantage of Mexicans who are trying to enter the United States illegally.

In today's paper there was a story about a young seventeen-year-old Nicaraguan who bought a *cédula* from one of these coyotes. The *cédula* is the ID card that every Costa Rican citizen carries. It contains the person's age, birth date, etc., and a picture of the owner. It is a sort of internal passport and is used for everything from opening a bank account to signing a letter to the editor of a newspaper, and all else in between.

There is a brisk trade in counterfeit *cédulas* sold to the Nica immigrants. The young man referred to in the newspaper article was illiterate and consequently did not realize that the card being sold to him described a ten-year-old boy. The article said that most of the counterfeit *cédulas* are of such poor quality that they are immediately recognized as forgeries. Others have been stolen from Ticos who, in their turn, apply for new ones. The computer will quickly pick up the stolen card, and the poor Nica who has paid a significant sum for it will be promptly deported back to his country.

And now there are reports in the paper about police violence against the deportees. Today Nicaragua sent a formal protest through its ambassador to Costa Rica asking that the treatment of Nicaraguan deportees be humane.

Finally, for those who are rich and want to enter Costa Rica illegally, the Internet has two sites that will allow one to buy what are "guaranteed" to be authentic Costa Rican passports and *cédulas*. The prices are substantial. In some cases, one can even purchase a diplomatic passport with the right to change the name and photo every couple of years. The price for this "super package" runs over $125,000.

A new area concerning international relations has just begun to attract interest here with the appointment of Juan Carlos Hernández Padrón, the first Cuban consul in Costa Rica since 1961. This is particularly current because on January 7 of this year, Costa Rica granted political asylum to twenty-one Cuban refugees who arrived here on a small fishing boat. When asked about these people, Hernández Padrón said that "This is obviously an act of piracy," because the boat was stolen. But then he added, "This is the official position," and the only way it will be resolved is through diplomacy. He seemed to be trying, in the interview, not to come across as a hard-liner. Costa Rica has a Cuban colony of between twelve thousand and fourteen thousand people (who, by the way, guaranteed the financial security of the refugees), and Hernández Padrón says that a great deal of his work will be involved in dealings with the Cuban community.

## Martin's Head

And the last bit of news is that Robin shaved my head for me the other day. Wow, does it feel a lot cooler. And everyone says that but for the little pointy spot on the top on my skull, my head is nicely shaped. They also say it makes me look younger.

Obviously, much of what I've written here is based on a short acquaintance with the country (and probably also on an imperfect understanding of what I read in the Spanish-language newspapers). We're still a few days shy of being here only three months. So many of our observations are, of course, subject to change as we get to know Costa Rica and its people better. We just thought that you'd perhaps like to know about what goes on in the country day to day as far as we can tell at this early point.

Best regards,
Martin and Robin

# CHAPTER EIGHT

## January 21, 2001

Hi, family and friends!

### Learning Spanish

It's been a long time since I've learned a language, and although I sincerely believe that Robin and I are making great progress, we nevertheless fall into every stupid trap out there waiting for us.

Here are some of the dumb things I've said in Spanish:

> To Marvin the cook who is raising chickens at the *bodega* on our building site: "Are you going to use those chickens for Thursdays?" (Instead of eggs.)
>
> To someone who was saying that my shaved head looked good: "Since I cut my hair, my head has been very soft drink." (Instead of cool.)
>
> To the contractor: "I will do that yesterday." (Instead of I did that yesterday.)
>
> To a taxi driver in San José: "Are you going to watch the big football juice?" (Instead of game.)
>
> To the person who asked me how I was feeling: "I'm really married!" (Instead of tired.)
>
> To a guy who came to the door to sell cosmetics: "I'm sorry, but my wife is a real disease." (Instead of is very sick.)

And of course then there was the tim          e I asked Kiki, our contractor: "Will it be very expensive to build the died?" (Instead of wall.)

And then, the very worst of them all:

Placing an order for Robin and me with the handsome young waiter at a restaurant we often go to but probably won't patronize anymore, I said, "She'll have tacos and I'll have you." (How this happened I don't know, and I don't want to think about it. It was hard to tell whose face got redder, his or mine.)

Then there are all the things we say incorrectly and never do find out what we said wrong but know that we made horrible bloopers by the look of confused incredulity or total lack of understanding on the faces of our interlocutors.

Sometimes when Robin talks to Seidy—the young woman who does some work for us a few times a week and who speaks no English at all—we can see on her face that it's all she can do to keep from breaking out in a huge guffaw. The same is true for Minor, who also speaks no English, especially the time I asked him if he would cut the guest for me. (Instead of the grass.)

The list of such stupidities is virtually endless. I always tell people that no matter what your method for learning a language is, you have to pay your dues. I guess I forgot just how many dues there were to pay!

## The Beach

I've been putting off writing about the beach here because I despair of even beginning to convey the awesome beauty that is so evident everywhere.

So I'll begin with a more or less realistic and factual description and see where that takes us. The beach on the South Central Pacific shore extends hundreds of kilometers. And although you can't walk it for that kind of distance because there are frequent spits and points and rock formations that jut out into the ocean all along the coast, there are areas between these protuberances that extend for many, many kilometers at a stretch.

There is ready access to the beaches all along the shore, and as far as I know, none of them is private. The state has made many efforts to preserve the country's natural beauties for its citizens.

When you drive off the main north-south coastal road to go to the beach, which might be anywhere from one hundred meters to three or four kilometers off the road, you almost always take an unpaved road through the jungle. At the end of the road you'll usually find a thick stand of mangrove and palms. You park your car, walk through the mangrove, and reach the beach.

During the dry season, the first meter or two between the mangrove and the sand is a layer of beautiful, smooth small stones and rocks. They look like river stones and rocks, and perhaps they are. Hundreds of rivers come down from the mountains that line the coast to empty into the ocean. For some reason—and I haven't had a good explanation yet—during the rainy season, these stones and rocks are spread out over a much wider area of the beach than the one or two meters during the dry season, which I mentioned above.

The sand here is a dark tan and relatively fine—that is, it is not powdery, but neither is it coarse. If you get to the beach at low tide, you are amazed by its width. I would say that it's a good 150 feet wide on average.

So we walk out a hundred feet or so onto the beach. We look north and south, and almost always, as far as the eye can see, there are either no people at all or two or three here and there. What a splendid feeling. Naturally there are places, for example, the beach at Manual Antonio State Park—one of the country's big tourist destinations for foreigners and Ticos alike—which are often crowded. But where we are, the rule is long, wide stretches of beach, empty as far as the eye can see.

And these beaches are for the people's enjoyment. It is strictly prohibited to drive vehicles on the beach, and that is good. But at the same time, there are no restrictions to having your dogs with you or riding your horses along the shore.

When you look along the beach, the view often ends far, far in the distance where a small cape or point either juts or curves out into the ocean. And at that distance, the fine spray from the waves breaking on the rocks shrouds the vista with a delicate, softening fog, giving you a feeling of looking at some kind of magic doorway far in the distance.

Robin and I take the dogs and go for a two-kilometer walk several mornings a week. Lately it has been at very low tide. The beach is wet and the sun glistens in wavy paths everywhere you look. There are crazy-quilt tracks of the tiny crabs that scramble sideways everywhere. And there are the trails of the sea snails, which are exposed at low tide, which make the most amazing patterns: circles, curvy lines, and mazelike spirals that seem as though the snail who made them must have been hysterical.

There must be a dozen different kinds of birds, always walking on the beach, just skirting the tops of the waves, or soaring high over the water. The dogs never tire of trying to catch the birds that are on the ground, though they never get closer than ten meters to them before the birds take to the air.

The water, unlike the Pacific we know in northern California, is always warm, but never hot. The temperature is perfect for walking out into the sea without having to hold your breath at the sudden chill or to dive in to get wet quickly.

You can't swim everywhere. There are many places where the surf is very high and extremely rough, with strong riptides. For this reason, the area around us is a surfing haven rather than a swimming destination. But there are other places here where, due to the curve of the coast or rock formations, the waves are small and gentle, and the tides not dangerous. These are the places where people go to swim.

This morning, while walking with Robin and the dogs, I happened to look down at my feet. The sun was bright and the beach was glistening almost electrically. Then I noticed that I could see under me the reflection of the clouds, which extended far to the left and right, and far ahead. And it was easy to imagine that I was actually walking above the clouds, looking down at them, and from time to time, where they were broken, I was able to see the warm dark tan beach below the clouds.

## The *Casita*

We've decided to refer to the *cabina* now as the *casita*, for it is much more a small house than a *cabina*. Work this past week has been extremely rapid. Once the beams were finally in place, not a trivial undertaking, things started moving at an astonishing pace. The ceiling and roof went up in three days (except for the tiles, which will be mounted during the coming week). All the cement was poured for the inner floors and the outside terrace and walkways in two days. During the coming week, the final layer of *repello* will be put on the interior walls, the septic tank will be finished, the cement floors and walkways will be smoothed, and the tiles put on the roof. This past week, too, all the electric wires were run through the conduit, which had been placed earlier. The week after next, the windows will be installed and the beautiful Italian and Spanish tile will be put down. We're really on schedule for February 15!

## Casa Pacífica

During the week, when the workers are at our site, there is, of course, a great deal of hustle and bustle and noise. But when they leave for the weekend, Robin and I drive up there and are able to feel what it will be like to live there after the construction is over. And the words that come to mind first when we're there alone are beauty, calm, and peace. The beauty is everywhere the eye looks, from the ocean and surf far below to the long curving shoreline to the north, from the mountains and valleys lush with tropical growth on three sides to our own property with its hills and trees.

Although there are many people living in Lagunas and you can see their houses far across the valleys, you never see or hear the people themselves. The only sound is the rustling of the almost-continual soft breeze in the trees and bushes and the calls of the many birds hidden in the jungle or soaring along our hill's edge almost at eye level. There is a sense of profound calm that accompanies the quiet, which, in turn, gives us a feeling of solitude and security. It's as though we are living in a Garden of Eden, guarded over by some benevolent force. All of this makes us strongly aware of the deep sense of peace that seems gently to enfold us as we gaze at the surrounding vistas while standing on the veranda of our house to be.

And for this reason, we have decided to name our house Casa Pacífica.

Every day we are growing to love our little piece of Costa Rica more and more. Now that we've become a little more used to being surrounded by the jungle and ocean and are more aware of the wonders that are just beyond the tree line, we take our time and focus more closely on the vignettes contained within the masterful painting that is our environment.

## Going on an Outing

Yesterday, we went to a secluded waterfall with a large pool at its foot. This enchanted place seemingly deep in the jungle is but less than a kilometer off the main road and not more than four kilometers from where we live. Here, too, you will encounter few people. Robin packed a lunch and she and the dogs and I drove there in just a few minutes. We descended from the road down to the pool on natural stairs formed by the roots of a huge ancient vine-covered tree. Once at the bottom, we went out over the smooth rocks into the middle of the small river that runs off from the pool at the bottom of the falls. We waded in the pool, took pictures, ate lunch, and played with the dogs who loved to swim in the pool. The pool is surrounded by many tall old trees, but the pool is just wide enough so that the canopy does not extend over its middle, thus enabling the sun to shine down into the pool's center.

On the way home, Robin, who is now always watching the trees when we drive, spotted two magnificent toucans. We stopped the car in the middle of the road—something that is not at all foreign to the culture here—got out, and looked at them closely. I only saw one of them. Its brilliant black, white, red, and yellow colors were spellbinding. And then you realize that you're not in a zoo, not looking at a copy of *National Geographic*, and not watching television. But this is where you live, a place that every day brings you something you've never experienced before.

All our best wishes,
Martin and Robin

# CHAPTER NINE

## January 29, 2001

Hi, family and friends:

### Batboy and Robin

Many of you who know Robin also know that she is a very gentle, sympathetic, indeed empathetic person who loves virtually all animals dearly and who will do almost anything to save an animal's life or ensure its comfort. With that as prelude, I'll tell you the saga of Batboy and Robin.

Three days ago, our neighbor, Kate, who lives in a little house next to our rental house, came over with a newborn Jamaican fruit bat in her hand. How did we know he was newborn? He still had his umbilical cord attached. How did we know it was a he? He has a tiny, little penis, naturally. He wasn't more than hours old. It seems that Kate's cat, Leo, brought the baby bat home. We don't know if Leo attacked the bat's mother or if the mother happened to drop the baby. At any rate, Leo brought him home not too much the worse for wear. A couple of small punctures in his tiny wings were all the damage that was visible. Kate, too, is very caring of animals and didn't want to throw the baby away. By the same token, she couldn't keep it in her tiny house with Leo around. So Robin became the mother of Batboy, which is what we have named the baby.

How do you care for a brand-new infant bat? Who knows? But that didn't deter Robin. Without going into a lot of detail, she spent hours on the Web looking for information about how to care for him. She was determined to rehabilitate him so he could survive. (Robin volunteered at a wildlife rehabilitation center in Palo Alto and also has a couple of years' experience as a vet tech.)

Although she was able to find a wealth of information on the Web about bats, her main problem was that she couldn't find information on the Internet that told her how to feed and take care of a newborn bat. And the care and feeding of bats, as is the case with all living things, depends on the species it belongs to.

But she did find contacts with phone numbers and e-mail addresses as well as an online bat group. Then she began to write many e-mails and to make phone calls all over Costa Rica and to the United States. The best contact she has made so far is a well-known bat specialist who lives in the northern part of Costa Rica in Monteverde, Richard Laval. He has given her a lot of advice, and they've exchanged phone calls and many e-mails.

Yesterday, Richard told Robin that if the bat had survived thus far, she is well on the way to becoming a first-class bat mother. Well, not only has the bat survived thus far, but also he's actually thriving!

But it's no accident. Robin fed him—warm, cream-enriched milk with an eyedropper—every two or three hours around the clock. Now she's feeding him, additionally, vitamins and some water on the advice of another specialist she's contacted. She carries him in her hand a lot to keep him warm. He sucks on her finger when he's not being fed. It turns out that a baby bat spends all day attached to its mother's teat. It feeds on demand, which is one reason why information about how much to feed an infant bat is so difficult to come by. Mostly Batboy takes about .5 to 1.0 cc at every feeding.

Robin has constructed a nest with soft material for lining and fine screening along the sides for Batboy to hang from. She wipes his little mouth when he's feeding and has him hang on the fingers of her cupped hand for security and warmth. She puts a little hot-water bottle under the nesting material so that Batboy will stay warm—he chills very easily.

There have been three attempts made to reunite Batboy with his mother—something Richard suggested. Robin hangs screening from the clothesline for Batboy to hang from. Underneath that, she places the nest, very close to the screening in case he loses his grip. She also puts him out at about the time he should be feeding in the evening, so that he will get a little stressed from hunger and the night air. This is so that he will call out. It seems that a bat mother can pick out her child from among literally thousands of other baby bats by its call. Clearly, was the mother to fetch Batboy, his chances for survival would be the strongest. But unfortunately, she has not come for him, and now it looks as though it's not worth trying anymore.

So Robin will be Batboy's mother for about eight weeks— that seems to be the time it will take in order for him to mature enough to be able to go out on his own. In the meantime, he's getting more and more active; yesterday he stretched his little wings for the first time. He's also moving around much more in Robin's hand and in his nest. He had no hair at all when Robin got him, and now he's beginning to develop fine hair all over his body. I think it's amazing. I would have bet that he wouldn't have survived for twenty-four hours after she took him in.

As for me, initially I was appalled at the idea of nursing a baby bat. Like most people, I had all the misconceptions about bats that are "common wisdom." However, in only three days of Robin's telling me everything she has learned, I realize that my "understanding" of bats was indeed made up of misconceptions. However, I must say on that first morning, I was anything but sympathetic. I agreed with one of our friends, the first person whom Robin called after getting Batboy. She asked him what advice he could give her. His reply: "Flush it!" Interestingly enough, he was not the only person to give her that same advice.

But after a day and a half, as I saw how she and little Batboy were truly bonding, I couldn't help but to begin hoping that he'd make it. There's no doubt that Robin loves the little thing. And he seems to know her well by now. To see her sitting at the computer typing with one hand while he nestles in the other, gripping her finger and sleeping soundly, is a truly tender sight. And every time she moves, he tries to grip a little harder, as though he doesn't want her to put him down.

The final softening of my heart came yesterday morning when I awoke to find Robin asleep on the couch in the living room—because she didn't want to wake me after a late-night feeding—with Batboy sleeping in her curled hand. And it seems to me that with his strong will to live, the fact that he is surviving and even thriving against such odds, no one could do anything but root for him to make it. Maybe we should have named him Rocky. But, on the other hand, how could we not call this dynamic duo Batboy and Robin?

The fight is still far from over. Robin will have to learn how to adjust his feeding as he grows. She'll have to help him avoid dehydration. She'll have to figure out what to feed him after he outgrows the enriched milk and water. Other questions will be how to house him as he grows and when he'll be able to survive on his own. But he's off to a great start due to gentle Robin's empathy, love, and effort.

### The *Casita* and Casa Pacífica

Wednesday, January 24, was a big day for *casita* progress. They put the *repello con color* on the outside of the walls—they'll use paint on the inside. The outside color is a beautiful and very light terra-cotta almost golden. In fact, the name of the color is *oro* (gold). The final *repello* coat is almost done on the inside walls, and the floors have been finished in preparation for the laying of the tiles, which will be done sometime in the coming week.

All the walls on the inside will be painted white, except for one wall in the living room which we've decided to paint a vivid sun yellow, and one wall in the bedroom which will be a brilliant bluish turquoise, as close to the color of the ocean when the sun is shining on it as we can get. The idea for this color scheme really stems from the Mexican interiors and exteriors I've seen and which have influenced me so greatly.

They have also begun building the framework for the counters and sink in the *casita*'s kitchen. They've poured the cement for some of the counters on Saturday morning. The counters will all be tiled on top of the cement. Unfortunately, they've cemented the opening where our stovetop is supposed to be! That was one of the last things they did on Saturday morning before they left and which we didn't see until Saturday afternoon. We'll tell them about it first thing on Monday morning, and I'm sure that the answer will be *"no hay problema."* They'll probably just knock it out with a sledgehammer and redo the edges. The workers here are very resourceful, and I don't mean that sarcastically at all.

A really big step this week was deciding on the orientation of the rear façade of the big house—Casa Pacífica—with iron poles and string. Robin, Edgar Rojas our architect, Marvin the foreman, and I spent about an hour or so together trying to find the best orientation for the view from the rear terraces over the ocean.

We think we have it placed in the best location. However, we can't say that this is the final location yet, because we need to consult with the swimming pool builder. The back of the house, which, as I mentioned, looks out onto our view of the ocean, will have the swimming pool between the house and the edge of the *plantel*. We want the pool to be as close as possible to the sharply dropping hill in the back in order to create an horizon pool. The problem we encountered is that we don't know how far back from the hill's edge the pool will have to be. What we don't want, of course, is to wake up one morning during the rainy season to find that our pool is resting peacefully on the valley floor! Things like that have happened here to people who were not careful in locating structures on their sites. One person we've met is spending a hundred thousand dollars to shore up the side of his hill, most of which washed away in a heavy rain, and which, by the time it fell three hundred meters onto the main road, took most of that out also. Fortunately, the house didn't go sliding down the hill with the tons and tons of earth that did.

Either where we've placed the house will be fine, or we'll have to move it back more to make more room for the pool. In either case, we can keep the orientation we've worked out.

## The Workers

We never cease to be amazed at how hard the men on the site work. And also, how much is done without the aid of machines that are so common on construction sites in the United States. Behind the *casita* there is a large hill (more about that later when we talk about the garden). The back of the *casita* is very close to the hill, and there's always the danger of a slide. So we decided to build a wall along the curve of the hill that extends from the side of the *casita* all the way to the edge of the site overlooking the ocean. We're talking about a very long wall, ninety meters when it is done. In the meantime, we're building only the part that extends around the *casita*, about thirty meters.

The bottom half of the hill, which is about twenty meters high at this location behind the *casita*, is solid rock. It slants out toward the *casita*. It needed to be reformed so that the slant at the bottom is gone and so that a ditch about .5 of a meter could be dug for the wall's foundation.

For three solid days, about six of the men broke the rock up with pickaxes; loaded the rock, dirt, and debris by hand into wheelbarrows; and pushed the wheelbarrows across the site to a hill, down which the material was dumped. Later this hill will be compacted and then planted over.

This is some of the most backbreaking work I have ever seen. And they were doing it from early morning until sundown! To make things worse, it was one of the hottest weeks we've had recently. The sun shone intensely all day.

Another example: while the wall preparation was going on, some of the men were working on the floor of the *bodega*. Because it will eventually be a stable, we decided to construct the floor the same way Bob and Bea did for their stable. They had the dirt floor dug out to a depth of about .5 meter. Then they filled most of that space with stones and covered the rest with hard-packed sand. That way the horses' urine will sink into the sand and the stones will act as a sort of drain field, much like the drain field of a septic tank. And of course, you don't want the horses standing on concrete all the time for all the obvious reasons, many of which have to do with sanitation and dryness, not to mention mucking the stables much more.

So, in typical fashion, the dirt floor was dug out by hand and the dirt carted away in many, many wheelbarrows. Then the stone was dumped in front of the door, a large dump truck's worth. You would expect at that point, given everything I've written so far, that they would load the stones by hand into wheelbarrows and then wheel them into the *bodega* and dump them. Almost. But the stones have to be graded. They are all smooth round river stones, but there are large ones and medium ones, and small ones. And there's an order in which they should be laid in the drain field. So first, the two young men doing this job sort the stones by hand into the three sizes. Only when that is done do they load them, by hand, one size at a time, into the wheelbarrows and then push the wheelbarrows into the barn, dump them, and spread them.

But what's even more amazing is that many days some of the guys, after supper, will play soccer on the *plantel* while others lift weights! They need exercise?! It's almost too much to believe. Unlike many U.S. construction crew workers, the Costa Rican men are not very big and burly. In fact many of them are almost petite. And all of them are extremely slender—except one new worker who has the tiniest bit of flab on him and whom Marvin calls "*El Gordo*" (Fatso). But as small and slender as they are, their endurance and strength is simply astounding.

## The Garden

On Tuesday, January 23, 2001, we met with Edgar, a very accomplished landscaper, for our first garden-planning session. Obviously we can't do anything on the building site until construction is finished. However, on the south side of our site, there is a very high hill, the face of which is bare because it was cut in two to create the *plantel*—it's along its face that we're building the wall. On the top of the hill there's about an acre of land, the underbrush of which has been cleared. Here we've intended all along to create a lush, tropical hilltop garden. We recently realized that we could start working on this immediately because the construction will not affect it.

What we have in mind is a dense planting of tropical growth, very green and broad leafed, splashes of vivid color, and very cool. Also we foresee many palms and several types of other flowering trees. There will be paths wandering through the garden and places to sit, rest, and contemplate. Also, very close to the highest point of the hill, we will be building a very large cistern or water tank for a backup water system. (I'll go into more detail about the building of water systems here in a later letter.) We're going to sink the tank, which is a concrete rectangle into the ground so that its top will be flush with the surface. We'll then use that for the floor of the *rancho* or *palapa*, which we'll build there so our guests and we can sit, relax, and look at the sea.

In our consultation, we also focused on the hill leading from the *plantel* down to the road on the north side, the one we've named *Avenida Miramar*. It is very important to plant this hill quickly in order to prevent erosion during the rainy season. In general, much of our planning for buildings and gardens takes the question of erosion into account very seriously.

Edgar is very good at what he does, and he has much experience in our area of the country. His sister calls him an artist. We've seen many gardens he has created and have found them extremely attractive. He's going to get back to us with a drawing and a proposal in about a week and then the planning will really be underway.

## People

Marvin the foreman. I've mentioned Marvin several times already. He just keeps growing on us. He and I are spending more time just chatting than we've done so far. Because he speaks no English, these bull sessions are also a great way for me to practice Spanish. And as I believe I once mentioned, he's very careful to speak slowly and to use circumlocutions when he sees that I'm not getting what he's saying.

Marvin wants to go to Virginia where his three brothers live and work. His idea is to stay there for about two years, save as much money as he can, and then return to Costa Rica perhaps to go into business for himself. He had planned to do this after the *casita* was finished. But Kiki, our contractor, asked him to stay to finish Casa Pacífica, too. Much to my relief, Marvin agreed to this. He clearly has the respect of all the men on the job. In addition, our architect has told us how he thinks that Marvin is a great foreman. Angelo, our U.S. neighbor and master electrician, who is doing our electrical contracting, also recently told Robin and me how impressed he is with Marvin.

The other day, when I was telling Marvin how pleased Robin and I were with the work on the *casita*, he replied that it was not bad, but Casa Pacífica will be much better. They'll go more slowly, take more care, and the finishes will be much more fine. Obviously, we were extremely pleased to hear this.

In general, the men are very happy that this is such a big project, one that will take at least a year in all. They know that for this year, they will have employment and won't have to worry about finding other work.

Frequently in our chats, Marvin tells Robin and me about what he calls "the Tico way." Usually these are funny stories about Tico life and culture. What makes them funny, and this is what Marvin focuses on, is the difference between the Tico way and the way of the *Norteamericanos*. Recently, for example, we told him that we were going to build a temporary area for the dogs, surrounded by a chain-link fence. As soon as the house is finished, we're then going to create something much more attractive on a spot below the main level of the *plantel*. Not only will it be more attractive, it's a much more pleasant spot for the dogs.

So Marvin asks us if we're really going to make it temporary. We were surprised at the question and answered that of course it was going to be temporary. It's not going to be very attractive, and we don't want it there any longer than possible. In response, Marvin said that this was not the Tico way. He elaborated that when the Tico builds something temporary, it stays there one year, then another, and eventually remains until it either falls down or the builder dies. They just discover more important things to do, or more interesting projects, or they just get bored, or they decide that the project just isn't worth any more effort. His telling was very funny. Of course he's not really talking about the Tico way, rather the way of certain people all over the world. Nevertheless, he spins a good tale.

Meli and family. We recently met a very young family from Tulsa—Meli; her husband Lars; and their two children, a little girl of four, Skye, and Forest, their eight-year-old son. I became acquainted with Meli through the CostaRicanLiving online group. She mentioned that she and her family were coming to Costa Rica for a few months. This is the second extended trip for them. This time, however, they were coming to our part of the country, whereas previously they visited other parts. She had several questions about things here, and I answered her and tried to help. During the course of our e-mail exchange, I gave her our phone number and asked her to give us a call if she got to Dominical.

The place they are going to stay is called *Cascada verde*. It's located near Uvita, about twenty kilometers south of Dominical. It's more or less a big old house divided into separate rooms with a communal kitchen and shared toilets and bathrooms. It's the brainchild of a young man from Germany named Patrick. From what Meli and Lars told us about it when we met them and from a brochure I read, it's a very New Agey kind of place.

There is a strong ecological orientation, as is the case with many places here where tourists stay for extended periods, also a strong emphasis on growing organic things. They are trying to become entirely self-sufficient and want to get energy from methane, build everything from what's available from the jungle, etc. Not unlike the how-to articles I used to read in the *Mother Earth News* back in the late sixties and early seventies. (Incidentally, now that we own a farm I've subscribed again to *Mother*.)

The deal that Meli and Lars worked out with Patrick was that in return for lodging, they'd do some computer and photography work for him. They did, however, have to pay for meals. The cost was high, five dollars per person, per meal. Meli and Lars are operating on an extremely tight budget, so this quickly became a burden.

They had the option of cooking their own food in the communal kitchen. But by the time we met them, they had been there a month and were clearly disillusioned. They said that the people who used the kitchen never cleaned up after themselves and the place was a mess. In addition, Lars was fed up with what he clearly felt was a great deal of hypocrisy, especially on the part of Patrick. He referred to *Cascada verde* as a rich German kid's toy. On the one hand, he said, "They want you to cut the soles from the bottom of your shoes and sit in the tree playing a pipe." On the other hand, Patrick has no hesitation flying wherever he wants to go, driving his car through the jungle, and using computers.

By now, Lars was saying that the only thing that kept it from being a complete loss was that they had beer there. Without a car, it is virtually impossible for them to do anything. Just to go to the beach for the day with the family meant an hour's walk. And the return route was uphill.

The day we met them, they had decided to come to Dominical by bus. We met them there, bought them lunch, and chatted a lot about their experiences at *Cascada verde*. They were hoping for a break. It seems that there's a large tourist development near where they're staying, some kind of hotel resort that is closed.

Supposedly, the owner, a foreigner who lives in Europe, was going to give a guy—whom they have met—some money to try to resuscitate the place. According to Meli and Lars, this guy in Europe was so rich that he didn't really care what happened to the place. So, Jim, the guy they met, was going to hire them to help him open the place again. As I said, they're very young, and their naivete was so apparent in their hope for this break that they seemed quite touching to Robin.

We finished talking and having lunch at about three. Their bus wasn't due until six. So Robin and I gave them a ride back to

*Cascada verde.* The exciting thing about the ride was that we saw a scarlet macaw flying low overhead. What a gorgeous sight! They've become very rare and are not often spotted.

A couple of days later, we had a message from Meli on our answering machine saying that they were moving on and that they'd perhaps be in touch later. I guess the deal with the hotel didn't work out.

Róger. I've mentioned Róger before. He's our "chopper." Almost anyone who lives near the jungle and can afford it employs a chopper to clear paths, to cut the high grasses on the sides of the roads, which obstruct driving, and to clear underbrush. Choppers are amazing: they work entirely with a machete and a stick. They use the stick to lift the grass or brush. This accomplishes two things: first, it means they don't have to bend so far, though they're almost always bent, and second, it means that they'll probably spot snakes that are hidden where they're cutting. A friend of ours tells about seeing a chopper working by the side of the road who swung his stick and threw a large snake clear across the road.

Róger is extremely dependable—he's always there when he says he will be. Right now he's working for us two days a week. He's not a boy. I think that he is probably in his mid-forties. He puts in a ten-hour day, seven and a half hours chopping and clearing—talk about backbreaking work—and two and a half hours walking to and from the job. That's right. He lives on top of a mountain. It takes him an hour to walk down the mountain to work, and an hour and a half to walk home. I just don't know how they do it.

The Americans. Speaking of people, I was reading a story the other day in *La Nación* about a tourist guide. Here's what one passage said (in my clumsy translation):

> [Sergio had] to admit that the simplicity and generosity of the North Americans was preferable to the close-fisted Germans, the disorder of the Spanish, or the loutishness of the Italians. The

Yankees allowed themselves to be led docilely. Everything seemed marvelous to them, and at the end, they always awarded his services with tasty tips. In addition, their questions were simple and they seemed satisfied with any explanation at all.

It's better than the Ugly American, isn't it?

## Facts and Prices

From the same article, a couple of interesting facts about Costa Rica:

> "[In] a territory smaller than that of Maine, Costa Rica shelters more species of birds than the entire United States, double the butterflies found on the African continent, and 6% of the world's biodiversity."

Finally, some more prices: Friday morning we bought the following from the fruit and vegetable truck that stops at our house twice a week: a cantaloupe, two mangos, twelve bananas, twelve tomatoes, two onions, a pint of strawberries, and a bunch of cilantro for six bucks.

Our best personal regards,
Martin and Robin

# CHAPTER TEN

## February 9, 2001

Dear family and friends:

### The Continuing Adventures of Batboy and Robin

The adventure continues. At midnight of the day, I sent the first installment of the adventures of the Fearless Foes of *Phyllostomidae* Family Flatulence. Robin woke me and said, "We have to go to San Isidro. Batboy's dying!" Batboy was clearly dehydrated, and we already knew that dehydration is probably the number one cause of death of bat pups in captivity. So we called Adrian, our vet in San Isidro, and told him we were coming. He lives right at the office so there wasn't much of a problem for him to see us, other than dragging himself out of bed at 1 AM, which would be our expected time of arrival.

Whenever possible we tend to avoid driving to and from San Isidro in the dark. The road, unlit, curvy, and mountainous, is often shrouded in dense fog as you approach the summit of the mountain before descending to the town. But the gods were watching over Gotham City that evening, and we made it in the usual forty-five minutes instead of the hour we had expected it to take. I was particularly glad that there was no fog as we were driving back from San Isidro at 2:30 AM, and I could barely keep my eyes open.

Adrian was waiting for us. The first thing was to give Batboy reglan by mouth and then a subcutaneous injection of Lactated

Ringer's solution, or, as we've learned, *Ringer con lactato de sodio,* which is basically an electrolytes and saline solution.

I won't go into all the details in the order they took place, but essentially, since I last wrote, Robin has been the mother of a sick infant, nursing him to health. There was a pneumonia scare, there was a problem with his eyes, and there were formulas that were not exactly right. The main problem is that, although Robin's intuitive understanding of what Batboy needed was almost always exactly on the money, there are so many complicated things about raising an infant bat in captivity that she couldn't possibly know them all.

For example, she had no problem at all giving Batboy the ongoing subcutaneous injections, but how often to give them was a shot in the dark. Eventually, she finally made contact with Susan Barnard, a woman who had written a book on raising bats in captivity. They began exchanging e-mails every day (and still are). At one point, after Robin told Susan how often she was giving Batboy injections, Susan wrote back, "You're drowning him!" You can imagine how that made Robin feel. Susan is a very busy woman and doesn't have time to write anything that's not directly to the point. Nevertheless, she's been investing a great deal of time helping Robin learn what needs to be done to ensure, to the greatest degree possible, that Batboy survives.

Then there was the feeding position. Robin was feeding Batboy from the syringe while holding him right side up. Susan wrote and said that he had to be upside down when fed, otherwise he'd contract pneumonia. Of course, Robin looked up the symptoms of pneumonia in bats and decided that Batboy had them all! As it turned out, fortunately, he had no pneumonia.

Sometimes the things Susan recommends are extremely difficult, if not impossible, to do or to find here in Costa Rica.

Thus, for a formula Robin was using Simulac, without added iron, as had been recommended. But then Susan said she should switch to Good Start formula. Robin and I ran all over San Isidro, and I ran all over San José as well, looking for Good Start. Not to be had here.

Then, Susan said that Batboy must have two special vitamins, usually used for birds, but recommended for bat pups with eye trouble, which Batboy seemed to be developing. So Robin called all over the country to probably a dozen pet supply and veterinarian supply houses, only to eventually learn from a vet she reached that these two vitamins are not imported into Costa Rica. So we ordered them online and they should have arrived in San José today. What kind of trouble they'll have getting through customs, we don't know. The very good news, however, is that Batboy's eye problem seems to have cleared up.

And the schedule! For over a week Robin was getting up every two hours through the night to feed Batboy and to give him water. Now, his feedings are not quite so close together, but she still gets up several times a night to either give him water or to make sure that the heating pad that lines his little improvised cage is at the right temperature.

Susan told Robin that she should carry Batboy inside her shirt. So Robin attaches a bandana with safety pins to the inside of her T-shirt and then lets Batboy hang on the bandana, protected by the T-shirt in front of him. He seems very, very happy there.

The fantastic news is that Batboy is now in great shape! Yesterday, February 8, 2001, Batboy had his birthday—two weeks old. His weight, twenty grams, seems to be just right. He is still slightly dehydrated, but not to any life-threatening degree. The reason he's still dehydrated at all is because of his diet, which can never be duplicated to the extent that it is exactly what he would have were he being raised by his mother. But between Robin and Susan, everything that can be done is being done. As he gets weaned from the formula and goes totally to fruit (remember, he's a fruit bat), that should help greatly. He ate his first piece of papaya today along with the formula.

Batboy has been stretching his wings for quite a while now, but yesterday, Robin says that he flapped them for the first time. According to what Robin has been reading, they don't usually do this until they're three weeks old. Thus, it appears we have an exceptional bat here. I'll try to enroll him in the Costa Rican

School for Exceptional Bat Pups, though I understand there's a long waiting list.

In the meantime, we have to get a flying cage ready for him. He'll probably need it in about a week. Robin and I just returned from the building site where we had a conference with Marvin who is going to build the cage for him. This is not just some box, of course, and also not a standard bat house like the various kinds people put in their gardens. This is a real home in which a captive bat pup will be raised and where he will live for a while and learn to fly. The specs for the house are complicated and include a little house within a house, suspended at the top of the cage and open from the bottom, the sides of which have to be grooved. Anyway, Marvin is going to build it for us.

Marvin is a great guy and, as I mentioned, likes to joke. He told Robin that frequently, while building houses, bats nest in them—usually in the rafters—and make a terrible mess. In fact, before the windows were up in our *casita*, some bats got in there. So eventually, Marvin and the guys have to get the bats out. He couldn't resist telling her that the best method they found for removing the bats involved a vacuum cleaner. And did he howl when he saw the expression on Robin's face and saw her protectively cup her hand over her upper chest where Batboy was hanging between his bandana and her T-shirt!

Batboy has really changed our life—not absolutely for the better, either. When I say that it's exactly as though we had an infant, I am not exaggerating. It really is. We have to plan our outings—business, pleasure, shopping, whatever, around Batboy's feeding schedule. And that really can cramp our plans. Then there's the frequent anxiety that Robin has had about Batboy's health, though that is letting up somewhat and, of course, the sleep deprivation that Robin has experienced over the last two weeks. But now, as the time between feedings is extended, he's at the point where he'll sleep through the night. Wow, just read that last sentence, and it brought back the joy from when my children slept through the entire night the first times. See what I mean about "just like having a baby"?

## Never a Dull Moment Department

Two paragraphs ago, Robin came over to me while I was typing and said, "There's a tree on fire next door!" And sure enough, right next to the wall that divides our property from the neighbors, a tall palm tree was burning. We weren't very surprised because our neighbors, a rather poor Tico family in a little house, always burn their trash. You see that frequently here because many families can't afford to pay for garbage and trash pickup. So I dashed over to the neighbors and told them about the tree on fire. The woman of the house cheerfully answered that this was because everything was so dry. I was a little nonplussed at that rather simple and obvious explanation, so I explained (eventually) that I was worried about the fire spreading. She answered pleasantly in a torrent of words, the only ones of which I got were that I shouldn't worry. Everything was OK. She also told me that they have a great deal of trash to burn and would like to do it when Robin and I aren't there and did I know when we'd be going out. I had to tell her that I didn't. These folks moved in about a month ago and burn their trash about every two days, mostly, it seems, when the wind is blowing toward our house and we have laundry hanging on the line. Not much fun, but we should be in the *casita* in about a week. We'll hold out that long.

### Pura vida

The national slogan of Costa Rica seems to be *Pura Vida*, which I thought meant "pure life." However, now after some research I've discovered that it's better translated as something like "It's a perfect life" or "It's a beautiful life." Anyway, you see it on all the tourist publicity, of course. And I noticed that many of the North Americans who live here, especially in their e-mails to the CostaRicanLiving list, tended to use it a lot. My sense was that the phrase was just something that was used for promotion and picked up by the foreigners. So I avoided using it.

But as it turns out, we quickly learned that the Costa Ricans really do use this phrase all the time. It's a very standard greeting. When I go up to the site, for example, most of they guys just say *pura vida* when I wave to them, usually accompanied by a thumbs-up sign. It's also frequently used in answer to the question: *¿Cómo le va?* or *¿Cómo está?* (How are you?) Robin and I love it and now use it all the time.

## Sexism in Costa Rica Revisited

In a previous letter I talked about the sexism that was so apparent here when one read the want ads. And I guess one expects it in a macho Latin country. But the other side of the coin is that there are a great number of women representatives to the general assembly, and it seems women also fill some of the higher governmental positions.

For example, there's Elizabeth Odio, who is the minister of the Environment and Energy; Mónica Nágel, minister of Justice; Lineth Saborío, director of the OIJ, which is the National Police Criminal Investigation Division. There is also a position here on the national level called the *Defensor*, or in this case, *Defensora de los Habitantes,* the exact equivalent of which in the U.S. or European governments I'm not sure of. At first I thought it was the Ombudsman's Office, but now I don't think so. It's also not the Home Office. Anyway, a woman occupies this position, too: Sandra Pisk. Her name is figuring in the papers every day now. It seems that she has made some very strong charges of corruption and mismanagement against the *Caja* or the CCSS—*Caja Costarricense de Seguro Social.* The *Caja* is a huge part of the government and handles all social security and public health functions of the nation. It has a vast budget and a very entrenched bureaucracy, which is already up in arms in a big way. I think if the guys in the *Caja* spoke Yiddish, they'd be saying, "Sandra has a really big 'pisk' and we need to shut it!" (Pisk is "mouth" in Yiddish.)

## A Dilemma

In my last letter, I told you why Robin and I had decided to name the house we're building Casa Pacífica. Now, however, I'm in a bit of a quandary.

I've been able to get to my books at last because all our stuff is finally here now that the *bodega* is finished. The first ones I grabbed were *Casa California, Mexican Design,* and *Mexican Tile.* These are books I'm using for ideas in creating the finishes for the big house.

*Casa California* is a wonderful book that focuses on the Spanish Revival houses built, mostly in Southern California, in the 1920s and 1930s. So I'm going through it and I come across a house built in the 1920s, the name of which is Casa Pacífica. Well, that's no big deal, of course. But then as I'm reading about the house, which is one of the most beautiful in the book, I read that in the 1960s Richard Nixon bought the house. It served as the Western White House during his tenure as president.

Well, with sincere apologies to my many Republican friends who read my letters, I've developed great doubts as to whether I can name my house the same thing as that of a house that Richard Nixon bought and lived in. That's what happens when you're a "Yellow Dog Democrat." (A "Yellow Dog Democrat" is someone who is such a die-hard member of the Democratic Party that he or she would vote for the Democratic candidate even if it were just a yellow dog.)

We haven't made our final decision yet, but in the meantime, I'm thinking of alternatives. The one I like most so far is *Casa de los Sueños Pacíficos* (or just *Sueños Pacíficos*—Pacific Dreams).

## *Casita* Update

The day is drawing close. We should be able to move into the *casita* a week from today! The progress since a week ago today (which was Friday, 2 February) has been fantastic. Almost all the tiles are on the floors, counters, and walls, also on the outside patio and walkways. We're simply crazy about the way it has turned out. Some of it contains designs that we created with help from Omar the Tile Maker—more about him some other time, and Marvin, who has a real creative streak. The ceilings, which are beautiful wood planks and beams, received coats of marine shellac and are even more stunning than before. The fixtures—plumbing and lighting—will go in early next week, and then the walls will be painted. The last step is to bring up and put in the appliances and we'll be ready. The whole process has taken just under three months!

## Dangers of Living in Costa Rica

In fact, there are lots of dangers, as there are almost anywhere. But I realized the other day that after living here only a little over three months, Robin and I personally know three people who rolled their cars. That seems like a lot. But it's easy to understand after you've driven here for a while.

## The Census

A couple of quick notes about the results of the 2000 census in Costa Rica, which were just announced. The population has reached 3.8 million and has grown almost 3 percent per year since the last census in 1984. The average number of children per mother is 2.6. The province of Limón, on the Caribbean Coast, has had the biggest increase in population, although the paper notes that this is most likely because many of the thousands of illegal Nicaraguan immigrants tend to go there.

Our province, Puntarenas, has grown by 34.59 percent; the population of our district, San Isidro de El General, is 41,711 and is among the country's six largest; and our Canton, Aguirre, has a population of only 20,180.

The division between sexes is almost exactly equal: 1,910,683 women and 1,913,910 men.

In the last fifteen years the number of households has almost doubled from 500,788 to 937,210, while the average number of inhabitants per household has dropped from 4.8 to 4.1

There are eight million tales in the *Naked Jungle;* this has been only one of them (for those folks who were watching TV in the '50s and maybe early '60s).

Our very best personal regards,
Martin and Robin

# CHAPTER ELEVEN

## February 23, 2001

Hi, family and friends:

It's been longer than usual since the last time I sent everyone an update on our Costa Rican adventure. And, in fact, this one has been done for more than two weeks, and it has taken me that long to edit it and send it. That means that a lot has taken place since I wrote this, so I'm planning on sending a follow-up to this very shortly.

### The Continuing Saga of Batboy

Yesterday, February 22, Batboy was four weeks old. I'm happy to report that he is truly thriving. It's also somewhat unsettling to report that I'm growing fonder and fonder of the little thing myself. Speaking of little, he's about four inches long now and weighs about an ounce. His growth and weight seem to be right on target.

He's down to eating only four times a day now, twice fruit alone, and twice formula and fruit. He's being gradually weaned successfully. We did have a little scare when his joints began to look a bit swollen. Susan wrote that this was because he didn't have the vitamins we ordered from the States. But they've finally arrived and he's getting them regularly.

It's really fun to watch him eat his little pieces of fruit and vegetables. Robin feeds him banana, papaya, strawberries, apples, mango, dates, cilantro and other greens, and his all-time favorite, avocado. Susan wrote that he shouldn't eat avocado because it will make him too fat. But we couldn't cut him off altogether.

What to me is the most interesting thing of all is the way that Batboy and Robin have bonded so closely. It's so obvious how much she loves him. She carries him with her almost all the time we're in the house. He doesn't have to stay under her shirt anymore, so he hangs from her shoulder, with his little feet in the threads of her shirt. She talks to him—both people talk and baby talk—croons to him, pets him, kisses him. And he is extremely responsive.

He now has a real flying cage. It's about four feet long and two feet deep and two feet high. (Man, is this going to cramp our little *casita*.) It's a frame box with the tops, sides, and bottom made of metal hardware cloth of one-fourth-inch mesh.

It also has a small box suspended from the top that is closed on all sides except the bottom. Its insides are grooved at one-fourth-inch intervals. He can go into his bat cave and hang when he needs privacy or more darkness. But whenever Robin opens the cage now, he scrambles across the mesh as quickly as he can to get into her hand. He knows, of course, that she is either going to feed him, play with him, carry him around, or all three.

However, one day recently, Batboy started to show some independence. For a while he wouldn't come to Robin's hand. It was a shock for her, and she showed clear signs of empty bat-cave syndrome. Seriously, Robin was experiencing some unpleasant emotions, perhaps even a feeling of being rejected. One has to remember that for the past four weeks, her life has revolved almost exclusively around first, saving his life, and then around his care.

According to Susan, the bat expert, this closeness with Robin is very good for Batboy. At about this age he would be learning to socialize. But, of course, he has no roostmates, so Robin serves as both mother and roostmate in the process of his socialization.

Right now the big challenge is to get him to eat his fruit and drink his water from the cups that are in his cage. He much prefers to have Robin hand him the pieces. When Robin wrote Susan about this, she replied that he's just spoiled! I really got a kick out of that. We have a spoiled bat brat. But most of us spoil our children, so why should Batboy be any different?

He should start flying any day now. That's the reason for the large cage. First he spread his wings, which he continues to do. Now he's engaged in static flying—that is, he is actually flapping his wings at least once a day. One day very soon, he'll do that and start to fly. That ought to be a great feeling for him. And that's also why we've ordered a bird net. He's sure to get out of the cage someday, and we'll need to catch him.

And speaking of that, some of you have written and asked what he's going to do for a companion (female) and when he'll be able to be released. Regarding the companion, we're raising Batboy for the priesthood, and thus he will spend his life celibate. As far as flying away, it looks like he's going to be with us for as long as he lives (usually a fruit bat lives about ten years in captivity). He just won't ever be able to survive alone in nature. He spent no time with his natural mother and, thus, learned nothing about being a bat. And his adoptive mother is unable to teach him the things he needs to know to survive in the real world. The upside is that at least I won't have to pay to send him to college.

One more tidbit. Probably everyone who's reading this has at least once spilled coffee or water or soda or some liquid on his or her keyboard. The other day, while Robin was typing on her laptop with Batboy perched on her shoulder, he simply went and peed on the keyboard. A unique experience so far as my knowledge of the annals of computing is concerned.

## The Ministry Everyone Loves to Hate

MOPT (*Ministerio de Obras Publicas y Transportes*), the Ministry of Public Works and Transportation, is the butt of many jokes and a lot of hostility here in Costa Rica. Not only do people blame MOPT for the poor condition of so many roads, but MOPT is also the equivalent of the highway patrol. So I'm sure that many thousands of people throughout the country got a big charge from reading an article in the paper about MOPT being fined twenty-five million *colones* by the Ministry of Environment and Energy. (For those of you who want to know how many dollars that is, the current exchange rate is 320 *colones* per U.S. dollar so it's $78,125.)

It seems that MOPT took it upon itself to build a road which entailed cutting down over two hundred trees. In order to do this, they would have had to have permission from the Ministry of Environment and Energy. But some lower-level MOPT official gave the project the go-ahead without the proper processes, and someone who lives on land adjacent to the road turned them in.

The interesting thing about the fine is the way it was computed. First the value of the trees was estimated to be over a million *colones*. Then that figure was multiplied by twenty, which is the number of years it will take the trees to reach the same maturity as those which were felled. Rather a neat way to assess a fine.

MOPT appealed the judgment, of course, but the appeal was rejected!

## The Roads Are a Jungle Out There

I know that I've mentioned at least a couple of times how dangerous the roads are here. Every week, it seems, dozens of people die or are severely injured. From the first of January to the twentieth of February, 2001, more than fifty people had already died on the country's roads.

Here's a good example of how some of the more bizarre deaths occur. Two weeks ago my friend Dave and I went to San José on a shopping trip. (Robin didn't go because she had to take care of Batboy. In fact, she doesn't get around much at all anymore.) On the way back, we were traveling on one of the better roads in Costa Rica—we went on another route rather than the Pan-American Highway, which is the way I usually go. The road was well paved, wide, and straight. We were doing about sixty miles per hour, the fastest I've ever been able to drive safely here.

A few hundred yards away, we saw some guys standing on the left side of the road—not at all unusual; there are always people on foot on the roads. When we were about one hundred yards away, one of the guys started slowly to wave his arm at us; in fact, it looked as though he were greeting us. At that moment, a huge tree began to fall from the left side of the road directly across our path! It hit the road just as we were about thirty feet away. Had the tree been about ten feet taller or the road a bit narrower, we would have plowed right into it. As it happened though, I was able to swerve to the right and miss it. But what a shot of adrenaline!

It seems that this was a group of workmen out cutting down trees. There was no barrier on the road, no "men working" signs, nothing at all other than this fellow slowly waving his arm at us. I think that driving the roads of Costa Rica needs to be included as an event in one of the new extreme sports meets.

## Errata

When writing about women in high office, I spoke about the *Defensora de los Habitantes*. I said that I wasn't sure of the translation, but it wasn't ombudswoman. As it turns out, ombudswoman is exactly what this office is.

## The Arrival of Batgirl or You Won't Believe This

I began writing this letter on February 23. Today is February 28, 2001. Yesterday, Robin was out on the hammock in the garden with her laptop, leisurely reading her e-mail (yes, it's a tough life here, but we can take it). Suddenly she hears a squeaking and looks down. Next to the hammock, on the ground, our puppy, Bug, has a (it's so hard to write this) baby bat in her mouth, playing with it. With a start, Robin jumps up and gets the bat away from Bug. She is petrified that Batboy somehow got out of his cage and into Bug's mouth. She looks closely at the bat and is sure that it's not Batboy. Nevertheless, she runs into the house and checks. There's Batboy, nice and secure, calmly hanging from the roof of his cage!

Who, then, is this? A quick check shows that it's a girl. Upon more inspection, she seems to be just about Batboy's age, judging from size and development. However, she is very thin and looks dehydrated. She also has a hole in her wing, evidently the most common injury for bats that wind up in rehabilitation. But she also looks different from Batboy in other respects. Her face is longer and her bones seem longer, too.

So Robin brought her in and began the process of nursing her back to health. We have her in Batboy's old cage, the one he used before he moved into the new bigger one. She is, of course, much farther along than Batboy was, who was one day old when found. She seems to be half-weaned already and is eating both formula and fruit. Because of her dehydration, Robin has to give her injections, as she did to Batboy.

Who would ever have thought that all the hard-earned knowledge Robin has gained over the past five weeks would have come in handy again so very soon? But there is very good news! Susan says that Batgirl (what else) has had enough time with her mother so that she can be successfully released back into nature. We're waiting to hear from Susan about when and how. We hope soon and easily.

## A Unique Experience in Mexico

A week ago I had to go to Mexico City to a meeting for my company. I really love to go to Mexico; it's one of my very favorite places. As it turned out, because of my current visa, I had to stay out of Costa Rica for seventy-two hours after leaving before being able to return. When Benjamín Beja, our Latin American regional manager, heard this, he invited me to spend the weekend with him, his sister Claudia, who also works for GlobalEnglish, and his wife at a *hacienda*, which is about an hour or so from Mexico City, and which has been in his wife's family since about 1930 when her grandfather bought it,

The *hacienda*, however, is extremely old, the first part, which is still standing and occupied, was built in 1710.

Although this is not an original line, I have to say that I've never been in a place like this without first paying admission. It is truly a magnificent museum; however, it's a museum that still functions as a house and one in which people still live, and thus, the sense of ongoing history is much greater than any I've ever experienced in a museum.

The name of the *hacienda* is Tecajete, and it is located right outside of a small town called Zempoala. Zempoala is a very interesting little town, which looks as though it could have been the place where *El Mariachi* or *Desperado* was filmed. It also has a church that was built in 1517.

Tecajete was once the home of a Mexican president for a few years. I'm not going to try to describe it in any detail at all, because it's just beyond me. I did take dozens of pictures, however, so that I can share the experience with Robin and my friends.

The *hacienda* is very large, both the house and attached buildings, and the land on which it stands. Though it doesn't have nearly as much land as it once did, which became the case with virtually all the *haciendas* after the agrarian reforms.

It's surrounded by walls with towers, has a huge entry courtyard, then a smaller one that is in the center of the *hacienda* proper. As is traditional, the inner courtyard is square, surrounded by corridors—what we call verandas—on all four sides. The doors on the verandas lead into bedrooms, the living room, the kitchen, dining rooms, etc.

But one of the amazing things about this place is that everywhere you look there is an astounding antique something or other. How far back the oldest things go, I don't know, but I suspect that the objects—furniture, paintings, art objects, dishes, trunks, lamps, etc., stretch from the eighteenth through the twentieth centuries.

Of special interest to me, at a time when I'm getting deeply into the design of our new house's finishes, were the amazing border paintings on the walls, the sensational tile work, the plantings, the ceramics, the cabinets and shelving, and so on. All the details that turn what is essentially a bunch of rooms built around a square courtyard into a magnificent, comfortable, aesthetically exciting dwelling.

One thing that sets Tecajete apart from a museum is the fact that it is still occupied and used. The business of the *hacienda*, the making and distribution of *pulque*, an alcoholic drink made from a plant, continued until just two years ago when prices fell so low that production costs could not be recouped.

Tecajete is currently occupied by a family member, Tío Jaime, at fifty-eight the youngest of the six children who inherited the *hacienda*. Along with Jaime, there are about forty other people living there, all from a family descended from old retainers. A few of them are still employed by the family; the others have jobs elsewhere but live on the *hacienda* free of charge. The oldest worker, and I'm afraid I never learned his name, is in his nineties, the father of eighteen children with his wife, and according to legend, the father of most of the children in the town who were born during his fertile years.

He insists on working, and mostly he sits in the outer courtyard dozing in the sun, and opening the gate and greeting arrivals in their cars. Particularly of note was the way he always doffs his hat whenever approaching a family member or guest. Some old ingrained habits will never die, of course.

Almost every weekend, family members and friends come to the *hacienda* to spend the weekend or to stay for several days. While we were there, about twenty guests had arrived for a four-day visit. It was delightful meeting these people, all of whom were friendly, gracious, and welcoming. Both Claudia and I were there for the first time and, thus, were meeting everyone for the first time.

For me, personally, I felt strongly the sense that I was at a Russian or English country estate in the eighteenth or nineteenth century, where guests were all invited for a country weekend, virtually every weekend. The activities, horseback riding (there are extensive stables at the *hacienda* with many horses), walking, playing board games, much eating and drinking—both formally in the huge dining room and informally outside in the grassy center of the courtyard—exploring, and having long lazy conversations were exactly as I had imagined them on such an estate from my extensive reading of Russian and English literature. And the food! When it comes to Mexican food, some of you might only be familiar with Tex-Mex. But most of you probably know that Mexico has a truly sophisticated and original native cuisine with outstanding regional specialties. I had about four meals at the *hacienda*, each one more interesting and exciting than the previous one. These meals were among the best I've ever had in Mexico, and that is saying a mouthful.

Knowing that this time at Tecajete was no novelty and that people had been doing just what we were doing in this very place for centuries gave me a sense of being part of a reenactment of some historical tableau, perhaps something like being one of the actors at Jamestown, except this was not acting. This was life continuing in many respects the way it had been going on for centuries.

There's much more that I could tell about this visit, but I'll stop with just two more related things. First, Tecajete is very close to the great pyramids at Teotioacan. Not too long ago, Tío Jaime discovered a small pyramid on the *hacienda's* land. It still remains covered awaiting the state's archeologists to work it. Nearby, however, is an open, stone-lined pit. It seems that there was an Aztec ritual that occurred every fifty-something years in which they would break all their pottery in such a pit and then remake it from scratch. Walking the land around the buried pyramid and the hole, one sees pottery shards right on the ground that are at the very least eight hundred years old. Benjamín told me that knives and arrows and spear tips are also easily to be found.

The next thing is that, as most of you know, I'm sure, the Aztecs made many things of obsidian. The obsidian mine that supplied the settlement at Teotioacan is very close to the *hacienda*. One time some of the family members went to the mine with a small truck and came back with hundreds of pieces of obsidian which were not of the highest quality and which the mine owners just throw away. They give it away gladly to people, so that they don't have to dispose of it. Jaime gave me a beautiful piece, which I brought back with me. The thing about the mine, though, is that it has probably been in operation for a thousand years and is still a working site.

This was a unique experience for me. Jaime invited me to stop at the *hacienda* with Robin any time we were in Mexico City. This is something we will be sure to do, especially because we are planning a couple of buying trips to Mexico for the house in the near future.

## The *Casita*

The *casita* is virtually finished. Of course we were supposed to move in on February 15 and today is February 28, but we'll be in there by the end of the weekend at the latest. I guess missing by two weeks isn't so bad. Were it not for Omar the Tile Maker, or Omar the Cemetery Man (his tile shop is next to the cemetery in San Isidro), we would have been in on time. But he's one of those guys who promises the moon and delivers a piece of moldy cheese. We bought not only our tiles from him but also the bathroom fixtures and all our faucets. These came in drips and drabs (pun intended). We will not be using him for Casa Pacífica. The *casita* is absolutely lovely. It's everything we'd hoped it would be. Its design is traditional, clean, and simple. The tile work and the colors make it extremely comfortable and cool.

## Casa Pacífica

I guess that in spite of Nixon, we're going to stick with this name for the big house. We both love it. Work has started on the house already. All the foundation trenches were finished today. Now all the rebar is being put together, and I imagine they'll begin pouring the foundations next week.

Robin and I will be much more involved with the building of Casa Pacífica than we were with the *casita*. There are hundreds of details to attend to: endless design decisions to be made; finishes to be selected; doors, windows, cabinets, hardware, etc., to be either ordered from suppliers or, in many cases, created by local craftsmen and artisans. It's extremely exciting. Often it's even hard to sleep, going over so many details while in bed, trying not to forget anything, making notes in the middle of the night of some thought that popped into your mind and woke you up.

While the house is being built, work will be starting Monday on the first part of creating the huge hill garden I've mentioned before. Edgar presented his proposal to Robin and me today for the first phase of the garden. This deals primarily with the shaping of the hill, the paths—major and minor—steps, landings, rest areas, etc. It should take about two weeks to complete this part of the project. After that, we will begin to select the garden's trees and plants and work on their placement. Edgar has already done a preliminary plan for this, too. However, we will have a detailed presentation after the first phase is completed.

We also should have our decision made by the end of next week concerning the contractor for our pool as well as its shape and placement. We're waiting on the results of a soil test that we had an engineering firm recently do.

What an exciting time this is!

## Angelo's Infection

A cautionary tale for us North Americans. I've mentioned our neighbor Angelo before. I believe that I told you he's a master electrician and did the work on the *casita* and will do the work for Casa Pacífica.

A couple of weeks ago, while working on our job and on a job in Quepos, Angelo cut himself a few times. As he tells it, on the job back in the States, he just "dresses" his injuries with a napkin and some electrical tape.

So, needless to say, he didn't pay much attention to the cuts he got on the job here. This was a tremendous mistake. There are viruses and bacteria here that we North Americans have never in our lives encountered. Many are airborne. Our immune system is not capable of dealing with these bugs at all.

In a short while, it became obvious that some of these cuts were getting infected. In particular, a wound on his knee was beginning to look quite nasty. After trying to treat it a bit himself, he eventually, at the urging of friends, went into San Isidro to a pharmacy. Many pharmacies here have licensed doctors available to make examinations and prescribe treatment. In fact, at one time Robin had a very bad viral infection of some sort, what the Ticos call "grippe," the same thing we called the grip when I was a kid and which we call the flu now. We took her to the doctor at the San Martín pharmacy in San Isidro where she got a shot and some medicine and was better in two days.

Well Angelo got about four shots at the pharmacy and a lot of medicine. But evidently he had waited much too long, for the infection just got worse and worse and began running down his leg. At that point, he and his wife took off for the *Clínica Bíblica* in San José. He got there just in time. He already had blood poisoning, the danger of blood clots, and several other complications. He had to stay at the hospital for four days before he was out of danger of either dying or losing his leg.

I don't imagine that any of us North Americans here in Lagunas are going to put off treating a wound ever after seeing what Angelo went through. I assume that we'll eventually build up immunity to some of these new bugs—if we live long enough.

By the way, now with Batgirl boarding with us for a (short, I hope) time, I guess I can't speak of the Dynamic Duo anymore. I'll have to refer to the Intrepid Trio.

All our best wishes,
Martin and Robin

# CHAPTER TWELVE

## March 14, 2001

Hello, all:

Here's the follow-up I promised in the last letter to bring you more up to date. Today is March 14.

### The *Casita* and Ongoing Construction

As of March 3, we've been living in the *casita*. Hooray! It's truly a lovely little place with great views. It's so much cooler than down on the flatlands where we were living. And when construction is not going on, it's paradisiacally tranquil. All you hear is the buzzing of the insects, the tinkling of the wind chimes, the rustling of the breeze, and the sounds of the birds. And wherever you look, there is either a view of the mountains and jungle valleys or of the Pacific.

As I type this, I'm sitting on our covered porch, looking out at the mountains across the valley in front of me—and also being deafened by the sound of a huge bulldozer and a backhoe working not more than a hundred yards from the porch!

In addition to living in our beautiful *casita* in the mountains, we're also living on a huge construction site. There are eighteen men working on the house proper, another six or so working in the hill garden, and the bulldozer and backhoe working to shape our lower hill to get it ready for planting and avoiding erosion.

Our day usually starts when the men come out of the *bodega* where they sleep and then begin working at shortly after 5 AM. I'm almost always awake by then and Robin manages to sleep—

or at least rest in bed—a little longer. Of course it's light out by a little after 5, so they get an early start. They work through the day until about 5:30 PM. They barely rest at all: one break in the morning, lunch, and another break in the afternoon. I've gone into detail before about how hard they work, and I can say that nothing has changed.

The foundations are already completely poured; the tons of reinforcing rebar are already in place; and as of a couple of days ago, the first three courses of block were in place. Now there's much more. According to Kiki, by the end of the week all the walls for the first floor will be in place. It's just amazing, especially when one considers that the walls also include those of a huge winding staircase, the most dramatic architectural detail in the house.

Of course when the block for the walls is all in place, the process slows down quite a bit while the many coats of *repello* (stucco) are being applied. The goal is to have all the walls and the roof in place by the beginning of the rainy season—May—so that work can go on uninterrupted inside under cover.

## The Hill Garden

Meanwhile, the hill garden is taking shape. It will be a true highlight of our location. I have already given you an idea of its size. Now that huge hill is filled with steps (dug in, not finished off yet), long winding paths, places to sit and rest, many special places for contemplating the views, etc. All of this is just roughed in at this time. They'll continue to work on the shaping for the next week. At that point, we'll make final the plans for the planting, and work will start immediately on that.

## From the Annals of Cultural Differences

Here's a story, which was related to Robin and me a couple of days ago by our friends Dave and Liz. It seems that in a local bar two men—whom we all know—were into their cups. There is a strong animosity on the part of man A toward man B. Eventually, man A accosted man B. The altercation was soon broken up. However, it turns out that man A goes around armed—a pistol in his fanny pack. Man B thought he ought to report what happened to the police and that they should talk to man A before he did something rash.

There are several police organizations in Costa Rica. There's the border police—the most military of them all in this country without armed forces. Then there's MOPT, about which I wrote in my last letter, which acts as the highway patrol. There is also the OIJ—the criminal investigation organization. Then there's the regular police, *Fuerza Pública*, and finally, the rural police force.

In almost every small town there's a tiny police station, usually manned by one or two policemen of the rural police. And this is the case in Dominical, where the altercation occurred. And this is the place man B went to file his report.

It seems as though the rural police rarely have cars. They cover their beats on bicycles. For those of you who are aficionados of cozy period English mysteries of the Miss Marple type, as am I, you'll be familiar with the local constable in the villages going about on his bicycle—I don't know if they still do this or not in England, but this is the first time I've been anywhere that happens.

At any rate, since man A lives up the mountain, the rural police weren't going to ride their bikes up at night. However, in order to strike while the iron was hot, all man B had to do was to pay their way up there and back by taxi. Which he did. As far as the outcome, I haven't heard yet. Rather a novel and creative way to get some help.

## More about Batboy and Audrey

Who, you might ask, is Audrey? In the last letter I told you about the arrival of Batgirl. But as it turned out, the next day Robin decided that Batgirl had such beautiful big eyes that she wanted to call her Audrey after Audrey Hepburn.

I expressed my joy in the last letter that Audrey would be able to return to nature after being nursed to health again. Alas, I spoke too soon. It seems that Susan, the bat expert, assumed that

Audrey could already fly. In fact she can't. In addition to that, Audrey wasn't as old as Robin had thought. She's probably two or three weeks younger than Batboy, which means—as you've already guessed—that Audrey is here for the duration as well because she, too, will not be able to survive in nature.

At this point Audrey and Batboy are living together in the big new cage. However, I have not forgotten my pledge to keep Batboy celibate, and as soon as he pubes, the little bugger is going to be castrated by our friendly vet. There will be no Batbaby!

Robin's work with the bats is not quite so intensive anymore. Batboy is totally weaned and Audrey is almost there. That means, other than spending quality time with them to assist their process of socialization, mostly Robin's work consists of preparing cut-up, fresh fruit each morning and then giving them a coop-cup of it three times a day.

## Batboy Flies!

Yep, Batboy is flying. It's been really funny. About a week ago, in the evening, we heard *flap, flap, flap, plop!* We rushed to the cage, and there he was, spread-winged and flat on the cage's floor. Then he scrambled up the side of the cage, rushed around to get in the proper position, and *flap, flap, flap, plop!* again. He had managed to fly about two feet before losing altitude and crash landing. He tried once more, and then gave it up, exhausted, and went to sleep.

Thereafter, every evening, between about 8 and 9 PM it's been the Batboy Show. For a while the results were the same as the first night. But after a few days, he made it from one side of the cage to the other, about four feet, without mishap. After that, he spent more and more of his evening hours soaring around his cage with an occasional pause for sustenance—a piece of papaya or mango—then back to the flight line. Audrey seems to pay no attention to him at all, but Robin's convinced that he's showing off for her.

Last night, however, he had a big adventure. Around the usual flight time, Robin closed the door to the room Batboy and

Audrey live in then opened the cage and reached in for Batboy. He jumped right into her hand and then, as soon as her hand was clear of the cage door, he took off! What a time he had. Of course two times he flew into the room door and went tumbling to the ground, but not at all any worse for wear. Eventually Robin got him in her hand again, and he settled down for the evening. I assume that Robin will let him fly around the room a bit every evening.

It seems the bats get along rather well together in the cage. The only problem is that Audrey has taken to hanging with her head in the food bowl while sleeping, and Batboy has to get her out of the way frequently so he can eat. He usually does this with squawks of indignation and nudges. More often than not, however, Audrey snuggles up right next to Batboy, and they seem to sleep contentedly, nestled together.

## The Rest of the Story

Upon rereading much of what I've written in these many letters, I realize that I've never—other than in the letter about our first day here—spoken much at all about daily trials and tribulations. It truly is as wonderful here as my writing has implied; however, there are many frustrations, sometimes daily, about which I ought to write, so that you get a fuller picture about what daily life here is like.

As far as the most current trials and tribulations are concerned, I thought I'd include the following paragraph from an e-mail that Robin just sent to her mother and sister.

"The last week has been an interesting experience to say the least. The *casita* has no curtains, no towel rods in the bathroom, no rack to hang clothes in the closet, the screen door won't stay closed, and the front door knob has stuck twice so that we were locked in the house. I didn't really have any idea what it would be like to live on a construction site. Right now there are seventeen guys building the house, plus the contractor and their cook, six guys working on the hill garden, two guys with bulldozers terracing another hill, and the electrician and his assistant are working. The noise is constant. They have two or three cement mixers going from about 7 AM to sunset. About three or four times each day, huge dump trucks drive up with loads of gravel, sand, and other stuff. Everything is dirty and dusty. We don't have a fenced area yet for the dogs, so it's a challenge to keep an eye on them. They wander around in the construction, where I worry they'll hurt themselves; they eat the chicken bones that the workers throw on the ground; they bark at everyone who comes up the road; they wander off into the jungle with the neighbor dogs. Of course, since we don't have any curtains yet, the workers can see right into the house, so there's no place to go to hide. The bathroom was private, but this morning I noticed that two of the guys working up on the hill garden could look right down into the shower. I decided not to take one. That was OK because the water wasn't working anyway. At least the electricity has only gone out once. We've been trying to get the *casita* fixed up and find a place for everything. Meanwhile, since they've finished pouring the foundation of the house, we're meeting with the builder daily to go over details of the construction."

So that's the way it is right now. Two points that Robin mentions, the electricity and water deserve a bit more amplification.

First the electricity. Electricity and communications, as I've mentioned, are all the domain of a government monopoly known as ICE, *Instituto Costarricense de Electricidad*. Part of ICE is RACSA, the *only* ISP allowed in the country. There is no competition in any area of telecommunications, and as a result, Internet access is very limited in terms of reliability and speed; people wait years for telephones in some outlying areas and frequently never have any. As far as cell phones are concerned—that is, the lines, not the physical phones—there is presently a waiting list of over 210,000 people. And the list is that "small" because at the current rate of delivery—about eighteen thousand per month—it will be more than a year at the least before you might get a cell phone account, so many people aren't even putting in an application.

Currently there is much acrimonious debate going on about ICE's plan to acquire four hundred thousand new lines. The three providers they're using, Alcatel, Lucent, and Ericsson, are publishing full-page "public information" ads in the national papers about how one or the other is playing unfair and how the company placing that specific ad is operating totally within the law, regardless of what the other competitors are saying. And they are threatening one another with lawsuits in their competitive fervor. Whether or not these lines, which were supposed to be acquired months ago, will ever be available is anyone's guess.

On the electricity side of ICE, there are still areas of the country—quite remote to be sure—that have no electricity. But for most of the country, electricity is readily available. The problem is that it's notoriously unreliable. The downside is that you might lose your electricity, at least where we live, once a day. The upside is that it's usually never out for more than about two to ten minutes. Except for the other day when there was some big catastrophe and the entire country was without electricity for from one to three hours, depending on where one lives.

Last March, when Robin and I were here on vacation, the entire country was in an uproar. It seems as though the government had proposed allowing competition for ICE. The plan was called the Combo. This resulted in ICE and other government entities, groups with vested interests such as the unions, and thousands of students taking to the streets in protest. Traffic was virtually shut down for days until the government finally capitulated.

Since then, the government seems to be looking for some type of compromise to improve the competitive climate; however, privatization is no longer an option for any government, which doesn't want to throw the country into chaos again. Part of the extremely hostile reaction on the part of the people to the breakup of ICE in any way—and I'm not talking about vested interests here—is due to an emerging country's fear of globalization and what the people perceive as globalization's resulting in a selling of the country to big international interests.

All of the people's fears about privatization might not be totally far-fetched, however. The analogy is to be seen in what has happened in the United States in many cases and many industries when deregulation has been instituted. Nevertheless, if Costa Rica, an emerging country, wants to continue to emerge, it is going to have to do something about this monopoly in electricity and telecommunications. The present system results in retarded economic and social development and growth.

The water situation. Costa Rica is blessed with abundant fresh water. The metropolitan area of San José and most towns of almost any size at all have "city" water—that is, there's an agency responsible for providing good, pure water to the citizens. And the system works rather well. Indeed, compared to the rest of Central America, Mexico, and much of South America, Costa Rica's water supply is excellent.

In the more rural areas, such as in Lagunas where we now live and where the house is being built, there is abundant water. However, the local communities take responsibility for delivering it to the local inhabitants. Even where water is supplied, such as in Dominical or in Barú—where we rented our house before moving to the casita—at some point it's the homeowner's responsibility to get delivery from the main line into the house.

In the house we rented, for example, there was a ready supply of water from the street line outside, but the house itself has an electric pump to finish the job. Three times in the four months we lived there, we had trouble with the pump, and there was no water for a day or two until the pump could be fixed. So you quickly learn to have many large containers of water stored away to take care of those emergency times.

Here in Lagunas the situation is a bit different. I don't pretend to know all the details at all, being such a new arrival, but essentially the situation is as follows. Water to Lagunas has its source in two or three springs high in the mountains. The water is pure and untreated with chemicals. At some point in the past, that water was tapped and it flows into tanks that the community, through its water committee, regulates. There are a series of pipes coming from the holding tanks and going throughout the community. These tanks are the primary means for delivering water to the houses.

Some people, however, have their own tanks that are cistern-like systems, which are filled through the collection of water during the rainy season. Thus, if there is a time when the water is shut off—which does happen—these people have their own supply. Robin and I are building such a tank as part of the house's construction.

In any event, there are often times here in Lagunas when the water is shut off. Mostly this happens for two reasons. Often there will be a ruptured line somewhere and the water leaks out. The ruptures frequently occur because built-up pressure will blow out a coupling, or a bulldozer working on a *plantel* for a new building will cut the line. When this happens, a man who has lived here all his life, who knows the system like the back of his hand, and who is employed by the water committee, will walk the lines, accompanied by other members of the committee until the leak is found and then repaired.

The other main reason the water is shut off, during the dry season especially, is to allow the tanks to refill. Thus currently, the water is shut off almost every day from about 8 PM, after most people have finished eating and doing the dishes, until some time during the night. I understand from neighbors, however, that this did not happen so regularly last year, and there is a lot of water committee and water subcommittee meeting going on now. The chief problems seem to be that there might still be an undetected leak, and that the growing population of Lagunas is beginning to require a bit more water than the current sources can readily supply in abundance.

But there are a great many more untapped sources readily available. As far as I know, the committee has already received an estimate and proposal for tapping into a new source, which should then result in very abundant water for the foreseeable future.

Of course that presupposes a meeting of the minds among not just the members of the water committee but also all the other residents of Lagunas, for it is the residents who have to pay the significant bill for tapping into the new source. I have a feeling that reaching a decision will not be easy.

Just as in any group or community, there are a great many disparate opinions and personalities. There are personal animosities, large egos, social and economic inequalities, etc. The longer we're part of the community, the more we learn about the existing personality conflicts, little enmities, long-standing disagreements, etc., that have developed over the years within the small often mutually dependent group. It will be kind of fun, I think, to watch the group dynamics unfold over the next couple of weeks as the community tries to reach a consensus about how to deal with the water problem.

One interesting side note is that the law in Costa Rica guarantees every citizen the right to tap into any natural water source to provide herself and her family with water. The problem is, of course, that it can often be very expensive to do if one is located far from the source. Nevertheless, for the people in Lagunas, although I've never discussed this with anyone, it would probably be possible for a couple of people—especially the more affluent—to tap into a source and create their own water system, independent of the rest of the community.

## Learning Spanish

Our knowledge of Spanish is increasing rapidly. When we first got here, we had a teacher, the wife of a friend of ours. We'd meet a couple of hours a week. But as time passed, it became increasingly more difficult to meet with her because she and her husband travel extensively and because often Robin and I would have a meeting associated with the building projects that just couldn't be postponed.

So eventually we started to do it on our own. For my part I spend a minimum of an hour per day reading the newspaper, often two hours. This has done wonders for my passive knowledge. In addition to that, I have a great workbook called *Spanish Verb Tenses,* through which I'm making my way fairly regularly.

But our greatest progress comes from the fact that we have the opportunity every day to speak lots of Spanish with Seidy, the young woman who works for us; Marvin, the project foreman; and Kiki, the contractor. Also, other than a clerk at a hardware store in San Isidro, none of the merchants we deal with regularly speaks English.

For a language professional like me, it's really fun to observe myself learning. Of course, as we all know, the learning process is so different when you learn in an environment where you have the opportunity to speak with native speakers every day as compared to learning entirely in a classroom environment. What's really fun is when you suddenly use a word that you didn't know had entered your active vocabulary, or when you come out with a verb tense form you didn't know you knew, or when in a conversation the person you're talking to comes out with a long, complicated series of sentences, and you realize you understand it all.

It's also fun when you realize you're learning regionalisms. When I was in Mexico a couple of weeks ago and talking about learning Spanish with Benjamín, I was surprised to learn how many words I know are different from those used to express the same things in Mexican Spanish.

But don't get me wrong. I still speak haltingly with innumerable errors and have far to go before approaching anything like verbal fluency. Nevertheless, considerable progress is being made, and I still hope to reach my goal of being reasonably fluent at the end of our first year here.

One last thing about learning languages. I find it terrifically interesting to see the differences between Robin and me when we engage in a conversation with a Spanish speaker. I, because of all the general knowledge I have about languages, am extremely aware of reaching a point in a sentence where I am absolutely sure that I can't say what I want to. Consequently, I pause for a long time while my brain works furiously, trying to either figure out the forms I want or trying to find a suitable circumlocution. Robin, on the other hand, perhaps because she does not have as much experience as I do in speaking foreign languages (although she is fluent in American sign language), just plows ahead, as indeed she should. If she doesn't know the tense form she wants, she just uses one tense form for that verb that she does know. If she only knows the infinitive or the stem, she uses that. And invariably she is understood, which obviously is the purpose.

I always used to tell my students, "Just speak, and don't worry about errors while you're learning." Easy for me to say, difficult for me to do. But Robin's a champ. No long pauses for her!

So at this point I think we've caught you up well with where we're at in our ongoing adventure.

We miss you all and hope that every one of you is well.

Martin and Robin

# CHAPTER THIRTEEN

## April 17, 2001

Hello, friends and family. Here's the latest from Costa Rica.

### More Great Spanish Bloopers

Recently, a few minutes after Lydia, the woman we usually deal with at the plant nursery, finished complimenting Robin on how good her Spanish has become, Robin was telling her how she makes guacamole. In the course of telling her, she said that she always puts some eye in the guacamole. (*Ojo* instead of *ajo*, eye instead of garlic.)

And then, a few days ago, I was telling Alejo, the proprietor of *La Choza de Alejo*, one of our favorite restaurants, that he really needed to attract more of the tourists from Dominical (about twenty minutes away). The way to do it, I suggested, was to warn them about the restaurant. (*Advirtir*, to warn, instead of *anunciar*, to advertise.)

But all in all, our Spanish continues to improve. I've just read my first book in Spanish, a collection of stories by the English mystery writer, Ruth Rendell, translated into Spanish. I'm also reading in Spanish, *Cuando Fui Mortal* (*When I was Mortal*), a collection of stories by the Spanish writer, Javier Marías. I had previously read the book in German translation and am using that as a pony. I'm doing the same thing with Isabel Allende's *Hija de la Fortuna*, for which I have an English translation. One of the really nice things about learning Spanish is that I am also beginning to read Spanish literature, of which I've only read some novels by Carlos Fuentes. Since we got here I've read, in English, Gabriel García Márquez's *Love in the Time of Cholera*, which I enjoyed tremendously. I'll soon buy a copy in Spanish and use my English copy for a pony.

## Trés Tico

In one of my previous letters I was making some generalizations about the Ticos. I mentioned that they would frequently tell you what they think you want to hear. The reason for this is the Tico's desire that everything and everyone *quedar bien*—that is, "be nice," which is also a reflection of their non-confrontational society.

Here's an incident that, as Robin pointed out to me, is probably a prototypical example of how this works. The members of the Lagunas Water Committee still believe that there's an undiscovered leak in our water system. It seems to many people that the amount of water being used cannot be explained simply by the residents' excessive usage. So they decided to do a test. It was agreed that no one in Lagunas would use water on a recent Saturday afternoon between the hours of noon and 4 PM. During that period, the meter that shows how much water is coming out of the holding tanks would be watched. If no one in the community is using any water but the meter spins, then chances are 100 percent there's an undiscovered leak somewhere.

The reason that Saturday afternoon was chosen was because by noon, there is no construction going on at our site on Saturdays (there are at the moment no other construction projects under way in Lagunas). And because we're at the stage in construction where we're using tons of cement, we're also using a great deal of water.

So at 12:15 that Saturday afternoon, I suddenly realized that most likely no one had told the weekend site guard about the test and that he shouldn't be using any water during these four hours. Consequently, I walked across the site to the *bodega* where the men live (all the other men had left for the weekend) and explained to him what was going on and asked him not to use any water from that minute until 4 PM.

He asked me about spraying the walls of the house. The concrete in and on the walls has to be kept damp, and so it is sprayed with a hose every two hours. I told him it would just have to wait until 4 PM. And of course he said OK; he wouldn't use any water until 4 PM.

So, I walk back to the *casita*—probably not more than a hundred feet—and tell Robin that everything is OK. Two minutes later she cries out to me, "There's someone spraying the walls!" I just couldn't believe it, and from where I was standing, I couldn't see anyone. But she affirmed that from the bedroom she could see him clearly.

My first thought was that on that day—as is sometimes the case—there were two guards, and the worker I had talked to hadn't told the other. So I go running back and lo and behold—there's the guard I had just talked to spraying the walls. I start waving my arms and shouting, "No, no, we can't use the water until four!" So he bends the hose to stop the flow and says, "But the walls have to be sprayed every two hours." So once again I explain to him about the test, the monitoring of the meter, etc., etc. Then he says, "OK, not until 4."

As I walked back to the house I was thinking, "Could it be that I just messed up the Spanish?" But what I said was really simple and straightforward, and I was convinced that I didn't make any mistakes or say anything other than what I had intended to say. And because I repeated the same thing in the second conversation and he clearly understood, I was simply at a loss as to why he just went ahead and sprayed.

Robin, however, got it immediately. She said, "Trés Tico." It was clear to her that this was the perfect example of *quedar bien* and being told what you want to hear. According to her, he most likely thought something like the following, "OK, I won't use any water personally, won't turn on the faucet for a drink, won't take a shower, won't wash my hands. But I've got to do my job, so I'll just spray the walls every two hours." I think Robin was right, trés Tico, indeed.

## A Bit More about Water

In my last letter, I wrote about water problems in Lagunas, and the rural water systems, and the fact that the country was rich in plentiful water. The very next day I read an article in *La Nación* that in certain neighborhoods in San José, water was being rationed—that is, service was being suspended during the night. The two hottest months of the year in Costa Rica are March and April, just before the beginning of the rainy season in May.

Water usage in these neighborhoods has been extremely high and the authorities became worried. Evidently, two weeks before they began to ration, they informed these neighborhoods that this would happen if the residents didn't voluntarily reduce their usage. They didn't do so and consequently the authorities acted.

But what I wondered was, if water is such a plentiful resource, how could there be the threat of a shortage. Well, it turns out there are two reasons. First, the rainfall during the previous rainy season was considerably less than normal so that reserves in the metropolitan area were down. The second reason is that we're expecting El Niño during the coming year and that means that we can again expect reduced rainfall.

Then in today's paper, I read an article that begins: "In addition to being one of the country's most abundant resources, water is also one of its most neglected. Until now there has been no national policy for managing it adequately and no interagency cooperation. Neither have there been any studies completed concerning the state of our water resources." Looks as though Costa Rica has become aware of another impending ecological, social, and economic problem. The article went on to say, however, that a major study is now under way and that, with luck, the politicians will institute some kind of water policy in the not-too-distant future.

## Some Prices

Other than quoting the prices of fruits and vegetables a couple of times, I haven't talked much about the cost of living here in Costa Rica. In one respect it's the same as anywhere else—that is, one can go to the most exclusive and expensive restaurants, stores, hotels, etc., and pay a lot of money for things. Even with groceries there's a wide spectrum. For example, if you seek out North American products, thousands of which are readily available here, you will end up paying a great deal more than if you buy Tico brands or others imported from Mexico, Central or South America.

You can stay at a super hotel in San José for $200 per night, one that caters to foreigners—which is still cheaper than some dumps in San Francisco—or you can spend $60 a night at a quite-lovely hotel in the same good neighborhood as the first one. With a little care you can go on a vacation here, stay at very, very acceptable hotels and not spend more than $50 per night. And if you look a bit further, $40 per night in a nice place is quite easy to find.

With clothes, however, I've not been able to find what I'd call medium-priced articles. Either you go to a big mall in San José and spend top dollar for brand names as in the States, or you go to one of the thousands of clothes *tiendas* and buy very cheap items that won't last very long. But you can buy five pairs of shorts, for example, for the same price as one pair at Tommy Hilfiger's in the Multiplaza Mall in an upscale section of San José.

Friends have told me, however, that there are, indeed, plenty of places where you can buy medium-priced clothes. The next time I go shopping for clothes, I'll seek some of these places out.

But the thing that I find most amazing and attractive are the fantastically reasonable prices that one pays for custom-made things such as furniture, windows, doors, etc. Also incredible values are to be found in services such as gardening and landscaping, small construction jobs, and the like.

Here are three examples: There was no landscaping at all around the *casita*, of course. That is something we had to do. On one side of the house, between the house and the Great Wall of Lagunas (that's what we're calling that wonderful ninety-meter wall we built), there's an area of about five hundred square feet.

We wanted to get it covered with sod. When we spoke to Edgar he proposed covering the area with sod and including a two-head sprinkler system (manually operated). We asked him for a price and he quoted us two hundred and sixty-six dollars! Obviously we had the work done. (See what a little job like that would cost you in Silicon Valley.)

Warwick and Barbara Lowe, friends of ours over on the next ridge, have what is probably the most beautiful house in Lagunas. I believe I might have mentioned it before. It, too, as will be ours, is in a Southwestern style. Their front door is all glass with a magnificent wrought-iron grill in front of it, fashioned to their design. The door is huge. A local craftsman in Dominical made it. The quality of the iron's finish is as high as anyone could possibly demand. The price? Eight hundred dollars.

The last example has to do with a couple of cabinets and some open shelves that Robin and I had built. The fellow who built all our closets, drawers, and cabinets in the *casita* is named Nicolas Núñez. He does the cabinetry for most of the projects that Kiki builds. He has an excellent reputation throughout the area, and deservedly so. His work is truly of the highest quality. And he'll build anything you can describe. The price of the *casita* included all the below-counter cabinets and drawers in the kitchen, a large pantry, a small cabinet under the bathroom sink, the four doors in the house, and a beautiful extremely large closet in the bedroom.

What was missing was a wall cabinet hanging in the kitchen and one hanging in the bathroom as well as some open shelves in the bathroom. So Robin and I contracted with him to build these for us. They were just installed today. The craftsmanship is perfect; the finishes are beautiful. The price for the two cabinets and the shelves made to order? One hundred and twenty-six dollars. Yep, that's right. It's just so hard to believe.

## Wages

It takes a while to come to terms with wages for workers such as Róger and Seidy. The fact is that wages are very low here.

And your first reaction, or at least the first reaction for Robin and me, was a strong sense of guilt.

We inherited Seidy from the woman from whom we rented our house before moving to the *casita*. At that time Seidy was paid 350 *colones* per hour. At today's exchange rate, that's $1.12. When Róger began working for us, his rate was 400 *colones* per hour. That's $1.25. We've raised Seidy to four hundred *colones* per hour and Róger to five hundred.

To those of you back in the States reading this, you, too, unless you've had experiences in developing countries, must feel shocked just as Robin and I did. But that's the reality of wages here. On the other hand, the thing that distinguishes Costa Rica from so many of its neighbors is the strong safety net that supports these workers. Private employers are responsible for paying each month, in addition to the salary, the costs for health insurance. In addition to that, the workers are guaranteed a month's paid vacation and a Christmas bonus equivalent to a month's wages. They are paid double time for working on holidays. There are strong price controls here as well on things such as gas, milk, electricity, and many other necessities of life.

So the result is that, in general, manual laborers in Costa Rica enjoy the highest standard of living in the entire area, even at wages that seem infinitesimal by comparison to everything we know.

The thing that bothers Robin and me is that many people will take advantage of the workers—that is, will not pay higher wages even if they can afford to do so, will not pay the insurance fees or the bonuses or the vacation. There are also maternity benefits to be paid by the private employer, which I forgot to mention. One frequently reads in the paper of cases where workers are ruthlessly exploited; fortunately, that doesn't seem to happen too often with North American employers, though on occasion it does.

Nevertheless, last week when we happened to mention to a couple of our neighbors for the first time that we had raised Róger's wages from four hundred to five hundred *colones* per hour, we were told not to tell our other neighbors because they'd get angry with us. The difference between those two rates is 31.25 cents per hour. There is no one in this community who couldn't afford to raise whomever they're paying four hundred *colones* to five hundred. The reason for the resistance to the increases seems to be people's fear that such raises will inspire some kind of upward spiral in wages. The fact is that many people are desperate to work, and only extremely rarely will they ask for higher wages.

The reason that so many workers here endure the obvious exploitation that they often do—that is, not reporting employers who fail to pay them wages on time or who fail to pay all the additional benefits they're entitled to—is because they are afraid of being fired. There are even laws here governing termination of employment that highly favor the worker. But either they're unknown to the workers, which isn't likely, or the workers are afraid of getting the reputation of a troublemaker and not being able to find ongoing employment, which is more likely.

Naturally Robin and I will continue to raise Seidy's and Róger's wages and those of anyone else who works for us as we desire and as they deserve, whenever we want to.

You can see, however, why with wages like these so many North Americans with limited retirement budgets move to Central America.

## The Great All-Costa-Rican Fruit Festival

Last Sunday, Robin and I went with our neighbors, Angelo and Maryanne, to a town about two hours away from here to attend its annual fruit festival. We didn't really know what to expect, but we very much like to go to Tico festivals whenever we can. (Some of you might remember my writing about the ox-cart festival we went to a couple of months ago where I discovered how far ox doo-doo could splatter.)

What we found was almost identical to a small-town county fair in the States. Even the building looked like a 4-H club building. In the building itself, there were dozens and dozens of stalls with local farmers showing and selling their fruits and vegetables. There were many stands offering food and snacks for sale. There were beer booths, a small carnival, a small disco where the kids were dancing, crafts booths, talent shows, plant sales, a fruit festival queen, and fireworks. Had it not been for the fact that everyone was speaking Spanish, I felt as though I could easily have been back at the Knox County Fair in Knoxville, Tennessee. Angelo sensitively told Robin that it was probably a good thing that she missed the annual bat-bashing contest. I, on the other hand, entered her in the annual prune-eating contest, but she chickened out.

Robin discovered a tasty dish at one of the booths—mango cerviche—and was also able to buy some bee pollen, something she's been trying to find to add to Batboy and Audrey's diet. On the way back, we had dinner at a fantastic seafood place right on the ocean near Jacó, a resort town about seventy or eighty kilometers north of here. Someone had told Angelo that it was the best seafood restaurant in Costa Rica, and after dinner, I thought that person might have been right.

## More about Food

In general, Costa Rica does not have much of a national cuisine. The most famous national dish is *gallo pinto,* rice and beans with peppers and lots of seasonings. It's most often eaten for breakfast with eggs but is available on lunch and dinner menus as well. Other than that, there's nothing much that one would call part of a national cuisine, quite unlike, for example, Mexico with its many fabulous regional cuisines.

On the other hand, if you look at Central America as a whole, I do think one can talk of its food as a distinct type of cuisine. All of the Central American countries have their specialties, and because of the geographic and climatic homogeneity of the region, the ingredients of these dishes are available everywhere in Central America.

When Robin and I got here, we were amazed at all the fruits and vegetables we'd see in the markets which were completely foreign to us. We'd ask the names but they still meant nothing to us in terms of what they tasted like, how they were prepared, what other foods went well with them, etc.

But recently Robin made a great find. She bought a book written in English and published in Costa Rica called *Sabor! A Guide to Tropical Fruits and Vegetables and Central American Foods* by Carolina Avila and Marilyn Root. From this book we learned all about those—to us—exotic fruits and vegetables that we've wanted to sample and cook for these past six months now.

The book describes dozens and dozens of fruits and vegetables readily available here, tells in many cases where they originated, describes the different ways of preparing them, and has many dozens of super-tempting recipes from all over Central America.

One thing we've discovered with the aid of the book is the *guanábana* fruit. It's interesting looking: dark olive green with what look like prickly spines on it. The spines, however, are not prickly at all and give at the touch. The fruit is elongated and fatter at the bottom, about eight inches in circumference and about six to eight inches tall. It has a very pulpy flesh. But the juice from it is just fantastic! I've never tasted anything quite like it. The taste is like a combination of lemon, grapefruit, and pineapple, but not at all acidic! Mainly it's used to make drinks, ice cream, or popsicles. There's also a recipe for guanábana cake that sounds very tasty.

Another thing we've discovered is the bewitching aroma of guava fruit. We have a guava tree directly in front of the patio of the *casita*. At the moment, it's full of fruit. I've taken to keeping a few on the table on the patio, where I spend a lot of time reading. The fresh, citrus-type scent they send out is wonderful. Also, after eating a piece, your mouth continues to have an extremely fresh taste in it for quite a time after.

So now with the help of the book, we'll start experimenting regularly with all the new fruits and vegetables available to us. I'm anxious to make, for example, the recipe I have for chicken, yucca, and mango salad, as well as pineapple salsa, sweet potato soup, *zapallo* omelet (*zapallo* is a summer squash), and warm garbanzo and green mango salad. And that's just the beginning.

Just the other night I made a new dish from a Spanish (Spain) recipe I found. It's called tortilla, but it's not what we, in the United States or here, think of when we talk about tortillas. In fact, the first time I had it was on my visit to the *hacienda* in Mexico, about which I recently wrote. The way it's best described is as a potato and onion omelet. It's thick and you cut it like a cake. It can be eaten hot or cold. We've tried it both ways and found it delicious either way.

But another of the joys of eating here is that even the most common things seem to taste better than they did back in the States, for example, tomatoes, and onions, and pineapples, and cantaloupe, and bananas, etc. And the reason, I think, is very simple. Virtually everything here is tree or vine or bush ripened before it gets to the markets and fruit and vegetable stands. And the difference in taste between naturally ripened and artificially ripened foods is so very perceptible. It's this difference that so enlivens our everyday meals.

Unfortunately, not everything is healthy. For example, yesterday for breakfast I made fried plantains for the first time since we've been here. They are so good! But they can't be too healthy, I guess. We'll have to use some real restraint not to have them too often.

## Update on Batboy and Audrey and Other Animal-Related Things

I'm happy to report that both young bats are doing just fine. As they are getting older, they're falling more and more into a routine. They've reached the point where they spend all day sleeping in the dark "cave box" in their cage, and then, around 6 PM begin to get very active for the evening and night. They come out to eat and then begin to fly about the cage. Robin still spends "quality time" with them every day, taking them out of the cage in the evening and holding them and letting them crawl around. They still tend to fly into doors and walls when they take off from her hand, so she doesn't keep them out of the cage too long.

Robin is also expanding their diet with the help of a list of additional foods she got from Susan, her bat expert mentor. Among the more exotic things they're eating are hibiscus and geranium flowers.

It seems as though they've probably had a calcium deficiency in their diet, however, because they've started to lose some of their fur. We're waiting for a shipment of RepCal from the States, which Susan says is very important for them. But in the meantime, until it gets here, we've got some oyster shells that we're grinding into a powder and mixing with their food. Susan suggested that this would be a good stopgap until the RepCal gets here.

Robin is spending more and more time horseback riding with her friend Bea. Bea is going to give us two horses. After Casa Pacífica is done and we convert the *bodega* into a stable, they'll live here. In the meantime, they'll stay at Bea's. Meanwhile, Robin is studying several books that Bea has lent her and is practicing what she's learning on her rides a few times a week.

The construction site is much quieter than it was last week because the men are working on shaping the rebar in preparation for pouring the concrete for the house's second floor. And I think that it's this quieter atmosphere that resulted in our having toucans in the trees around our house the last two days.

Their call is quite distinctive, so that we can recognize instantly when they're in the neighborhood and come out and look for them. There are certain trees that they're attracted to because they like the fruit that grows on them. Robin and I have heard the name of the tree a dozen times, but we just can't seem to get it into long-term memory yet, so we refer to them, as do many people here, as toucan trees. We have about six or seven of them on the property, so we're hoping that the toucans will be regular visitors. (Checked with some friends and the tree's name is Cecropia.)

The other day we were riding on the road from Dominical to the turnoff to Lagunas, and Robin spotted a troop of capuchin monkeys. We stopped the car and watched them. It was a real treat. They had just crossed the road, but there was one of them who hadn't yet crossed when we arrived. So he just continued to stay on his side of the road, watching us very carefully and, clearly, waiting for us to move on before he joined his companions.

Our best regards and fondest wishes,
Martin and Robin

# Chapter Fourteen

## May 20, 2001

Hello, all:

### The Web Site

I've finally got around to getting our Costa Rican dream Web site up and running, at least version 1.0. If you go to http://www.homeincostarica.net you'll be able to see lots of pictures of the many things Robin and I have been telling you about in these letters. We're adding material regularly and there's still a lot that we have that isn't up yet, but there's a lot to see now, too (including a great picture of Batboy).

### An Anniversary and *Chorizo*

Tomorrow will be seven months since our arrival in this beautiful country. And to mark this auspicious date, Robin and I have been informed that our applications for residency have been approved. We're now legal residents and will have a residency card. This means that we no longer have to have our tourist visas renewed every three months, that we don't have to carry our passports anymore, and that when we go places that have tiered rates, a lower one for nationals and a higher one for foreigners, we pay the lower rate. It also means that we will eventually be able to apply for permanent residency.

On the downside, it means that when we go on trips outside of the country, our departure tax is $70 instead of the tourists' $15. Seems like a small price to pay, though, given all the benefits.

(Now, three years later, the departure tax has been reduced for foreign residents.)

I'm also under the impression that the cops treat foreigners a bit more nicely during routine traffic stops if they show a residency card rather than a passport. In fact, I noticed that after I got my Costa Rican driver's license and showed that instead of my California license, the police didn't bother to go through the rest of the routine stop checks.

There are a lot of what are called "perpetual tourists" here, that is, people who come here to settle and who have been here for many, many years but who never get residency papers. From things I've read in the newspapers many native Costa Ricans resent that, and from time to time, the government—that is, the immigration department—cracks down and deports people who just keep getting their tourist visas renewed.

Because it's necessary to leave the country for seventy-two hours in order to have your visa renewed, there's a thriving business at some of the border crossings where for a "nominal fee," some obliging official will do all the necessary stamping without your having to leave. Just part of the normal life here with its "*chorizo*." I recently saw a neat bumper sticker: "*Donde hay permiso, hay chorizo.*" (Where there's a permit [to be obtained] there's bribery.)

The latest scandal involving *chorizo* has to do with MOPT again. I mentioned them before in relation to a tree-cutting scandal. Part of their duties includes being what we in the States call the Motor Vehicle Department. It turns out that for about sixty thousand *colones* ($180), you can buy a driver's license. And because the people who are selling them are the same ones who issue them legally and enter all the data into the computers, there doesn't seem to be any way to catch the people who have bought licenses. Just what we need here where a person dies on the roads every fifteen hours.

## The Accident

So before I tell you about the accident, let me say that everyone is just fine, honest—that's the truth! About two months ago, Robin and I were out on our ATVs. I mentioned in an earlier letter that we got a couple shortly after arriving here. They are absolutely wonderful for getting to places that you can't get to by car and are too arduous to walk to. Usually other than an ATV, the only way to get there is by horse.

So that day, Robin was showing me one of the beautiful places where she and Bea often go horseback riding. It was about 4 in the afternoon because we wanted to wait until the heat of the day had passed before setting off.

We were riding in single file, Robin ahead, along a winding, rocky and, in places, muddy path that led down to a creek, which we crossed, and then up again, maybe twenty feet above a winding creek that paralleled the road. We were deep in the jungle, and I was simply awed by the beauty and quiet Robin had been telling me about. The path at that point seemed to be rather level. As I looked at Robin, driving about ten feet in front of me, she suddenly and simply disappeared!

I immediately jammed on my breaks and jumped off the ATV while screaming her name. I heard the crash of trees breaking and looking at the place she had disappeared, I saw her ATV going end over end in the air with no sight of her anywhere! Rarely in my life have I been so scared.

I was running to the spot where I had last seen her and then heard her calling, "I'm OK! I'm OK!" She knew of course that I must have been petrified with worry and, immediately, began to reassure me that she was all right.

When I got to the edge of the road, I saw a trail of broken small trees leading down a very steep hill. At the bottom was the creek. In the creek, right side up, was her ATV. And she was sitting on the bank of the creek.

Her helmet was off, and she called up that she had lost her glasses. Robin literally couldn't see a foot before her face without her glasses. (I say couldn't because now she can. More about that later.) She kept saying, however, that she was OK, only scratched. And she did indeed seem to be OK, as unbelievable as it seemed to me at the time and as unbelievable as it still seems to me.

Our immediate problem was how I was going to get to her. The incline she had fallen down was so steep that we were afraid that if I went down that way, we wouldn't be able to climb back up. She was so shaky and beginning to get so sore, not to mention the fact that she was virtually blind, that we didn't think it was a good idea for her to try to climb up without my help.

At that point I remembered that we had crossed the creek just a little way back from where the accident happened. So I told her I would walk back there, then come up the creek to where she was, and then lead her out. And that's what we did.

Our next problem was how to get out of there. It was only about an hour before dark, and the last thing we wanted to do was to be stranded in the jungle after dark. We hadn't brought a flashlight with us, though we did have a large bottle of water that Robin had insisted on taking after I said that "We don't need no stinking water." Thank goodness she hadn't listened to me.

We didn't think that we could get her ATV out of the creek. Even if it still ran, there was no way we could follow the creek on it because there were just too many places where the boulders were too large to ride over. I did not want to ride her on back of my ATV because there were many places where we had ridden where there were also large boulders and I was afraid we wouldn't get through.

Finally, Robin said that Bea's place was not too far, and we could walk there and try to get there before dark. This turned out to be a fifty-minute forced march, uphill all the way. I had to lead the way with Robin very close behind me because she couldn't see. With my not being in the greatest of shape and having high blood pressure, Robin became frightened that I'd stroke out. And it was a tough hike. Thank God for the water Robin had brought along.

Eventually, just before dark, we made it to Bea's house. What a welcome sight! Of course Bea, her husband Bob, and the four houseguests they had immediately made a fuss over us. We examined Robin's scratches and emerging bruises carefully and then got her into the shower quickly. After she showered, Bea gave her some muscle relaxants (Bea's a nurse and always has a stash of really useful medications), and then Robin went to rest in bed for a while.

When we had begun to walk out of the jungle, Robin said, "What about the ATVs?" My answer to which was: "#*%& the ATVs!" But Bea was quite concerned about them because there are locals who walk that road, and she was convinced that they'd be gone in the morning. We all tried to talk her out of going after them, but she insisted, and so she and Bob set out to retrieve the ATVs, and this after dark!

We figured it would take them an hour. By the time an hour had passed, the six of us still at the house began to get worried. We recalculated the time and thought then that it really would most likely take an hour and a half. We then began to form plans about what we'd do if they weren't back by that time.

We decided that we'd drive over to Denny and Gail's, our neighbors, alert them, and then go across the road from their place to Steve and Kim's, some other neighbors. Denny and Steve are the community's most fearless ATV riders and know the area very well. We thought that if anyone could find Bea and Bob at night in the jungle, it would be they.

An hour and a half passed and I had just walked out the door with some of the others to get into a car and go off to Denny's when the dogs (Bea and Bob have six of them) began to bark. And there they were, Bea driving my ATV with Bob on the back. There was no way that they could get Robin's out of the creek at night.

What a relief it was to see them safely back! Then Bea said that she and Bob would go back at the crack of dawn and get the other ATV. They gave us a ride back to our house so that Robin could go to bed.

Sure enough, early the next morning, Bea and Bob went back to the creek and brought the other ATV back to our house. They said that it wasn't difficult after all because on the other side of the creek there was an old unused road that they were able to drive along and work their way back.

The night of the accident I said to Robin and everyone else that the first thing the next morning I would put up a notice that the ATVs were for sale. Robin really didn't want to sell them, but I was absolutely firm. There was no way that we were ever going to go out on them again.

As it turned out, Bea and Bob bought them from us the next day after they became convinced that I was not going to change my mind. And a couple of our other neighbors, Warwick and Barbara, also wanted to buy them had Bea and Bob not been first.

It probably took Robin about two weeks before all the aches went away. She had a lot of scratches, none of them very deep, but also several abrasions that burnt quite a bit. She had so many black and blue marks that she looked like a rainbow. But if there are such things as miracles, the fact that she didn't break anything, or worse, certainly counts as one in my book.

When Bea went to get Robin's ATV out of the creek, she took a close look at the path where Robin went over the side. She told us that in fact, the path did slant some toward the creek at that point. Probably Robin just hadn't noticed the slant, and when the wheels on the right side of her ATV were on that spot, the whole vehicle just began to slide sideways because the dirt was very soft.

## All's Well That Ends Well and the Satellite

So, we sold the ATVs. And we decided to use that money to pay the outrageous charges for what RACSA, our friendly Costa Rican Internet access monopoly, calls *Internet Directo*, that is, VSAT wireless satellite access. As you know, now that we've moved to the *casita* in Lagunas, we have no telephone access. In order to use the phone, we have to drive about fifteen minutes down the mountain and mooch from Liz and Kent at South Coast Realty. If it weren't for them, most of the folks in Lagunas would be completely without communications. There are some folks here who have cell phones, though the reception is only good at certain sites on the mountain. And some of the folks with good reception use their cell phones to connect for e-mail. Web browsing is pretty much out of the question because of the slowness of the connection.

As it turns out, our site has pretty good cell reception; the problem is that we're so far down the waiting list for a cell phone that it will be at least a year before our number comes up. Ordinarily, we would never have been able to afford *Internet Directo* ($500 per month), but the money we got from selling the ATVs will give us enough connected time to last us until we get our cell line.

Also, there seems to be a good chance now that we'll get phones in Lagunas within the next four months or so, though it's a little tricky. It's a microwave system and there are only thirty lines. There will be about forty of us signed up, but only thirty at a time will be able to talk or connect. But it will certainly be better than nothing—and a hell of a lot cheaper than *Internet Directo*. (As it turns out, Lagunas finally did get that system, but not until 2004. It also appears as though many people there still can't get the system because they are not in a direct line of sight with the transmission tower.)

In the meantime, we have great Internet access—seems to be just about the same speed as our cable modem in California, which was really fast. I've set up a hub, and Robin and I are networked and can both access the Internet at the same time. In addition, since our connection allows for a LAN with four users, our friends can come over and use the connection, too. Just yesterday, I installed an Ethernet card in Bea's laptop and configured her machine to work on our network and give her fast access. We'll have to put a sign out soon: Marty Mañana and Off-Road Robbie's Internet Café.

One of the things that we thought we'd do when we got connected here was to use Net2phone or Dialpad to call the States. Well, it turns out that we're having some trouble getting it to work. I did use Net2phone successfully from a regular phone hookup and called Baker and my son David. But there seems to be some difficulty with the satellite connection, and I'm working to get that resolved. Actually, if we can get them working, we can call the States with Dialpad at no cost. And Net2phone is only about fifteen cents per minute. On the other hand, making a call within Costa Rica will cost us about forty-two cents per minute. Go figure.

## The Rainy Season

The rainy season has started! And it's welcome by everyone. Of course it's not good for tourism, so the tourism industry refers to this as "the green season." And it is indeed the green season. It's difficult to imagine without seeing it how everything begins turning deep green and shoots way up after but two or three rains. It's so beautiful.

Generally, during the rainy season which lasts from about the second week in May through mid-December, it rains every day, but in a wonderful way. Usually the mornings are sunny and it stays that way until about 3:30 to 4:00 when the clouds start rolling in. Then it'll begin raining anywhere from an hour to most of the night. Again, the next morning, the sun shines again.

There's also a period of about 2 weeks in June when the rains stop. This time of the season is called San Juan Summer.

Of course there are periods when it might rain for two to three days in a row without stopping, but those periods are much fewer than the pattern I just described.

When Robin and I arrived here at the end of October last year, we did experience about a month of the rainy season, and it was truly delightful. Roads do wash out; there are landslides; trees fall—the works—but it's still so beautiful that you just deal with the inconveniences.

## Language-Related Stuff—Don't Get Familiar!

I made an amazing discovery last week. In Costa Rica, people do not use the familiar *tú* form of the verb! I put the exclamation mark at the end of the last sentence because I was indeed so amazed to find this out.

Before we came here we had read that the Ticos don't use the plural familiar form, *vosotros,* but had heard nothing about not using familiar forms at all.

I had noticed that the workers used *usted* with one another, and that struck me strange, but I never asked anyone about it. But then, last week, Robin and I were in San José for eight days. When we're there, we use a cab driver, José, to take us around on our errands. He's really a great guy, and I wanted to do something nice for him.

Robin and I planned to go to the bird zoo one day that week, so I invited José to join us and to bring his little four-year-old daughter and his ten-year-old stepdaughter along. José is divorced and the girls live with his ex-wife. So we stopped there to pick them up. His ex came out and we chatted for a minute or two, and I noticed that José used *usted* with her. That seemed strange, but then I thought maybe it had something to do with the fact that they were divorced—kind of reaching there.

But I was really shocked when I realized that José was using the formal *usted* with his daughters, too. I didn't want to ask him about it in front of the girls, and I was thinking all sorts of crazy things, for example, maybe it's some kind of affectation among a certain class of people. I just couldn't figure it out.

Eventually, after we took the girls home, I asked him. He explained to me that people in Costa Rica just didn't use the familiar form, period. I'll talk to more people about this, but it really came as a shock. On the other hand, if I only speak Spanish in Costa Rica, there will be that many fewer verb forms to learn. Hurray!

Eventually I found out more about the use of the familiar form in Costa Rican Spanish. I won't go into it to any depth other than to say that when the familiar form was used much more in the past (and still today, though rarely) the pronoun was not *tú* but *vos.* I don't know about the history of *vos* yet, but I do know that it is used probably more than anywhere else in Argentina.

Our latest language gaffes belong to Robin this month:

She recently told a tico friend of ours that she had been onion-back riding (*cebolla* instead of *caballo*).

In Costa Rica, as in most of Latin America, when people greet one another, they usually kiss on the cheek. The other day, Robin was greeting Edgar, our landscaper, who happened to be unshaven. After touching cheeks, she said to him, jokingly, "That hurts! If you don't sharpen yourself, I'm not going to be able to kiss you anymore" (*afilar* [made reflexive] instead of *afeitarse*). Turned out to be more of a joke than she had intended.

Which reminds me of something that Edgar's sister once said, "When Edgar and I talk to gringos in Spanish, we've learned that the more they nod their heads 'yes,' the less they understand." By the way, "gringo" in Costa Rica does not have any of the negative implications that it does in Mexico. I don't know how it happened to turn out that way, but it's definitely not an insult here.

## The Bat Report

Batboy and Audrey are doing just great! The best news is that their fur is starting to grow back. It seems as though all the supplements that Robin's been adding to their food have begun to work.

What's really interesting to me is how different their personalities are. If you remember, Batboy had no experience whatsoever with other bats. Robin found him on the day he was born—his umbilical cord was still attached. Audrey, on the other hand, was probably about two weeks old when Robin got her, which, of course, meant that she had had two weeks with her mother and other bats. That's also the explanation, we're sure, of why she is so much bigger than Batboy.

We also think that this is the explanation of the different personalities they display. In short, Batboy is extremely tame and loving. When Robin opens the cage, he comes scurrying over to her immediately and jumps into her hand. He'll snuggle up on her chest while she pets him, scratches behind his ears, and coos to him. His eyes start to close and he begins to purr. Yes, bats "purr." It's not so much that they make the noise cats do when they purr, but their bodies vibrate just like cats when they purr.

Sometimes, when Robin takes her siesta, she'll get Batboy out of the cage and hold him while she naps. He'll nap right along with her for an hour or two.

Audrey, on the other hand, seems wild in comparison to Batboy. She doesn't particularly like to be held, though occasionally she'll permit it. When Robin reaches into the cage, she never comes hurrying over the way Batboy does. She's also much more active, that is, when Robin does take her out, she never cuddles up but is constantly active, scuttling around all over her without stopping.

She'll also display her displeasure by biting—never very hard, and never breaking the skin—just to let Robin know that "we're not amused" by the attempts at affection.

Batboy, on the other hand, never bites, unless he thinks your finger is food. The other night I had eaten some peanut butter. A bit later, I was holding him and he started licking my finger like mad and then started to bite it—very gently—but nevertheless perceptible. He does this with Robin, too, after she's prepared their food and then starts to hold him or pet him.

They're both getting better at flying. Now when we let them out a bit before bedtime to fly around the bedroom, they no longer fly full speed into the nearest wall. They do a neat circle to come in at the right angle so that they can land hanging upside down. The problem is that they haven't yet figured out that the smooth bedroom walls won't give them the purchase they need to hang, so they go sliding down the wall to the floor. Must be frustrating. We have bamboo blinds in the bedroom, however, and they're starting to learn that this is a great place to land.

Who would ever have thought that a couple of pet bats— bats?!—could give so much pleasure. They're so foreign that it's absolutely fascinating to observe them and learn about them.

From everything I've written before, you all know what a phenomenal job Robin did in rescuing them and caring for them;

all the sleepless nights, all the study and research. Yesterday, Robin got an e-mail from Susan Barnard, the bat expert who has helped her so much by e-mail in raising the little guys. Here's a quote from this latest e-mail:

> "You have been doing a beautiful job with these bats and can be very proud of yourself. You are a delight to work with because you see the natural balance we must maintain. You are factual in your reporting and make excellent observations. I sure wish I had you as a neighbor and part of the Basically Bats' Team. Dream on, Sue."

Praise truly well deserved!

An update: It is now June, 2004. Just yesterday Robin received an e-mail from Alvaro Herrera, Director of Researcher Relations at INBio Park, a recreational and educational park for teaching people about Costa Rican biodiversity and increasing their awareness about its value to society. They are considering building a bat display for teaching people about what an exceedingly important role bats play in maintaining this biodiversity. Mr. Herrera had been directed to our Web site by someone and came away impressed with Robin's experience. He has asked her to assist in the planning and design of a bat flight cage that will be part of the display. Needless to say, Robin is thrilled to be a part of this project.

## Robin's Eyes and No Redeeming Qualities

Above, when I was telling you about the accident, I mentioned that Robin couldn't see her hand before her face without her glasses. Now she sees perfectly without glasses! About a week and a half ago, Robin had laser surgery performed on her eyes. This has been something she's wanted to do for many, many years and has now finally done it. She is just indescribably happy with the results.

The entire process—she had both eyes done at the same time—only took about an hour, including the time she had to wait for her eyes to be dilated. The actual surgery only takes about ten minutes. However, we had to stay in San José for a whole week. That was so that we'd be near the doctor in case there were any complications (which there weren't) because we live a four-hour drive from San José.

Well, we had plenty to do there and kept busy the whole time. But on the way back home, Robin said that as far as she was concerned, San José has no redeeming features at all. Actually, there are a couple: a few good restaurants, the bird zoo, our friends, Darrylle and Ulises and their apartment, an oasis of civility in the midst of chaos, and probably a couple of more things that we haven't discovered yet.

But all in all, San José is an ugly, sprawling, polluted, crowded, crime-ridden city. It's hectic, indeed chaotic, with the worst traffic congestion, horrible smells, ugly buildings, and virtually no sense of history to be felt or seen by the visitor. One could easily get the impression that history began here in the mid-nineteenth century.

Nevertheless, we will, of course, continue to go there. That's the only place where we can buy so many of the things we need here. Most likely, we'll continue to go there once every month or two for necessities.

Oh, another redeeming feature was when we were there last week, we went to the movies and saw *Hannibal*. Lots of fun.

## Casa Pacífica

The house is making great progress. Now it looks as though we'll be in by October instead of December! All the walls and the roof are up, and the men are working on putting the stucco finish on the interior walls. The hole has been dug for the swimming pool, and the cement work will begin tomorrow, Monday, May 21.

Robin and I are very busy selecting tiles, light fixtures, plumbing fixtures, cabinets, etc. It's lots of fun and we're getting more and more excited as work progresses. You can see lots of pictures on the http://homeincostarica.net Web site.

## The Weight Report

Looks as though my weight has leveled off and now fluctuates between 180 and 185. A loss of about thirty-five pounds. Needless to say I'm delighted and happy about what that loss is doing for my health.

This has been a long letter, as usual, but it's been a while since we've written.

We miss you all,
Martin and Robin

# Chapter Fifteen

## August 8, 2001

Hi, friends and family:

It's been quite a while since the last time we've written, and there's been a lot going on. Here's a summary of what we're doing and what we're learning.

### A Do-It-Yourself Project Costa-Rican Style

I decided to build a rather large potting bench now that we're at a point where I can begin to garden. Most of my larger tools are still packed away, but I figured that I could get the guys at the lumberyard to cut to size what I needed, especially because we've bought loads of lumber for the house from them. Then all I'd need would be my drill, a hammer, and a bunch of screws to put it together. And indeed, they cut everything to size for me—a bit rough because they did it with a small chain saw rather than with a circular saw—but what the heck—it's a potting bench, not a piece of furniture. Then I needed a drill bit and a small square. I decided to buy these from our local small hardware store in Barú on the way home from the lumberyard in San Isidro.

So I told the man in the hardware store what size drill bit I needed. He told me that they only had that size in a bit that fit a manual drill, which meant, of course, that it wouldn't fit my electric drill. I was stymied. But not the clerk at the *ferretería* (hardware store). He suggested that we simply cut off the part of the drill bit end that wouldn't fit in the electric drill, and that there'd be enough of a shank left to use it in my drill. So that's what we did, and it worked perfectly.

Then I asked for the square. He had several hanging on the wall. All of which had the metal part (the bottom of the L was plastic) very rusted. The hardware store only has steel bars to close it up at night and on weekends, so everything is exposed to some weather and a lot of stuff is rusty. But I really needed it, so I bought it. Then, when I got home, I had to think that in the States I would have never bought it, but by the same token, I wouldn't have found a rusted-out square hanging on the wall in the hardware store in the first place.

I used it for the project and it worked just fine; I had to think that it really had made no difference at all that it was rusted, and I also realized how much my attitudes about so many things are changing in my new environment. I guess that it could all be summed up by saying that Robin and I are really learning "not to sweat the small stuff" in a way that I had never thought possible—at least in my case.

The drill-bit incident then made me remember something else that happened to me here, which also emphasizes the fact that necessity is indeed the mother of invention, especially when necessity seems to appear so very often here.

## How to Jump-Start a Car, Costa-Rican Style

When we were in our rented house, our neighbor came over to ask me if I could bring my car to her house so that a friend of hers could jump-start his car. I gladly obliged. When the cars were positioned correctly and the hoods were raised, I asked him where the jumper cables were. He said he thought I probably had some. I didn't.

Then our neighbor said, "Wait a minute," went around the back of the house, and returned with a long piece of heavy cable. So I'm looking at this thing and thinking, "What's that going to do?" But everyone else was nodding in a pleased manner. Then someone got his machete and cut the wire in half. Of course it still didn't have any clips. But naturally "we don't need no stinking clips," and they just held the four ends to the four terminals on the batteries of the two cars, and of course, it worked just like a charm.

I was a bit dazed and couldn't believe that my battery didn't short out, or my whole electric system for that matter. But you learn here to make do, and the consequences usually aren't too drastic.

Just yesterday I bought a weed eater in San Isidro. It was brand new, but all the accessories were in disparate plastic bags, and there was no box for the tool. I probably wouldn't have given it a second thought were I not writing this.

## More Making Do

The road from Barú to our house is, as unpaved roads go, in very good shape. That's due to the efforts and great job done by our Lagunas Road Committee. About twice a year the road is well graded. One of those times is at the beginning of the rainy season, which is now. The problem with this grading is that all of the rough surface gets smoothed out, and when it rains the first few times and you're going down the mountain, it's like going down a mountain covered with ice. What eventually happens is that the mud gets worn off, and the rocks and gravel buried by the grader start appearing again, and there's plenty of purchase for your tires when the road's wet. But, because of this, after the initial grading, the committee usually arranges for a few loads of rock to be dumped at what will be the most slippery places and then the grader smoothes it out.

So while this was going on a few weeks ago, I was coming up the mountain from Barú, went around a curve, and there smack in the middle of the road was a huge load of rocks that had just been dumped. But there was no grader in sight. The dump truck driver had jumped the gun. So "traffic" starts backing up; there are about three cars on the way up and a like amount on the way down.

Although the rocks were in the middle of the road, extending about one hundred feet along its length, there seemed to be enough room on the right side—heading up—to get past.

Because I was the first in line heading up, we all decided that the folks would direct me through. So I put the Jeep in four-wheel low and started slowly to go around watching the guys in front of me who are signaling which way to steer. And then my Jeep just slowly and inexorably started to slide to the right and came to rest in the gutter (unpaved, of course). At that point, my car was jammed firmly against the cut in the side of the mountain.

It was so slick in the gutter that there was no way I could drive out. What to do? That's easy, have someone drive down the mountain again to Barú and get our friendly backhoe driver up there with his backhoe to pull me out. There's no calling AAA on the road between Barú and Lagunas.

So in a relatively short time, here comes the backhoe. By now there are several vehicles stopped. About ten people are standing around, shaking their heads, seeing the humor in the situation, wondering how the dump truck driver could have been so dumb just to leave his load in the middle of the road, and, in general, having a good time.

Then it's unanimously decided that we can't pull the Jeep straight out because it's jammed so tight against the mountainside. If we were to try it that way, the whole finish would be scraped off. Seems the only way, according to the consensus, is to pull it out sideways. I'm seeing pictures of my Jeep back in the center of the road but minus its two right tires and half of two axils, which are still in the gutter. But you gotta make do, right?

So there's a lot of figuring and positioning of the backhoe. The backhoe legs are set down for stability, and it's time to go at it. Except no one has any chains to attach to the backhoe and the Jeep. And it's down the mountain we go again to get the chains. Eventually everything is hooked up and we're off. I'm sitting in the Jeep to steer, suddenly thinking, "How is this ever going to work? How are we going to pull the Jeep out sideways with the right side in a gutter that's about a foot and a half deep?"

But somehow they did it. Actually, they didn't just pull the whole thing out straight to the side. First they pulled the front out forward and to the side, then the back a bit, and I was able to get purchase after some of the rocks were thrown under the wheels. (We had tried to do that at first, but it didn't work without having part of the Jeep already out of the gutter.)

Other than a little dent in the right side of the car, it wasn't at all any worse for wear, and a good time was had by all.

## Gay and Lesbian Pride Day in Mexico City

Right now, I'm writing this in my hotel room in Mexico City. I'm here buying some stuff for the house. Yesterday was Saturday and shortly after I arrived at the hotel, I walked outside on the Paseo de la Reforma, one of the main arteries of the city, and there was a giant parade going on.

I then spent an hour and a half standing in front of the hotel watching the Third Annual Parade of Sexually Diverse Communities. It was an amazing Mexican Gay Pride Day Parade and was actually in the same league with San Francisco's.

There must have been ten thousand participants and a thousand gay and lesbian rainbow flags, some as long as one hundred feet carried by dozens of people. There were dozens of long flatbed trucks with hundreds of people on them.

Every contingent was represented. There were, of course, the typical gay construction workers, policemen, body builders, leathermen, transvestites, transsexuals, and lesbians of every possible stripe, including the *Grupo de Madres Lesbiana*. There was a contingent of gay Jewish guys complete with T-shirts in Hebrew and a Star of David flag. I even saw one blue-black-red BDSM flag.

Lots of nudity and the most outrageous costumes. All of this going down one side of the Paseo de la Reforma. And the amazing thing is that from the hundreds of cars that passed going in the opposite direction, I didn't hear one jeer or ugly remark. Quite to the contrary, lots of horn blowing in tune, *honk, honk—honk, honk, honk,* the way they always do here when there's some kind of big celebration going on, and lots of thumbs-up. Not the kind of goodwill one would expect in a country that most of us see as stereotypically macho because of its culture. It made me feel good to have that particular stereotype fall apart.

## To *Tú* or Not to *Tú* Revisited

You'll remember how surprised I was when I discovered that the Costa Ricans almost never use the familiar form of the verb. Today I was riding in a cab here in Mexico City and the driver and I were talking about Costa Rica. He was saying that he had had lots of Costa Ricans in his cab over the years and was impressed by how calm, respectful, and polite they all seemed. Then he said that they always used *usted.* I told him that the familiar form was almost never used in Costa Rica, upon which he asked if that was true within families as well. I told him that to the best of my knowledge that was indeed the case. In response to this he exclaimed, *"¡Qué bueno!"*

Of course it's very difficult for me to understand truly why this would make such a positive impression on him, though I did come up with a couple of theories. One of them has to do with differences in general. As I started learning languages with familiar forms, I always liked the idea of having a special way for speaking with special people.

Of course I eventually learned that in some situations everyone is addressed familiarly, at other times it can be used to insult, and of course, the native speaker isn't going to be conscious of its being so special most of the time because it's so much a part of his or her existence.

But then I thought that for the Mexican driver, using the polite form all the time seems special because it's so different from what he's used to. I guess the pronoun's always *mejor* (better) on the other side of the border.

## San José Revisited

Recently I wrote—in a not-too-favorable way—about San José, saying that there were only two redeeming features, the apartment of our friends, Darrylle and Ulises, and an Asian restaurant they introduced us to. Shortly after writing that letter, I was having lunch with Darrylle, and he expressed his displeasure at my depiction of his adopted city.

He pointed out that there are many beautiful parks, museums, a symphony orchestra, lots of good restaurants, wonderful farmers' markets, art galleries, etc. All in all, all the things that can make a city be a delightful place to live.

After that conversation, I spent some time thinking about what Darrylle said and decided that I'm sure he and Ulises have wonderful lives in San José. Not only are there all the things he mentioned, but I know that each of them has a circle of lovely friends, some of whom I've met and liked immensely.

But yet, I knew and know that San José is one of the last places on earth I would want to live. There are a lot of reasons for my feeling that way, but I think the one most overriding reason is because to me, it is one of the most aesthetically ugly places I've ever visited.

Most of the buildings are shabby. The streets are in horrible condition, as are the sidewalks. Probably for most of its existence, the city never had any zoning laws at all, and all the horrors of no zoning are evident everywhere. When you're driving or walking in traffic, which is virtually everywhere you go, the noxious fumes belching from the cars, buses, and trucks constantly choke you. Traffic congestion is abominable.

Yes, there are lovely parks, but the city is huge, and they're scattered, and unless you're near one of the parks, you never feel that San José is a green city. Yes, there are lovely views of the mountains, which surround the Central Valley, but frequently, dense clouds of black exhaust fumes coming from thousands of old vehicles, both private and commercial, obscure those views.

But worst of all, perhaps, is the fact that almost every house in San José and its environs, and I mean this literally—from the meanest to the most luxurious houses—is surrounded by bars, many of them topped with barbed or razor wire. Behind the bars and walls surrounding the houses, all the windows are barred. In a vast majority of cases, there is a barred gate before the front door. My reaction to this is one of depression. It's simply a horrible way to live from my perspective. I don't think the crime rate in San José is any worse that in most large cities, but perhaps burglary is worse. I just don't know.

Of course I can't help contrasting San José to where I live.

## In Love

I've always been crazy about Mexico City. Every time I come here, I enjoy it tremendously. I like the vibrancy of the city and I very much like the people. Indeed, if I ever get rich, I'll certainly buy us a little apartment in Polanco or a bordering neighborhood, the Woodside or Menlo Park or Palo Alto of Mexico City.

But, as I write this, I've only been gone a day and a half from our mountain valley and I miss it profoundly. I have truly fallen in love with the place and our life there as, of course, has Robin. There's a peace and calmness there that I've rarely experienced before. Even when we're having hectic days, and there are a lot of them with all the construction and projects going on, not to mention the occasional difficulties in the process of becoming acculturated, there is still that pervasive feeling of well-being.

Perhaps it has to do with the beauty of our surroundings and the absence of traffic and noise (except for the construction, of course, which has diminished considerably and will soon be gone). No matter where you look there's a beautiful view, a fantastic bird, some creature you've never seen before, a flowering tree glowing intensely, a bush with the strangest leaves, patterns of sun and cloud all over the mountains, the ever-changing ocean, and the sheer fun of learning new things about our adopted culture and the lives of our Tico friends and neighbors.

I sit on our front patio at the *casita* for hours drinking my fantastic *Trébol* (Clover) coffee and just gaze at the valley; watching the light patterns shift and change; focusing in on the unusual bushes, plants, and trees; being conscious of colors in a way I've never been before (even when I was painting every day for years); watching and listening to the birds; listening to the wind; planning our gardens; thinking about Spanish; reading a newly found literature and learning so many new things from it.

Several times a day I hear and see large flocks of screeching parrots flying virtually right in front of my eyes.

And, of course, there's much more: discovering new fruits and vegetables almost daily; attempting to cook things that I've never cooked before; learning about Costa Rican art; having people drop in unexpectedly for quick visits and chats; planning new things—now I'm getting ready to try my hand at pottery—watching Robin become more involved with her and Bea's animals and pets—yes—even learning to love our bats and getting an enjoyment from them that I never even dreamed might happen; feeling healthier and more fit than I can remember. And all of this in just nine months.

And we haven't even begun to explore Costa Rica yet. There are so many places we read about and about which our friends tell us which we're looking forward to visiting and getting to know.

We'll probably start doing this as soon as the house is done. And then there's the rest of Central America to visit and learn about. Here, again, our friends tell us about the experiences they've had and the wonderful things they've seen in Panamá, Nicaragua, Guatemala, Honduras, and El Salvador, and we're looking forward to having those experiences, too.

## House Update

Progress on the house is considerable. We've reached the point now where they've begun to apply the stucco to the outside. The ceilings are in place. Today (I've been back from Mexico almost a month now), they've begun laying the tile on the upstairs floors, a major development. At the same time they're also in the process of building the patio around the swimming pool. The red tiles are all in place on the patio roofs.

The garden, though far, far from filled in, is beginning to show growth. The lawn we've planted is doing very well and helping to take away the raw construction site feel.

I've been very delinquent in updating our Web site, but Robin has been taking pictures, and as soon as I've sent this letter off, I'll update the site and let all of you know.

## Buying Plants and Trees

I'm continually buying hundreds of plants and dozens of trees. And continually I'm still amazed at the prices we pay for these. Today, for example, I had delivered the following: two ten-foot livistone palms at fifteen dollars each; five navadeño palms, about six feet tall at twelve dollars each; two nice-sized hibiscus bushes at three dollars each; and nine heliconias, about four feet each with several in bloom, at seven dollars each.

How many hundreds of dollars would one ten-foot tree be at your nursery?

But, in addition to that, my neighbors Angelo and Maryanne went in with Robin and me to buy twenty yellow pipa palms with which to line our road. They are varied in size, but some of them are as high as twelve feet. The price for these twenty palm trees (delivered, of course) was $150.

Most of us refer to this place as paradisiacal. If you're in love with gardening, it's even more so.

## The Batboy and Audrey Report

They are absolutely thriving! They seem to me to be a couple of very happy bats. They have a new home, which they seem to be enjoying. Robin brought it back with her from the States. She's also decorated it with foliage and toys as well as nifty little hiding places for them. One of the toys is a set of jacks (minus the ball). Robin puts them in a coop cup, and they seem to love flying over to them, picking them up one by one, and dropping them on the floor of the cage.

They also have a string of colored beads hanging down from the top of the cage. At the bottom of the string is a little bell. They enjoy buzzing by the bell and making it ring.

Every day, once or twice, we open the cage door and let them fly around the room. They make endless sorties; they come flying out of the cage, go swooping around the room for several rounds, and then shoot back into the cage for a brief rest. They'll continue to do this until we either close the door on them or they just decide to take a snooze, at which time we close the door.

But there is a difference lately. Audrey, who has always been stronger and more active than Batboy, has learned that she can hang from the ceiling. So now she'll frequently rest up there rather than returning to the cage between sorties. This only becomes a problem when Robin and I are ready to go to sleep—and we often let them out right before going to sleep.

When it looks as though Audrey has decided to take a long rest at our bedtime, Robin gets out the bird net, climbs up on a small step ladder—our ceilings are very high—and coaxes her to fly. Then Robin stays in place so Audrey can't return to her favorite roosting place on the ceiling, and eventually Audrey will tire of flying around and return to the cage.

Currently, Robin is beginning to design the bats' new outdoor habitat to which we'll move them after the house is done.

## Bat Speak

One of the most interesting things Robin and I have learned about bats has to do with their communicative abilities. There seems to be a series of sounds they make to indicate such things as greeting, well-being, annoyance, and others. I have the impression, however, that not a great deal is known about these many sounds. Robin and I read an article recently about Mexican free-tail bats in which the author claims to have identified twenty-six different sounds. By the way, the author of that article is the woman who ran Battie School—more about Battie School below.

But it's clear that our bats do make sounds of greeting when Robin, and sometimes I, approach them in their cage. The sound is like a soft "backward" click, that is, it sounds like a click but a puff of air escapes from their mouths.

Also, when they cuddle with Robin, they tend to make a sound that Robin likens to purring. We both want to pay a lot of attention to these communicative sounds for they're extremely interesting. If we learn anything more of interest, we'll certainly share it with you.

## The Pasture

We have a new project going on. Róger and another worker are clearing a pasture area on the property and sowing it with seed. It won't be too long before the house is done—maybe two more months. At that time, Robin will bring Dorado, the horse Bea has given her, to our property to live in the barn we've built. With about four more months of rainy season left, the pasture should be in good shape for Dorado when he arrives at his new home.

## Spanish

Still making a lot of progress with Spanish. (I should hope so, given how little I knew when I started.) I'm learning more and more, but of course, I never know from day to day whether I'm going to have a good day or am going to appear to be an idiot. My ability is still so uneven. When I went to Mexico, other than a lunch I had there with friends where we spoke English, I spoke only Spanish for seven days. That resulted in a great deal of improvement.

My vocabulary is also increasing regularly due not only to my speaking practice but also to the extensive reading I continue to do in Spanish.

Robin's vocabulary development has fallen behind a bit due to the voracious reading and studying she is doing about bats, all in English, of course. But she still continues to speak as fluently as I.

As far as new language howlers are concerned, I think I'm repressing them, given how many I've made since the last time I wrote. But I'll start to write them down again, so you can all have another good laugh at my expense.

## Battie School

Most of you don't know that Robin went to the States a couple of weeks ago to visit her family in Tennessee and to spend a week in Mineral Wells, Texas, attending what we've come to call either Battie School or Bat Boot Camp. This is a very intense (from early morning to late at night) hands-on experience in learning about the rehabilitation of bats.

There were five other participants (enrollment is limited to six). The woman who runs the workshop is one of the best-known bat rehabilitation people in the country. This is not the other bat expert, Susan Barnard, who was so much help to Robin early on. This woman's name is Amanda Lollar. She is the coauthor of a book titled, *Captive Care and Medical Reference for the Rehabilitation of Insectivorous Bats.*

Bat Boot Camp was a fantastic experience for Robin. She gained an enormous amount of new knowledge (not to mention the fact that she was also able to virtually wallow in hundreds of adorable little batties).

Robin is seriously thinking about creating a bat rehabilitation center here on our property in Lagunas. As far as we can tell, there is no such facility in all of Costa Rica, in spite of the fact that at least one hundred of the approximately one thousand bat species of the world are native to this country.

## *La Negrita*

August 2 in Costa Rica is a national religious holiday that provides an amazing display of faith. It is the anniversary of the finding in 1634 of a very small black stone statue of the Virgin and Child called *Nuestra Señora de Los Angeles,* popularly referred

AT HOME IN COSTA RICA 167

to as *La Negrita*. *La Negrita* is the patron of Costa Rica. She is housed in a basilica in the old provincial capital of the country, Cartago.

Beginning several days before the second, thousands of people make a pilgrimage to the basilica. Many of these people walk as far as 150 kilometers to see the virgin as she is carried out of the basilica to be displayed to the faithful. This year the number of pilgrims was estimated to be between seven hundred thousand and eight hundred thousand.

## My Buddy, José

I recently mentioned José, the cab driver that Robin and I use as a chauffer whenever we're in San José. He's really a wonderful guy. I've got to know him much better than Robin has because I spend a lot more time in San José than she does.

For example, as I write this I have just finished spending three and a half days with him. The three full days we spent nine hours together each day—I've had a hell of a lot to do!

One of the great things about this is that José doesn't speak English. So all in all, I've spent literally hundreds of hours with him speaking Spanish. I know this has helped me a lot.

José is a young man—he just turned thirty-seven. He's big and strong and, unfortunately for his health, rather overweight. He's a native of the area—he was born in Heredia in San José.

His father and mother, also natives of the area, were both educators before they retired. His mother—whose name I don't know—was a high-school teacher and his father—Braulio—was first a professor and then the superintendent of the Heredia School District.

José has a brother who is an electrical engineer. He has a first cousin who is a veterinarian, and another first cousin who owns the largest slaughterhouse in Costa Rica.

José has a miraculous memory. If he hears a phone number once or sees a number on a piece of paper, he knows it forever. San José is a huge sprawling city, and José knows virtually every street in it. All the other cab drivers who work at the hotel we stay at in San José say that José knows the city better than any cab driver in it.

I've never asked him why he didn't go to college and how it happened that he became a cab driver. But one day I will.

José is a gentle, kind, and honest man. He was married once and divorced after eight months. He then lived with another woman with whom he had a little girl, Danielle. Danielle's mother and José are separated, but José supports the child and sees her almost every day.

His other big passions are horses and bowling. He once told me that he only works for three reasons: Danielle, bowling, and the horses. Ordinarily, he wouldn't be able to afford to keep horses, but among his seemingly limitless number of friends and relatives, there is a very wealthy cousin with a huge farm not far from San José. This cousin allows José to keep his horses there free of charge. He doesn't even have to pay to feed them. His only expenses are for tack.

Several times a year, José shows the horses at meets. He also participates in many bowling tournaments and bowls every week. In fact, just yesterday, he showed me his picture in the newspaper in a full-page ad announcing an upcoming tournament. There was a list of the top-ten-rated bowlers who were going to participate, and José was number one in the list!

His current romantic situation is quite complex. About six months ago he fell in love with a woman who has multiple sclerosis. It seems as though she's in an advanced stage of the disease now and has been hospitalized for the last two weeks. There had been previous hospitalizations as well. The woman has three children, eleven, fifteen, and nineteen. The oldest doesn't live at home, but the two younger ones do, of course. José has moved into their house and is caring for the children.

He works from about 7 AM until 5 PM. Then he goes to the house and picks up the kids and takes them to the hospital to visit their mother and stays there a couple of hours. Then they go home and he makes sure that they do their homework and get to bed at a decent hour.

Sometimes if he has something he must do in the evening, he'll run home, get the kids, take them to the hospital, and leave them there, then do what he has to, return to the hospital, and pick up the kids after visiting a bit himself.

As if that weren't enough, he has just discovered that his cholesterol is through the roof, and he needs to do something about that as well. Though I doubt that he will.

Still, he is never less than cheerful, fun, polite, and extremely helpful. When Robin and I need to get something that's not readily available, José will make endless phone calls and drive to dozens of places all over the city in an endeavor to help us find it. Usually Robin and I give up long before he's ready to.

I've learned much from José and feel fortunate to be able to spend so much time with him.

I'll try not to let so much time pass before I write again.

Our warmest best wishes to all,
Martin and Robin

# CHAPTER SIXTEEN

## October 22, 2001

Hi, all:

A long one again.

### More Spanish Boo-Boos

Marvin asked me if he could fly directly from Costa Rica to New Jersey. I told him that he'd probably get a flight with at least one stick—instead of stop. (*Estaca* instead of *escala*.)

I went to the nursery and said, "I want three bags of ground—instead of soil. (*Suelo* instead of *tierra*.)

Then I told José that I had to go to the department store and buy a giraffe—instead of *carafe* for my coffeemaker. (*Jirafa* instead of *garrafa*.)

And on and on it goes. Nevertheless, we're constantly improving. I was thrilled when I saw José after not having talked to him for a couple of weeks, and he remarked how much my Spanish had improved during that period. The fact is, I'm making more and more errors because I'm becoming more and more adventurous with my vocabulary and my grammar.

I'm reading about 250 pages a week of Spanish novels, and I still read the newspaper every day as well. Virtually every day, more and more things move from my passive to active knowledge.

As I write this today, October 20, 2001, it is exactly one year from the date of our arrival in Costa Rica! Hard to believe. Before we left, I said that I expected to be fluent in a year. Did I do it? Well, no, not in the sense I meant.

I do speak fluently and can confront virtually any situation I have to. I've reached the point where I frequently interpret for those of our neighbors who don't speak any Spanish. But I know that when I said "fluent," I had in mind the almost-complete mastery of the grammar as well as a huge vocabulary. I'd say that my vocabulary is quite extensive, but certainly not huge. As far as my command of grammar is concerned, it's growing steadily but is far from mastered.

I wouldn't say at all that I speak "broken" Spanish, but I know it frequently sounds odd. I'm conscious of the fact that I often say things that sound like, "I am being in this country already a far distance."

On the other hand, I probably have complete control over about six tenses and shaky command of a couple more. Recently I've begun using the subjunctive more, not just in circumstances where it's obvious, but where Spanish locutions require it, and where it's not required in the other languages I know.

But now, with a year under my belt, I see that it will be at least another year before I approach the kind of fluency I have in mind.

## About Spanish in General

For the many of you who get this letter and have a strong interest in languages, here are a few things I've gleaned from articles in the paper recently about the Second International Congress of the Spanish Language, held in Valladolid, Spain, beginning on October 16.

"Spanish is the mother tongue of 400 million people, the official language of 20 countries, and is the fourth most spoken language in the world . . . but it is threatened by . . . a certain lack of interest on the part of those who speak it and by its scarce presence on the Internet."

The articles were interesting in that it was clear from the reporting that there was a great deal of linguistic chauvinism expressed by some of the speakers, and a lot of idealism concerning the role of languages in a democratic world as well.

For example, Andrés Pastrana, currently the president of Colombia, is convinced that "ours is the language of the twenty-first century. Spanish is the language of the third millennium because it is the language of solidarity and peace." I love it! This is from the president of Colombia, one of the most divided and violent countries in the world.

On the other hand, famous writers such as the Peruvian, Mario Vargas Llosa, and academics such as the Mexican historian, León Portillo, spoke about the importance of the coexistence of languages as a "source of creativity."

As far as the Internet is concerned, only "five percent of the pages on the Internet are written in Spanish," whereas 68 percent are in English.

The congress also coincided with the appearance of the latest edition of the Spanish dictionary, published by the Royal Spanish Academy.

## Casa Pacífica

Now, perhaps, is the most frustrating part of building the house. We're so close yet still so far from moving in. We're at the point where every week we hear "only two more weeks now."

Basically, it's the time of the last details: decorative tile work; finishing the installation of the plumbing and fixtures; finishing the installation of the water system, the electrical system, the electrical fixtures; building the various drainage systems; installation of the doors and their hardware and windows as well as the cabinetry.

Once the doors and windows are all in place, the painting can begin. We can't paint the place before we can close it up every night because the bats in the area love to hang out there for a night roost, and they make a real mess of the walls.

And it's a great deal of fun to see this progress because many of these things are the things that are making our house into a home. But, by the same token, we're so anxious to actually live there that our frustration mounts almost daily.

But it really shouldn't be much longer now. My best guess is in about three more weeks at the most. *¡Ojalá!*

## Participatory Democracy and
## Robin's Great Adventure

I'm not quite exactly sure what participatory democracy is. Though I've read a few contradictory definitions, I know that it is not the formal definition of Costa Rica's democratic government. However, one often hears the term used here to describe what is happening when the people take to the streets to protest. Public protest is a time-honored tradition in Costa Rica when a great number of its citizens do not agree with the government's (any government—city, provincial, national) actions.

Robin and I got big taste of this phenomenon when we made our first trip to Costa Rica in March 2000. It seems that the government had proposed opening the electric and communications monopoly. The plan was called the Combo.

People took to the street by the thousands to block all of San José's main thoroughfares and virtually all of the main highways throughout the country. There were several days of severe disruptions until the government finally backed down, much to the dismay of many of us who would like to see some competition, which would result in better infrastructure and services.

For Robin and me it was a nightmare. We were going places where, of course, we had never gone before (just like Captain Kirk and his crew), and if we couldn't follow the maps, we didn't have a clue about how to get where we wanted to.

We might never have reached Dominical (and, as a result, might not have been living here now) if it hadn't been for a really nice tractor-trailer driver who told us to follow him around the blockade.

So with that as a background, I'll tell you about Robin's adventure. A few days ago, she was going to keep an appointment with a young veterinarian named Pedro Martínez at his animal rehabilitation center between Dominical and Quepos. (More about this project later in the letter.)

The road between Dominical and Quepos is the worst *major* artery in the country. It is forty kilometers of agony most of the time. It's unpaved and has potholes big enough to hide a cow in. Sometimes the potholes are so bad that you can't even dodge them; they're across the entire road.

But as bad as the road is, the many bridges, probably about fifteen to twenty in all on this stretch, are simply unimaginable if you haven't seen them with your own eyes. They're all single lane of course, as are the majority of the bridges in the country. But they are so dilapidated, so broken up, so rickety, so scary, that you almost close your eyes when crossing them.

The amazing thing is that this is a major truck route. All day and all night hundreds of eighteen-wheelers use this road. It is part of the main road from and to the Panamanian border. Also, this long road is one of the best in the country other than this forty-kilometer stretch, which, as I mentioned, is the worst.

In addition to the huge eighteen-wheelers, there are large buses that do the route between Quepos and points south, and a myriad of other trucks.

It is really only because one sees these behemoths crossing the bridges that one has the nerve to do it oneself.

But every once in a while, a hole will open on one of the bridges that makes it impassable for even the most intrepid truck or bus driver. At that point everything stops moving in both directions until some sort of Rube Goldberg fix is made. This usually means that someone fishes some planks out of the nearby irrigation canals and lays them down.

So Robin was on her way to Pedro's place and one of the bridges was out. Most of both sides of the road for about thirty of the forty kilometers are part of a huge (thousands of acres) palm-oil tree plantation. The people in front of Robin knew a way to go through the plantation and bypass the bridge. So she followed them and, sure enough, got past the bridge and was able to go to Pedro's.

A few hours later, after the meeting, she was heading back and the bridge was still out. So our fearless animal rehabber smiles to herself because she knows the way through the palm plantation.

The problem was, however, that someone had tractored a huge pile of dirt to block the alternative route.

Naturally she couldn't imagine why anyone would have done that. Her guess was that the plantation owners didn't want all that traffic going over their land and thus blocked the way.

There was absolutely no telling how much longer it would be before the bridge was open again, so she made the right decision and went back the way she came, all the way to Quepos, and took a hotel room for the night.

She called our friend Bea from the hotel. (Bea lives in Lagunas where there are no phones, but she has a cell phone.) Bea then came over to our place to tell me what was going on and that Robin was safe and sound and that I shouldn't worry. She expected to be home the next day, not exactly sure what time, and was just fine.

So the next day comes and around 10 AM I get an e-mail from our friend Liz. Robin had called her in Dominical. (Bea wasn't available with her cell phone.) It had turned out that there were now three bridges out, and there was absolutely no way to tell how many hours, or more likely days, it would be before the road was open.

This left Robin with only one choice. To make the four-hour drive up the costal highway from Quepos to San José, go through the city, and then head south for three and a half hours on the Pan-American Highway! All in all about an eight—to eight-and-a-half-hour drive with stops!

And that's what she did. She got home just before dark, quite tired, naturally, but in good health and spirits.

And here's where participatory democracy comes in. It turns out that the three bridges that were out of commission had essentially been torn down by the residents of the towns along the stretch between Dominical and Quepos. This was their way of protesting the horrible condition of the roads and bridges and of trying to force the government to do something about it.

For years this road has been scheduled to be brought up to the level of the rest of the costal highway. Once a few years ago, millions of dollars had been allocated for the job. But it seems as though some corrupt official did away with the money. I don't know if he or she embezzled it or used it for some other pet project. At any rate, thus far, there hasn't been any more money allocated.

Closing this road is not just a simple local action. It has repercussions that are truly extensive economically due to the fact that so much freight moves along it so regularly. Whether this will force the government to do something or whether the police will be brought out to stop the protest is still an unknown.

And a last note: the road through the plantation was blocked by the protesters, who brought in a tractor to do the dirty deed and to maintain the integrity of the protest, not by the plantation owners.

Now, in June, 2004, almost all of the bridges on this stretch of the coastal highway have been rebuilt and are a pleasure to drive. It also seems as though the road will finally be paved soon. Time will tell. It's only been twenty-five years since the project of paving the coastal road began.

## Trying to Pay a Bill

I've mentioned several times that paying bills here is often a horrendous waste of time due to the system's inefficiencies. Banking was the same horror for me until I was able to do online banking.

The way I pay my electric bill is to go to some little private home at the foot of the mountain. These people have all the electric bills for all the residences and businesses in our area. You go to the house, tell them your name, they find your bill, you pay them, they give you a receipt, and that's it for another month. Quaint, but it works. This is how it's done in all the rural communities in the country.

I should have paid my bill yesterday, but I had to drive to San José and, therefore, thought I'd pay it there at ICE's main office. I had my customer number and expected that they could just look up the bill on the computer (and they are computerized) and that would be that.

I knew that this would mean standing in line anywhere from fifteen minutes to an hour, but that was better than having our electricity turned off. Well it took about fifteen minutes until my turn at the cashier's booth. I told him what I wanted to do and gave him my number.

He then politely informed me that first I would have to go to another line (and that one was really long) in order to get a photocopy of my bill before I could pay it. I must admit that I didn't really understand all of that, only that he was pointing me to another long line.

However, I was lucky. The guard, who had seen me in line and realized that I had been in the wrong one, led me to a manager's office saying that this way I wouldn't have to stand in the long line. Needless to say I was very appreciative.

So I sat down and gave the manager my number. Instead of turning to the computer, he made a phone call and told me just to wait in his office for a few minutes. He then goes back to work on the computer. About ten minutes later, he says "I think it should be here by now." Of course at this point I don't know what he's talking about, but I stay seated as he indicated while he walks out of the office. He came back a couple of minutes later with a photocopy of my bill. Then I asked him to explain (slowly please) what the procedure was.

It seems that they can't collect money on a bill without having the bill, even if it's in the computer. Since my bill was down in Dominical, he called the IT people (in a different building) and had them print out another one, which they then faxed to him. Now I was able to take this fax and get back into the original line. Again the guard came to my aid and brought me to the front of the line, explaining to the people who looked a bit irate that—I loved this— I was an old man! They're truly considerate of the old and infirm here—*grrrr*. I almost told him to forget it and was going to go to the end of the line. But then I thought, well, if there's anything good that comes from being an old man, why not take advantage of it.

So I went up to the cashier and gave him the fax. He punched up the account on the computer. I gave him the money; he gave me my change. I expected him then to give me my receipt. Instead he called in a loud voice to his colleagues, "Who has the scissors?" I wait another five minutes while he goes off to find the (one pair of?) office scissors. He then carefully cuts out the bill and then cuts the part of the bill that is perforated on the real thing, so that he can stamp both parts appropriately and give me my receipt.

A year ago things like this made my blood pressure go through the roof along with my anger. But I've mellowed so much (my blood pressure is better than it's been in ten years) that all I was thinking about was how trés Tico, and that this would make a great story for my next letter from Costa Rica.

In addition, this is the culture in which we now live. Robin and I have made a great effort to forget about "the way we do it in the States." Part of finding happiness here, or in any other culture not your own, is clearly to adapt and to adopt your host country's way of doing things. And I think we're being more and more successful in our efforts. (Those of you who know us also know that it's been a bit easier for Robin than for me. But I am catching up fast!)

An interesting P.S. The next day I went to RACSA. I had to pay my monthly satellite Internet-connection bill. Here too, I only had my number, not the bill. There was no line (the line at RACSA is usually small) and I walked right up to the cashier. I told her I wanted to pay my *Internet Directo* bill and that I didn't have it but I had my customer number. At that point I cringed silently, wondering what horror she had in store for me.

She smiled, took my number, punched it into the computer, told me how much; I paid and she gave me my change and a computer-generated receipt, and I was out of there in five minutes max.

Go figure.

## Poor José

In our last letter, I told you about my friend and driver José. I just found out that he has had some very bad luck. When I came to San José the other day, I didn't see him at the hotel. The other cab drivers, almost all of whom I know, told me that he had had a bad accident with the cab. He wasn't hurt, but his cab was badly smashed. It got sandwiched front and back.

I called him right away. He confirmed that he hadn't been hurt, but his cab has been in the shop for two weeks and will be there a week more. And in addition, he has caught a bad case of intestinal parasites, and the doctor told him he had to stay in bed for eight days.

He must be hurting badly. His cab is virtually his only income except for some moonlighting he does from time to time. His parents are both retired, and I'm sure they won't be able to help him too much financially.

I'm going to call him again and see if I can lend him some money. He probably won't take it, but it's worth a try.

P.S. He didn't want the money, and when I saw him two weeks later, his cab was fixed and he was feeling fine. Ah . . . it's great to be young.

## The Birds

As there is less and less noise on our construction site, more and more birds seem to be returning. There is almost always birdsong to be heard. We hear many of them singing but don't always see them.

Among the ones we do see frequently are black grackles, green parrots, and, probably the most beautiful, swallow-tailed kites. These are large birds, black on top and white underneath, with black outlining on the bottom of the white wings and white outlining on the top against the black. They soar over the valley at about our eye level. They barely ever move their wings and just float majestically on the air currents.

Then there are hummingbirds. One came up on the terrace the other morning as I was drinking my coffee and just hovered in front of my face, checking me out. In general Robin and I have found hummingbirds to be fearless. That's the way they were at our house in California, too, where we had many at our feeders.

The other week one of the workers pointed out a hermit hummingbird to me. It was an adult and no bigger than two inches from tip of beak to end of tail.

And of course there are the amazing toucans that appear from time to time. They have a very distinct song, and we hear them a lot more often than we see them.

Then there are all sorts of other birds we haven't identified yet. We have a lot of trees with many different types of berries and fruits that attract them continually.

Watching the birds at such close range is one of the great pleasures of living here.

## Low Taxes?

Are taxes low in Costa Rica? In the United States, income from taxes is 32 percent of GDP; in the European Union, it's 42 percent of GDP; in Costa Rica, 12 percent.

## Costa Rica and Ethnicity

Many of you know that interesting cuisine is not one of the delights of Costa Rica. It's rather a generic Latin cuisine here. Yes, there are a few Costa Rican specialties, but not nearly enough to cause anyone to get excited or to inspire someone to visit here merely for the food, as could easily be the case with Italy, France, and Mexico.

I think one of the reasons for the rather uninteresting state of the culinary art in Costa Rica is the almost total lack of indigenous culture.

I recently read that from a population of four million people in Costa Rica, there are only forty-five thousand indigenous persons. And these people are the remaining representatives of what had been eight distinct indigenous ethnic groups!

There are very few traces of indigenous culture remaining in Costa Rica. There are some annual festivals; our favorite gallery specializes in all Costa Rican arts and crafts with a representation of indigenous objects, but there's really not much.

The most frequently heard or read news about the indigenous peoples here has to do with their poverty. Of course poverty, discrimination, and exploitation have been the lot in general of the indigenous peoples of Latin America. The unfortunate thing in Costa Rica is that because of the small number of people remaining, there cannot be much protest by them on their own behalf as there has been lately in other Latin countries.

So that's it for this letter. Hope you enjoyed it.

Our greetings and love,
Martin and Robin

# CHAPTER SEVENTEEN

# November 8, 2001

Hi, friends and family:

Lots of different topics this time around, which we hope you'll find interesting.

## Something Unique

Now that Batboy can read and write, we've set him up with his own e-mail address: batboy@homeincostarica.net. Be sure to write him. He loves to get mail. We think that he is most likely the only bat in the world with his own e-mail address.

## Minimum Wage

Every six months representatives of the Costa Rican government, the unions, and employers meet as the National Salary Committee to set the amount of increase in the minimum wage for the period. This period, the increase was 7.71 percent.

As one would expect, the employers proposed 6.92 percent, the government 7.71 percent (the amount finally agreed on), and the unions 9.05 percent. Although 7.71 percent sounds like a healthy increase, inflation this year from January until May was at a rate of 6.34 percent. Optimistic predictions are for an annual inflation rate this year of 10 percent. So no one is getting rich with this increase.

Here are a few of the new minimum wage salaries:

| | | |
|---|---|---|
| Kitchen worker | $9.21 | per day (Note: per day, not per hour) |
| University graduate | $476.71 | per month |
| Butcher | $9.21 | per day |
| Bus driver | $9.62 | per day |
| Cook | $9.62 | per day |
| Guard | $272.91 | per month |
| Messenger | $251.50 | per month |
| Unskilled worker (*peón general* in Spanish) | $8.39 | per day |
| Journalist | $704.68 | per month |
| Secretary | $293.20 | per month |
| Domestic worker | $145.40 | per month |
| Technician in higher education | $389.21 | per month |
| Health technician | $389.21 | per month |

Some things to note about this list:

This is the minimum wage scale and many workers are paid at a higher rate. For example, the unskilled worker that I employ to work on our grounds gets $15.15 per day rather than $8.39 per day. Most of my neighbors are paying $12.12 per day, still almost $4 per day more than the minimum wage.

I found the pay scale for a university graduate extremely interesting. I'm assuming that this $476.71 per month is the minimum for a new graduate, perhaps going into a management-training program.

And that brings up this personal note. In 1965 I dropped out of graduate school for two years and took a job as a management trainee for a large insurance company. I was hired in Miami where I was living at the time.

My salary was $375 per month. On that salary I was able to

buy a nice little house (a three-bedroom rancher in a middle-class suburban neighborhood) for under $10,000.

That was the United States thirty-six years ago. It's quite possible that an emerging country at Costa Rica's level is on an economic par with the United States thirty-six years ago. I'd have to do more research to find out.

And while we're on the salary nostalgia kick, in 1968, I was hired as an instructor (who had passed all his exams but had not yet finished writing his dissertation) at the University of Tennessee, Knoxville, at $9,000 per year.

I thought it was rather interesting that the highest salary on this list was for a journalist, but I'm not sure exactly what that tells us. Of course the list published by the newspaper and from which I'm copying, is just a sample, not the entire list by any means.

## Drop-Ins

In the last letter I mentioned how nice it was to have our neighbors to drop in frequently. It's a great chance to see people, catch up on things, get the latest gossip, and spend some time with people you enjoy.

However, Robin pointed out that most likely the main reason there is so much dropping in going on here is because none of us in Lagunas has a telephone. She then said that most likely when we do get phones—and we might have them by the end of the year—there will be a lot less dropping in going on. Talk about a mixed blessing. It will really be a great convenience to have a phone in the house, but we'll certainly be losing something, too, when that happens.

## More about the Indigenous People of Costa Rica

When I wrote earlier that there are but forty-something thousand indigenous people in Costa Rica, I was wrong. We just celebrated a holiday called Day of Cultures and there has been a lot in the newspapers about Costa Rica's indigenous population. It turns out that there are 63,800 in Costa Rica. The difference in numbers is that about forty thousand live in homogeneously indigenous villages, and that's the figure that is usually quoted. But with the new census, it turns out that there is another twenty-something thousand who live in communities throughout the country.

For those of you who might be interested, here are the names of the various indigenous groups: Bribris, Cabécares, Borucas, Guaymíes, Huetares, Malekus, Chorotegas, and Térrabas. Seventy-nine percent of these people live in rural areas. And unfortunately, as is the case with so many indigenous peoples who were conquered by colonial powers, the great majority of the people live in severe poverty, with attendant health problems and little access to education and social services.

## More about Learning Spanish

Here's a fun one for you: The other day, while talking to Marvin, Robin suggested that the upstairs guest shower walls have the *chalupas* to a height of two meters. *Chalupas* are what we call tostadas in the United States. So, when you come to visit us, if you're the first one to use our shower, you'll be able to dine on luscious tostadas while washing. Those of you who come later will just have to stand in the garbage while showering.

And here's one on me: The other day I got into José's taxi and asked him, "Did I sleep well, last night?" And, sweet guy that he is, instead of saying, "How the heck do I know? I don't sleep with you," he just answered, "Yes, I slept well, thanks." Then about a minute or so later, he said, "Did you sleep well?" giving me the correction in that gentle way of his.

And another fun experience. Robin and I have been buying thousands of tiles for the house at a store called Guadalajara in San José, which imports all sorts of great furnishings from Mexico.

The other day I was there doing some buying and asked the young saleswoman where Marco, the owner, was. She said he was in Dominical. I replied, "Why, that's where I live!" She remarked, quite impressed, that Dominical was really far from San José. I told her it wasn't too bad at all. We've been going to this place once or twice every two weeks for months now, so I assumed she thought that a lot of travel—which it certainly is.

Then, the next day, I was shopping in a San José supermarket where I ran into Marco and his wife. I asked him how he had enjoyed his trip to Dominical. He replied, "Dominical? We just got back from a business trip to the Dominican Republic." No wonder the young woman was so impressed. I don't hear that well in English, but in Spanish my hearing loss can be a disaster.

Robin and I were talking yesterday and realized that we had both noticed the same thing about our conversations with Ticos in Spanish. Very often we'll say something, and the answer will contain a word different from the one we had used. For example, recently I was talking to Marvin and said, *"No hay espacio,"* (there's no room) to which he answered, *"Sí, hay campo,"* (yes, there is room). I had heard campo used in the sense of space or room before, but the problem is that Robin and I never know whether we're being gently corrected or whether our conversation partner is merely using a synonym. Sometimes we ask, but usually in a conversation, we don't take the time.

As you know, I spend a lot of time reading in Spanish. I'm convinced that this is a great way to learn. I've been reading quite a bit of good literature, which, for me, is still difficult and slow going. So from time to time I read simple stuff such as detective stories. Right now I'm reading a novel by Mary Higgins Clark, whose books I detest.

But the other day I wanted to get something light in Spanish and saw this book. I remembered that once I was stuck in France with nothing to read in English, and I bought one of her books in French. As it turned out, I was able to read the whole thing and understand almost all of it—and my French is about as rudimentary as it gets—which gives you a good idea of how easy she is to read.

Anyway, I realized last night while reading this book that I'm learning a great deal from it. I hardly read a page without figuring out something that is not part of my active Spanish knowledge.

I saw some evidence of this new knowledge recently. I haven't had much need to use the past perfect tense in my conversations thus far—I tend to keep my sentences rather simple. But I see a great deal of this tense in my reading.

Then, the other day, out of nowhere, while talking to José, I used it when I asked, "And had your father been a professor before he got the job as district superintendent?" I realized the minute I said it that I had used the tense for the first time—and without even thinking about it! Just to be on the safe side, I asked José if it had been correctly formed. I got an affirmative answer and was a happy Spanish student.

Very often I've gained a common word, which for one reason or another, I had never learned and didn't even realize I didn't know it. This morning, for example, I read (in Spanish) "She stopped in front of the sofa." I understood it but realized that I didn't know how to say that. How I could be here so long and not know how to say "she stopped" is beyond me. But I didn't know and now I do. And, as I say, something like this happens with almost every page.

The context helps so much! Of course understanding all these new things does not make them part of my active language store, but the repetition eventually does help to move many of them from passive to active knowledge.

But I still make the dumbest errors. And that reminds me of a story my friend, Jim Falen, once told. Jim and I were in the army together and eventually wound up being colleagues teaching Russian at the University of Tennessee for about twenty-five years.

Jim is one of the finest American Slavists I've ever known. In fact, in September, he is getting a medal from the Russian government for his magnificent translation of Pushkin's *Eugene Onegin.*

Jim is the only American I've known personally who, from time to time, could actually pass for a Russian. Yet as good as he is, I remember him one day telling me about an error he made in conversation. The thing was, it was an error that students rarely make after completing first-year Russian.

His point was that no matter how well you know the language, because you're not a native speaker, strange, seemingly autonomous errors come popping out of your mouth, apparently with no rhyme or reason at all.

And a couple of days ago, I made the same type of error in Spanish, the kind a decent first-year student would never make. As many of you know, one of the verbs for "to know" is irregular *(saber)*. The first-person singular is *"sé."* I knew how to say *"yo sé"* or *"yo no sé"* even before I had learned any Spanish to speak of at all, long before I came to Costa Rica. It's the most common of locutions, and I've used it more times than I can possibly recall.

Yet there I was in a pharmacy, telling the woman who told me that I should take two of these pills every day, *"Yo sabe!"* I simply couldn't believe I said it. I turned bright red and repeated, "Yo sé" four times, giving the pharmacy clerk a good laugh.

There's never a dull moment while learning a foreign language.

## Laid-Back Is Good

One of the things I appreciate so much about living in Latin America is how very laid-back the culture is. Of course this is a horrible generalization. I've know many, many Latino and Latina business people who are every bit as neurotically driven as their counterparts to the North. And of course Latin America is just as replete with obsessive and compulsive people as are the United States.

Nevertheless, I frequently find a refreshing willingness here to relax the rules, which results in much less anguish and tension overall.

The first time I noticed this was once when Baker and I were on vacation in Los Cabos, Mexico. She was going to stay two weeks and I a week. One of the reasons I was going back early was to visit our best friend who was dying. Baker had just seen him while I had not seen him in a while. We both knew that this would be the last opportunity I would have to visit him.

So we go to the airport in Los Cabos and find out that there had been a schedule change because of daylight saving time. That meant that instead of arriving at the airport two hours before flight time, we arrived only one hour before. We were told that my seat had been given to someone else, and that I wouldn't be able to fly out until the next day.

Baker, who was so upset about our friend, just fell apart and, while crying and sobbing, explained to the clerk why I simply had to be on that plane. The clerk was obviously moved. He told us I could go if I sat in the flight attendant's jump seat at the back of the plane. (It was a very old small jet, and there was one jump seat at the very back, situated between the doors of the rest rooms.) When we took off and landed, the flight attendant squeezed in beside me and buckled us in with one of those seat-belt extensions that the airlines use for extremely large people.

Can you imagine a clerk at an American, United, or Delta counter allowing that, or for that matter, any North American or Western European airline? I'll always have a soft spot in my heart for Mexicano airlines.

## Mario the Mad Marauder

Baker and I experienced another type of "the hell with the job" attitude when we made our first visit to Costa Rica several years ago. We had decided that instead of flying from San José to Quepos (where we were spending our vacation and which is only forty kilometers from where Robin and I live now), we would take the bus and see some of the country.

Our travel agent—cursed be her name—told us that there would be big modern, air-conditioned buses leaving from the bus terminal every hour on the hour. Well, we arrived at the bus terminal and found out that we had a three-hour wait until the next bus. And rather than being big, comfortable and air-conditioned, it was an ancient converted school bus. (Not to mention the fact that the particular bus terminal we left from, the Coca Cola terminal, is one of the most dangerous places in San José.)

So we get on the bus with our driver, Mario, a young, good-looking charmer. Mario's buddy was riding shotgun—that is—he was sitting on the steps in the front of the bus keeping Mario company with unending conversation, which Mario seemed to enjoy a great deal.

I won't tell you much detail about the bus ride. You've already read much about the roads here and the way people drive. Except back then, the road that today is not at all bad was mostly unpaved, and Mario drove like a man possessed. If Baker hadn't kept her arm around me, I would have fallen out of my seat into the aisle countless times. And fortunately, the children behind us who kept throwing up did have plastic bags handy.

We finally reached the outskirts of town after four glorious hours. As we approached the first traffic light in Quepos, a driver passed Mario's bus, cut in front of it, and then jammed on his brakes as the light turned red.

Well, no one is going to do this to Mario and get away with it. He lets out a scream, opens the bus doors, tears off his shirt, runs over to the guy's car, pulls open the door, pulls out the driver, and starts punching him out. The driver is not going to take this lightly, so he begins to fight back with what seemed a great deal of gusto. Meanwhile people are running out of houses, restaurants, and bars to watch the evening's entertainment. Eventually the cops come along. It looks as though we're never going to get to our destination.

But Mario's buddy decides that the show must go on. So he gets into the bus starts it up, closes the doors, and just drives on, leaving Mario the Mad Marauder to his fate. We never saw Mario again, thank God.

I can't imagine this happening this way in the United States. Although on the other hand, I did once see two cab drivers get into a knock-down drag-out fight in front of the Ritz in Boston.

## MUSOC

Which brings me to what made me think of all this. I frequently go to San José on the MUSOC bus from San Isidro. These buses are, in fact, large, comfortable, and air-conditioned. It's so much easier going this way than driving, and so inexpensive—three dollars.

I was thinking during the trip, how accommodating the bus drivers always are. These are supposed to be nonstop, terminal-to-terminal trips from San Isidro to San José over the Pan-American Highway. There are about ten buses a day making the trip in each direction.

But the reality is that the bus drivers will stop virtually anywhere to let people get on or get off nearer their homes than the terminals are.

When you're riding the Pan-American Highway, you often see little schoolchildren who live far from their schools waiting for rides in the rural areas that line the highway. The bus invariably stops to pick them up and then drops them off at school or home a few kilometers away. And this is for free, of course.

Today something happened which I had never seen before. A woman came from the back of the bus to talk to the bus driver. (Well, that often happens—people are always talking to the bus driver on these trips.)

I happened to be seated in the first row, right behind him, so I could hear their conversation. She told him that she didn't have anything to drink with her and that her little girl was very thirsty. *¡No hay problema!* About a kilometer down the road, the bus driver stopped at a little store and told everyone that if they wanted to go to the bathroom or get something to eat or drink, they could. We were there about fifteen minutes, and the little girl got her drink. *¡Que bueno!*

## The Excitement Intensifies

Although the entire experience of building Casa Pacífica has been exciting, we are at a point now where the last details are starting to be done, and we can see more clearly than ever what our place will be like when it's completed

As I think you already know, Robin and I have spent a great deal of time working on picking the ceramic tiles. We've been in dozens of stores; we've visited some of them dozens of times. We've searched books for patterns, not of the tiles but how they would be laid. I've even traveled to Mexico to buy tile and bring it back.

And now we're getting our first glimpse of how all this planning will turn out. Thus far we're thrilled! I really think we are going to succeed in creating the feel, style, and atmosphere of a sort of combination of rustic Mexican country and traditional Santa Fe style home. But we're also trying to get the feel of the dramatic Mexican contemporary style as well. What I'm really after, I suppose, is an eclectic yet totally integrated style.

Nevertheless, there is still much to be done. The reason I'm in San José for the next few days is to select and purchase the last of the tiles; all the light fixtures; and all the sink, bath, and shower fixtures.

We're still working on the colors for the interior walls as well. We hope to get them right the first time around, but at least if we do make a mistake with the colors, that's an easy one to fix, unlike the tiles.

This week the men will pour the patio around the swimming pool. That's a big step because then we'll really be able to have a feel for how the pool relates to the house on the site.

Meanwhile we're buying plants by the hundreds and barely making a dent in the site. Creating these grounds will certainly be a multiyear project, and I can't say I'm sorry about it. It's a wonderful experience.

### What's in a Name?

Rice is a difficult one for the Ticos to get. I always have to spell it for them. I frequently tell them that it's English for *arroz*, and that gets a laugh, but as far as I can tell, no one in Costa Rica or, for that matter, anywhere else in the Spanish-speaking world is named *Arroz*.

So I've been thinking that it'd be extremely cool to have a very Spanish name. Thus far my favorite is Martín De La Cruz Santiago. Now, does that have a ring to it, or what?

I told José about it today, and he loved it so much that he began calling me Don Martín for the next hour. He said the name had that kind of effect on him. Then he told me it conjured up images of Mexican *hidalgos* with huge landholdings and thousands of *peones* (peasant workers).

I guess there are a couple of contradictions here: What kind of a name is De La Cruz for a Jewish kid from Philadelphia? and how does one reconcile one's decidedly leftist leanings with being an exploiter of *peones*?

On the other hand, I've always thought how I might have enjoyed being a big French plantation owner in Vietnam in the 1930s and 1940s.

I'll deal with these contradictions by remembering one of my favorite professors who often said that consistent people are boring.

P.S. Just the other day, after I wrote the above, I was talking about the name change to a Tico friend of mine who happens to be Jewish. He told me that, in fact, many Hispanic Jews are named Cruz and Santa María and Iglesias and all sorts of other very Catholic-sounding names. This comes from the time of the Inquisition when so many Spanish Jews converted in order to avoid being burned at the stake. And when they converted, they would frequently change their names to make them sound much more Catholic.

## A Novel Way to Learn a Foreign Language

The other day I was at an optician's in San José getting a new prescription filled. The first time I wasn't able to understand the guy who was waiting on me, he told me to wait a minute and came back with another guy who spoke English. I hate it when that happens.

Anyway, the second guy's name was Juan Carlos and his English was really excellent. So of course I told him how good it was and asked him where he learned it. I expected him to tell me he had spent some time in the States or had studied it in school for a long time.

Imagine my surprise when he said he had learned all his English by attending AA meetings. It seems as though the AA meeting places he went to had a lot of North Americans among the attendees.

He's been attending the meetings for two years now. For the first six months he went to two or three meetings every day of the week. Then he'd attend one or two every day of the week. And at this time he's still attending one every day.

He had indeed had a couple of years of English in high school but had never had the opportunity to practice. Now he was around North Americans every day and decided that it would be a really great thing if he could both control his alcoholism and acquire a new skill at the same time.

He then made it a point of speaking to these North Americans at every meeting, going out for coffee with them, and even, after a while, attending meetings at one chapter, which were held in English.

He achieved his goals. He hasn't had a drink in two years, and he speaks great English.

We used to joke and say learning a language by having a girlfriend who was a native speaker should be called the audio-sexual method of language learning. I guess you could call this the abstinence-social method.

## Cultural Differences in Policing

In a previous letter, I told you about the local police officers who asked someone who had a complaint to give them taxi fare so they could investigate. Now I've had my own unique police experience.

Not too long ago, Robin and I returned from a trip to San José, and Marvin told us that the police had come to the house wanting to talk to me. They asked if I would drive down to the police station in Dominical when I returned to see them. I asked Marvin if they seemed to want to arrest me, but he said no, they seemed fine.

So a couple of days later I went to the small police station in town—not much more than a shack near the beach. This is the rural police force, one of the several police organizations in Costa Rica.

I found an officer in the street outside the station and told him who I was and why I was there. He then took me inside and introduced me to a younger officer. That officer then explained to me that their car was in terrible shape and that they just didn't have the money to get it fixed, so they were asking people in the community to make a contribution so that they could put the car back into shape. In particular, he said, the tires were completely bald and needed desperately to be replaced.

I told them that I'd be glad to help and took a ten-thousand-*colón* note (about $26) out of my pocket and gave it to him. He thanked me and then said that he wanted to show me something. We went outside where the car was parked (and there truly was no tread on the tires). He opened the hood and showed me that the engine was covered with oil. I'm not sure what the problem was; I couldn't understand everything he was saying, but maybe a gasket was blown or something similar. He then started to bounce up and down on the fender to show me that the shocks were totally useless.

So, I took out another ten-thousand note and gave that to him, too. He thanked me profusely and I left.

Some of the local folks think that this is just a form of extortion. I don't agree. It strikes me as another example of the Costa Rican talent for "making do" when there is often a great lack of resources—much like the story I told you about the jump cables. The car was a wreck; there is no doubt about that. The roads here where the police have to go are almost exclusively unpaved and very rough. It would be extremely difficult for them to get around in that car.

And, in addition, looking at it realistically and honestly, I don't even care that much if it was a scam or not—though I really don't think it was—because it seems to me that in a relatively isolated area like the one we live in and with no telephone, it can't hurt a bit to have the local police know who you are and feel well disposed toward you.

That's it for this letter. Stay tuned—there's much more to come.

Martin and Robin

# CHAPTER EIGHTEEN

## April 8, 2002

Hi, family and friends:

I began writing this letter on November 18, 2001, about four and a half months ago! Does that tell you anything about the tropical indolence I once wrote about? But I'm not going to try to bring you up to date on everything that has happened here since then. You all have lives to lead that include more than spending a week reading a letter from me. In fact, though, this is a very short letter, especially compared to ones we've sent previously.

### Welcome to Some New Family Members

We're happy to report that Batboy and Audrey are the proud parents of a bouncing baby bat. Spencer was born on January 18, 2002, and is as healthy a little fruit bat as you ever did see. He's living with his parents in their new outdoor flight cage, which was finished a couple of months ago. You can see a picture of it on our Web site (also a picture of Spencer). Unlike Batboy and Audrey, we will be able to release Spencer into the wilds very shortly now, and Robin is preparing for the release.

Yes, I know that I swore there would be no Batbaby. I said that we'd have Batboy castrated. Well, obviously that didn't happen. Turns out to be a major thing to have a little fruit bat castrated, especially here. So, Batboy and Audrey get to live enjoying all the pleasures of adult life.

Fred and Ethel and their four new offspring, Rosie, Pearl, Merry, and Pippen, have joined the family. You might ask "who are Fred and Ethel and their kids?" Cute, little white mice. You might ask "why are they here?" Because Robin bought them to feed to the three opossums she was rehabilitating (who have been released already, thank goodness). Part of the rehabilitation process involved teaching them to catch and eat live prey. So one day in San José, Robin decided to buy some white mice to feed to the opossums. José and I told her when she bought them that she'd never feed them to the opossums. Her answer, "I *really* think I can do this!" Right. Anyway, they're very cute and don't eat very much. Unlike the Great Dane puppy that Robin's currently negotiating for.

### Abbott and Costello Learn Spanish

Before we moved into our new house, I had a conversation with my friend José which truly reminded me of Abbot and Costello's "Who's on first?" routine. I said to José (or at least I wanted to say), "On Tuesday we move all our things from storage in the *bodega* into the new house. Two workers with a truck are helping us." I used one verb *trasladar* for "to move" and he used another, *pasar,* but that wasn't the problem. He knew what I meant by *trasladar.*

Then the routine started.

José:     Will the things be in the right place already when you go back or will you and Robin have to put them where you want them?

Martin:   What do you mean? We move it on Tuesday.

José:     Right. Today is Saturday. You're going back to Lagunas on Monday. Will the stuff be all set up already?

Martin:   Monday? I said Tuesday. Look, you didn't understand what I said, right? I said it wrong? Right?

José:     No, I understood; you said it right. But you weren't there when they moved it, so how did they know where to put it? Did you tell them beforehand?

Martin:   It's not Tuesday yet!

José (with a shake of the head): It's Saturday already!

Martin:   Listen, José. The stuff is still in the *bodega*. We move
           it on Tuesday!

José:      If you moved it on Tuesday, how could it still be in
           the *bodega*? Oh, they only moved part of it, right?

For those of you who speak Spanish, you figured out right
away—I'm sure—that I didn't give him a marker to know that I
meant the Tuesday that was coming. For those of you who don't
speak Spanish, you need to know that the form I used, *trasladamos*,
is the same in the present tense as it is in one of the past tenses. So
he thought I was talking about Tuesday past, and I was talking
about Tuesday coming. Had I used a future tense or said "next
Tuesday," everything would have been clear. The more I learn,
the more of a circus it's becoming. But I love it! How else can
you have insane conversations like this? Most of my life currently
seems to be spent having these types of conversations.

## The Move

As you've probably deduced from the above, we will move
into Casa Pacífica on Tuesday, November 20, 2001. One year
and one month to the day from our arrival in Costa Rica. It's
hard to believe that we actually got it all done. Building a house
this way is not for sissies, but we wouldn't have missed it for the
world—at least I wouldn't have; I'd better not speak for Robin.
There's going to be a great deal of work involved getting
everything set up right, but that's a job we've been looking
forward to for a long time. And I'm sure it will take a long, long
time to get everything the way we want it, not even to mention
the gardens, which will take years. But we have a great motivation
for at least getting the first stage done quickly; we're throwing a
big housewarming party for about sixty people on December 9.
We've invited all our Tico and non-Tico friends from Lagunas,
Dominical, and San José.

(The above was written quite a while ago. As it turned out,
because of the party we did get everything done on time. The party
was a great success with about seventy-five people stopping by.)

## Costa Rican Art

Today is Sunday and I've been here in San José since last Monday when Robin and I drove here in order for her to leave for the States last Tuesday. Robin went to attend a wildlife rehabilitation conference in Orlando, Florida. I had a few days of errands to run, as usual. We decided that it was really silly for me to make the long drive back to Lagunas just for two days before I would have had to return to San José to pick her up. So I decided to stay. Because I had so much time, I took it easy and only ran errands for half days for the first four days. I spent the afternoons relaxing and reading more of my trashy Spanish-language detective novels. Yesterday, Saturday, however, I decided to finally get around to visiting some museums and art galleries.

There's one gallery that is housed in the beautiful old former airport building in Sabana Park. This gallery is devoted entirely to Costa Rican painters. The display is not large—the building is not very large—but there were some wonderful pieces there, especially one mural, which I thought showed a strong Diego Rivera influence, and which was spellbinding. In addition to the permanent collection—only part of which is on display at any given time—they also had an exhibition of leading contemporary Costa Rican women artists, which, overall, was simply outstanding. The works were all for sale, but the two I wanted were already sold. The prices, however, were unbelievably reasonable. They ranged from $350 to $2,000. As it turns out, the artist gets all the money, unlike in a commercial gallery where the prices would have been doubled. But even doubled, the prices would have been reasonable considering that the artists are all well known and highly respected here.

As far as I can tell, there does not seem to be a long tradition of art in Costa Rica (not including, of course, indigenous art). A few months ago I bought a lovely piece at a gallery called Gallery 11-12, which specializes in Costa Rican masters. There didn't seem to be anything there at all older than the beginning of the twentieth century. The owner, a really neat guy who is a poet and some of whose poems I'm trying to translate into English, told me that, indeed, there is no significant Costa Rican art—other than indigenous—from before the late nineteenth century.

Then we went to the National Gallery, which is housed in a really fascinating building. The building is the Children's Museum, which also contains the National Gallery. Until the 1980s, this building was the state penitentiary. And it looks like it: high walls, guard towers, crenellations, round, decorative towers, etc. Evidently, from the display inside about the remodeling of the building, it had been a very notorious place. There was much information about prison gangs and also tidbits such as the fact that when some of the walls were ripped down, human bones were found buried in them. It had been built to house 450 prisoners, but when it closed, it held more than a thousand.

But the remodeling was a great success, and it's a wonderful building with terrific exhibits in the museum and excellent gallery space. The current show featured five contemporary artists who work in varying styles. There were twenty-five works by a watercolorist named Max Rojas, which I thought were truly masterful. The subject matter is almost entirely the jungle and seacoast in loose, wet, classic watercolor style. There was one in particular that I just fell in love with when I saw it, but it, too, was already sold. I later noticed that it was one of the three works reproduced in the show brochure. Here, too, the prices were a steal. I want to come back before the show closes and get one or two of Rojas's pieces.

## Wildlife Rehabilitation

Robin has been involved with a very interesting project at the Savegre River Wildlife Conservation Center, which is located about an hour's drive from here. The center is run by a young veterinarian, Pedro Martínez, from Colombia who is doing a tremendous job with very limited resources. His funding comes mainly from the Savegre Co-op and a Spanish charitable foundation. Money also comes from volunteers who come from all over the world to work there. Robin donated the costs for a domain name and site hosting and has created a Web site for the center. It was her first Web site, and I think she's done a fantastic job. You can see her handiwork and learn all about the Savegre Center at www.costaricawildlife.org.

## Potting

I've done it. I've taken up potting. This is something I've wanted to do for a long time and finally decided to "just do it." I won't go into all the details about the difficulties I had getting started—that is, in getting clay, a wheel, a kiln, and materials for glazing. But we managed to get virtually everything I needed. I'm having a great time and learning so much. Everything I make is still really ugly, but we definitely see improvement. If I ever make anything that's not so ugly, we'll post some pictures on the site.

That's it for this time.

Warmest personal regards,
Martin and Robin

# CHAPTER NINETEEN

# May 14, 2002

Hi, all:

## Batboy and Audrey's Astounding Adventure

Thought I'd bring you up to date on the exciting lives of our bat family. I'm sure you remember that Batboy and Audrey had a son, Spencer. The plan was that when Spencer matured he would be released. To that end, we never handled him and he did, in fact, remain scared of us and never approached us the way Batboy and Audrey did and still do.

Robin designed and then had a fantastic flight cage built. You can see it on our Web site. It's really an outstanding environment for the bats. In fact, one of the experts who helped Robin with the design online told her that it was an environment that any zoo would be proud to have.

One of the key components to the cage is a small vestibule with a door leading to the outside and one leading into the cage proper. The idea is that the bat to be released spends some time in this smaller vestibule cage to get used to eating and roosting there. Then, when the release takes place, the outer door remains open, so that the bat has food and a refuge to which it can return until it decides not to. This is called a soft release.

We knew that the proper time to begin Spencer's soft release would be sometime after he was weaned and after Batboy and Audrey had excluded him from the family roost. And eventually that's what happened. Batboy and Audrey continued to roost together in their basket, and Spencer was hanging around outside of the basket.

So one day Robin decided to move Spencer to the vestibule. What a surprise she received when Batboy and Audrey wouldn't allow her to do it! Of course Spencer didn't want her to pick him up and clung for dear life to the mesh that lines the cage. What then happened was that while Robin was trying gently to pry his fingers from the mesh, Batboy and Audrey did everything they could—short of biting her—to prevent her taking him. They would buzz her head. Then they would literally put themselves between Spencer and her and cover Spencer's body with theirs. At one point, Batboy even put Spencer's neck into his mouth to make it harder for him to be removed.

In addition, Batboy made the hostile sounds and gestures that these bats make when angered or threatened. This was a truly different experience from anything we've witnessed before. Naturally Robin left Spencer in the main cage.

This episode made Robin feel quite sad. She felt that Batboy and Audrey perceived her as a threat to Spencer and would perhaps not trust her anymore or would continue being hostile to her. As I write this, I feel that it might be hard to understand Robin's sensitivity to the bats' feelings. Of course Robin anthropomorphized the bats from the very beginning. And eventually even I came to do this as well. But this goes beyond such things as wondering, "Do you think the bats wonder how we can stand upside down like this without all the blood rushing to our feet?"

We have to remember the strong bonding that took place between the bats and Robin. She saved their lives when they were infants. She fed them by hand for months, slept with them, doctored them, groomed them, studied intensely in order to become knowledgeable about their species, and observed even the most insignificant-seeming stages of their development. And of course she has come to love them deeply.

Robin then turned to her advisors on the Batline online group for explanations and advice. It seems that what had most likely happened was not that Batboy and Audrey were protecting their child, but rather one of their colony. These bats are very protective of one another, and having seen that Spencer was being threatened, they came to his defense.

During this conversation with the Batline group, a discussion was started on the possibility of releasing Batboy and Audrey as well as Spencer. This was something that we had not considered since Batboy and Audrey were infants. We had believed that bats, which had lived their entire lives in captivity, could never be released.

But the way that Robin structured their lives in the flight cage changed a lot of things. One of the most important things was that she planted trees in the cage and hung all the fruit they ate from the branches. Before, when they were in smaller cages, most of the fruit was peeled and cut up and put into coop cups.

In fact, one of the trees fruited, and we saw that the bats had eaten this as well, the first time that they had discovered and consumed fruit in a completely natural way. Because of these things, several of the experienced people on Batline felt that all three of the bats would have an excellent chance for survival were they to be released. But of course they also said that there would be nothing wrong in not releasing Batboy and Audrey as originally planned.

The release of captive wild animals is an extremely complex matter, not only in technical terms of preparing them for release, but in terms of the philosophy of release. There's a large divide, for example, in the philosophies of animal scientists and those of people engaged in rehabilitation. One hears things such as: "One day of freedom is worth a lifetime in captivity." My feeling about this is, "How the hell do you know?" Nevertheless, when one sees an animal released, one knows that this is what rehabilitation is all about; this is its sole reason for being.

But now Robin was faced with an extremely difficult decision: whether or not to release Batboy and Audrey as well as Spencer? And she agonized over it for two weeks. At one very important level, this decision was pitting her own feelings of love against what might be best for the bats. Naturally her love for them led her to know that what was best for the bats was the only decision she could make. And she had come to believe that giving them their freedom was in their best interests.

Her only nagging concern was for Batboy, who continued occasionally to indulge in a habit from his youth: he would still sometimes land on Robin's head or T-shirt for a quick hello. Such behavior could quickly get a friendly little bat killed by appalled and terrified humans!

Thus, Sunday evening (today is Tuesday), Robin decided to release all three bats. At dinnertime, 5:30 PM, we went into the cage to put out their food as usual. But when we exited the cage, we left both doors open. We walked to the terrace of our house, which is only about six feet from the cage's entrance, and waited. During a period of about ten minutes, all three bats exited the cage. What mixed emotions we had. Seeing them be free for the first time was exhilarating—flying free like this was what they were born for. At the same time, knowing that this might be the very last time we'd see them was so very, very sad.

I was so proud of Robin's having made this difficult, heart-wrenching decision. And it was so much in keeping with her extraordinary sensitivity and compassion.

It was, of course, difficult to tell who was who in the dusk, but for quite a while one or more of them kept flying around the area, even flying across the terrace where Robin and I were sitting. We joked about the fact that for their entire lives, all three of them had only flown in circles and perhaps would never figure out that they could fly great distances in a straight line. Finally we went inside and eventually went, saddened and hurting, to bed.

At 5 AM the next morning, I went out on the terrace as usual to drink my coffee. And there were the bats, flying around, coming over to the terrace to say hello, flying into the cage, and then back out as the day slowly lightened. I knew that there was more than one bat there, but I couldn't tell if there were three, and I certainly couldn't tell who was who.

A little later they had flown into the cage to roost for the day, and Robin came out to see them. There were only two, Batboy and Spencer. Audrey was not to be seen.

We closed the cage for the day. Of course we knew that there was no way that we'd know what had happened to Audrey. She could have found a mixed-sex colony of fruit bats and joined it; she might have joined a harem—which is one social structure in which fruit bats live and mate—or she might have joined a colony of only females, another common fruit bat organizational scheme. And of course she might have perished. There are innumerable predators of bats in the jungle. There was simply no way to know. I was thinking that she might have found and joined a female colony because she was pregnant. But of course that was only conjecture or, even more, wishful thinking.

Of course we were sad all day, but just kept hoping that the best had happened.

And so last night, Monday, it was time to allow Batboy and Spencer to be free again. We followed the same scheme. Put out the food, left the doors open, watched a bit while they flew, and then eventually went to bed wondering once more whether we'd ever see any of them again.

This morning at 5 AM, I went again out onto the terrace, and there were bats flying just as the previous morning. It made me happy and I went to tell Robin. I couldn't determine how many there were nor who they were. Robin went out to the cage. There was only Batboy there. We were thrilled to see him, of course, and glad that Spencer was free. But still, we were losing one a night, and our feelings had moved from sadness to light depression.

A little later in the morning, Róger was preparing to cut the grass in the flight cage. Before we do that, we close the little windows that allow the bats to fly in and out of the roost in the center of the cage. When Robin went to close them, she checked to make sure Batboy was inside the roost, which he was. But she also walked around the cage carefully, looking to see if there might be anyone else there, one of the bats we hadn't noticed.

And there was Audrey! Hanging on the mesh outside of the cage. We couldn't believe it. Why hadn't she flown into the cage? How long had she been there? Had she been hanging there since yesterday morning when Batboy and Spencer came home? We'll never know.

But Robin quickly saw that Audrey was not well. She slowly approached the bat and raised her hands to take her down off the mesh. Audrey has not allowed Robin to hold her ever since she learned to fly. But she came right into Robin's hands. She was clearly dehydrated—one of the first things that happen to injured or otherwise traumatized bats. And shortly thereafter, Robin noticed a discharge, which then, after closer examination, led her to understand that Audrey had had a miscarriage, as well.

So for the next two hours Robin nursed Audrey. She held her in her cupped hands to warm her—she was very cold, another sign of trauma; she fed her peach nectar to help rehydrate her; she petted her, groomed her, talked gently and quietly to her. And then it became apparent that Audrey was recovering quickly and well.

About a half hour ago, Robin put Audrey back into the roost with Batboy. This, too, was fascinating to watch. Batboy immediately leaned over to sniff her; she gave a start and flew out of the roost and around the inner roost house for several turns. Then she went back into the roost next to Batboy. At that point, for almost twenty minutes, they engaged in a behavior, which we had always thought was associated solely with hostility. They stared at one another, shook their arms with great force, and made very loud purring noises. But clearly this was not hostility, but certainly some form of extreme emotion. Eventually they stopped, and Batboy spent a lot of time sniffing her. Finally, she started to groom herself, a very healthy reaction.

Now they're sleeping in their roost, and that's the end of their release. It's now obvious that Audrey was not able to care for herself in the wild, and Robin is still concerned that Batboy might try to socialize with the wrong human. Thus, it now seems that captivity is in their best interests after all. They'll live a long (probably ten years), happy life in their state-of-the-art flight cage with catered meals each evening. Not such a bad deal at all.

Tonight and for the next few weeks, we'll put food in the vestibule and leave its door open in case Spencer needs some R&R for a while.

A very emotion-filled couple of days for the batties as well as their caregivers.

## A New Bat to Care for

And one more announcement: There's a new bat in the Rice menagerie: a baby greater white-lined bat. About two weeks ago we were having dinner at the house of some friends who live high in the mountains and quite a bit south of us. Nancy, our hostess, took Robin over to an old shack on their property where there's a large colony of bats. She wanted to see if Robin could identify them.

When they entered, Robin almost immediately saw a baby bat on the floor. Clearly either the mother had dropped it, or something had happened to her and he was an orphan. They got a plastic container and scooped up the baby, and later we took it home. Robin consulted her books and identified it as a greater white-lined bat, an insectivore rather than a fruit eater.

Having always assumed that someday she would have to rehabilitate an insectivore, Robin quite a while ago acquired some mealworms—which comprise most of a captive insectivore's diet—and has been raising them. The bat was under two weeks old because that's when this species learns to fly. Now he's old enough to fly but still isn't, most likely because he's in captivity. He's very small, not just because he's a baby but also because the species is quite small. He seems to be doing quite well, and Robin will release him as soon as he learns to fly.

To avoid becoming too attached to him, we only call him "the baby" and are not giving him a name.

(Unfortunately, a couple of weeks later the baby died. He just never gained enough strength to survive.)

So that's it from Animal Kingdom, Costa Rica.

Warmest regards to all of you,
Martin and Robin

# CHAPTER TWENTY

## May 19, 2002

Hi, family and friends:

Thought I'd bring you up to date on what's going on in Costa Rica recently.

### The New Government

A new government has just taken office here. A presidential election takes place every four years and a president can never be reelected. In fact, just last year, Oscar Arias, Costa Rica's Nobel Peace Prize winner, was part of a movement to amend the Constitution so that he could run again. The amendment was defeated. Not much chance of a dictator taking control in this country short of a coup. But without an army, the chances of a coup are quite slim.

In general, the two major parties, the Social Christian and the Liberationist, seem to exchange power every four years. But this year's election was quite different. A brand-new party, only a year old, the Citizens' Action Party, made a very strong bid for the presidency under the leadership of a relatively young man and caused a runoff election. But the Social Christians won in the second electoral round. The previous president, Rodríguez, was also a Social Christian. Thus, this party will have been in power for eight years by the next election.

The new president, Abel Pacheco, is a sixty-eight-year-old former psychiatrist who has been an active politician for many years.

The first big change is his commitment to cutting governmental costs and corruption. To cut costs, he's requiring every governmental department to submit a new budget with cuts of 40 percent, mostly in the area of abused perks: travel, consultants, cars, phones, etc.

(Now, in June 2004, halfway through Pacheco's term, it looks as though his presidency will go down as having been very weak and as having accomplished almost nothing of significance.)

A new proposed law, which looks as though it will pass easily, is similar to the referenda in California, in that the citizens can, with a certain number of petitioners' signatures, cause a law to be submitted to the congress.

The difference, however, is that the country will not vote on the new law, rather it will be voted on in the legislature. Right now, the debate is over how many signatures will be required. Originally the requirement was 5 percent of all registered voters, but some of the deputies are arguing for 1.5 percent.

(An interesting political note: It is my understanding that Costa Rica is the only country in the world where members of the Libertarian Party hold national office.)

## A Political Scandal

There are a couple of new political scandals brewing, which happen to be related. Nothing special, really, but I wanted to write about it because it's so illustrative of the stupidity of bureaucrats the world over.

There is a government agency called IMAS, which stands for *Instituto Mixto de Ayuda Social.* IMAS was created in 1971. Its charge is to take action to help alleviate the problems of the most extremely impoverished citizens of the country.

Until yesterday, the agency had been run since January 2000 by a woman named Roxana Víquez. However, yesterday President Pacheco fired her.

It seems that the Office of the Controller issued a report about great irregularities in the purchase of some forty lots that are to be used to build houses for poor families. The first irregularity was that the land was bought from a family named Salas, a member of which is Lilliana Salas, one of the country's legislators. It's possible that she used influence to make the deal happen. But that's another story.

The second irregularity found by the controller is that several of the lots are not even suitable for building. Because the purchase was made by IMAS, *La Nación* interviewed Roxana Víquez. When asked why she authorized the purchase she said—and I do not embellish— "I didn't read the documents; in fact, I sign lots of documents that I don't read. I have faith in the abilities of the agency's lawyers."

So the next day Pacheco fired her because of a "lack of confidence." But the best is yet to come. Poor Roxana agreed to another interview with *La Nación* yesterday. I'm going to translate it for you, because if I paraphrase it, you just won't believe me.

Why do you think the president relieved you of your charge?

What was written in *La Nación* did me a great deal of harm. It led people to believe that I was guilty of everything.

But what the paper published came from a report from the Office of the Controller, which you yourself characterized as grave.

Yes, but my name wasn't mentioned in those reports.

The Office of the Controller indicated that IMAS had not exercised sufficient controls in managing its resources. Neither did it give any warning about the poor conditions of the lots it purchased in San Ramón. Don't you believe that as the head of the institute that was your responsibility?

I have no responsibility for what others do. You know that they've already instituted administrative procedures to punish the truly guilty ones.

To what then do you attribute the president's decision?

It's because I have many enemies who want to see me out of IMAS.

Of what enemies are you speaking?

It's better if I don't speak anymore about this. It's gone far enough already. I respect Don Abel's (Pacheco's) will. My position was one based on trust, and if he now says that he doesn't have that trust in me, this is what he has to do.

If this is the way things are, then what do you think the reason for which you've been fired is?

I think they're laying blame on me for not watching over the institute the way I should have. But that is not my fault. I'm satisfied with the work I've done.

And what are you going to do in the future?

I'll return to my professional work. I won't want for work.

A situation no different from those on any day in any country in the world, and poor Roxana is not unlike so many of her bureaucratic colleagues the world over. Only she just seems to have even fewer oars in the water than the others. *Pobrecita* (Poor Little One).

## Car Inspection

The roads of Costa Rica are filled with tens of thousands of clunkers. People do not have a lot of money here, and the cars are kept running for decades and decades. And these old cars, buses, and trucks, especially the trucks, are horribly underpowered; belch terrible clouds of blue and black smoke; have burned out headlights, taillights, and break lights; smooth tires; and virtually no breaks.

There is an inspection here—called the *ecomarchamo*—which is required to get your license plates renewed, and which is supposed to pick up on these things. The only impact it seems to have, however, is to raise revenue. It's certainly not getting the clunkers cleaned up or off the road.

So a couple of years ago, the government contracted with a Spanish company to build six inspection stations throughout Costa Rica and to provide an additional two mobile inspection stations that would go into the most remote parts of the country.

The company has now invested twenty-two million dollars in building these inspection stations, which will test the vehicles in an eighty-point inspection. Each station will have at least twenty bays; all inspections are by appointment, and drivers get their vehicles inspected in the month that agrees with the last number on their license plate.

The inspections are scheduled to begin May 28, that is, in just nine days.

And now, suddenly, there is opposition breaking out all over the country. The chief reason, of course, is that people won't be able to afford to get these old dying vehicles fixed and, thus, fear for their livelihoods. Some of the opposition groups say this openly. But there are other reasons given for the looming protests as well, for example, the chauvinistic, "Why should this be handled by foreigners? There are plenty of mechanics and garages in Costa Rica which could do this." Of course that's not really so because the equipment required for this type of highly sophisticated mechanical inspection is not at all readily available here.

Then there's the complaint that this is a monopoly (more about that below). But in fact, before work was started on building the stations, the country's Supreme Court ruled that this was not monopolistic in that all mandated repairs would be made not by the Spanish company, which only does the inspection, but by the country's garages.

It seems that the group most loudly protesting the new system is the union of agricultural workers. They have demanded a meeting with President Pacheco next week and will get it. However, the union's leader has stated that if the demands are not met, they will bring out all their heavy vehicles and block the nation's main streets and roads. This is the typical Costa Rican method of protest and is fantastically disruptive.

Robin and I got caught in one protest when we arrived here. That was about the government's attempt to break up the state electric-company monopoly. It's interesting to recall that the people who protested breaking up the monopoly are now going to protest because of a perceived monopoly.

Then recently the rice growers tied up San José for several days.

And the nation's high-school students also tied up the country a few weeks ago protesting a proposed decentralization of the nation's educational administration.

Now MOPT is saying that perhaps the inspection start date will be postponed because the charges for the inspections have not yet been set. Hard to believe, isn't it? This has been going on for two years now and proposed charges have been published in the newspaper a few times already. But this might be a way for the government to buy some time to try and work things out with the people.

P.S. The day after I wrote this, the paper related that MOPT had postponed the starting inspection date for "at least a month."

## ICE

I've mentioned ICE, the nation's electric and telecommunications monopoly several times already. It is an extremely important national institution.

ICE really needs help. You might remember our ordeal about getting a cell phone (which, by the way, we finally got). As of today, there are about 320,000 cell phone lines in the country. But there are an additional 350,000 applications pending! And ICE has recently announced that it will probably be late in the year before any new lines are issued. Basically, the problems have to do with Byzantine methods of bidding by the chief suppliers— Alcatel, Motorola, and Eriksson, and changing technology.

There are consistently promises of the availability of hundreds of thousands of new lines to be distributed "very soon now," followed by lawsuits from the providers, stop orders issued by the Office of the Controller, a governmental watchdog agency similar to the United States' General Accounting Office, because of violations of bidding and purchase policies, etc.

The situation with landlines is very bad as well, which is why there is such a demand for cell phones.

And then there's Internet access, for which there is also a great demand. But, because it depends on phones, many people can't get access because they don't have phones, as is the case in the community where we live. And on it goes. It seems obvious, however, that for as long as ICE has the monopoly, things are not going to get better.

On the fifteen-point legislative agenda for this session of congress, there is an item concerning opening the country up to other access providers. Given the huge protests here two years ago when something similar was proposed, I don't hold out much hope for this to come to be.

## An Update on Spencer

In the last letter, I told you about Spencer's soft release. The first night he slept in the flight cage. The second night, Batboy was there, but Spencer wasn't. And he didn't come back to eat the food put into the vestibule for him nor did he the next night. But the last two nights, food has been eaten. There's no way to know, of course, if it's really Spencer coming by to eat, but the greater odds are that it is indeed he. *¡Qué bueno!*

## Letters to the Editor

One of the things I look forward to every day is reading the letters to the editor in *La Nación.* They're not very long—there's a sixty-word limit every day but Sunday. But they're a true cultural expression and so different from those in the papers back in the United States. Here the letters name names and name companies. And they're loads of fun. For example, a typical letter will say something like:

> "Yesterday I went shopping at the Multiplaza Automercado [a large supermarket chain]. The cashier, Ms. So-and-so, was exceedingly rude to me. When I inquired about a special I had read about in the paper, she said that she didn't know anything about it, and it was up to me to bring the paper with me. Is this what the company calls good customer service?" (Sixty words exactly.)

Or "I have to take the Superduper Bus Company bus every day from Cartago to San José. The bus is never on time. Either it comes very early and I miss it or very late and I have to wait. I'm frequently late for work and my boss is getting angry. The bus company doesn't care about its customers, only about getting rate increases."

Almost every day there are letters complaining about ICE, RACSA, and MOPT, of course, and about the AyA (the water company), or the lack of courtesy either in stores or on the streets, the horrors of the roads, about false advertising—again, naming companies—bad doctors, incompetent lawyers, lazy bureaucrats, etc. I just love it. By the same token, one frequently reads letters praising this or that hospital or governmental agency, or business or individual who went out of his or her way to help someone.

I think that one of the reasons you don't see much like this in the United States is because of the newspapers' fear of litigation. There's not that kind of fear here because it's not a part of the social fabric the way it is in the United States and many other countries around the world.

Also, it's fun a couple of days later to see a letter from the manager of that same Multiplaza Automercado expressing his or her sorrow at the customer's bad experience and asking him or her to come back to the store for a special present so that amends can be made.

## The Rainy Season

The rainy season is here again (*whoops,* the Green Season— *pace* Costa Rica Tourist Board). It's so very, very lovely. The days generally are beautiful, sunny with temperatures in the mid to high 80s. Then, beginning around 4 PM every day, the clouds start to roll in over the mountains; it grows dark, and the rain starts. Sometimes it's gentle, sometimes quite heavy with thunder and lightening. It lasts anywhere from a half hour to several hours. And in the morning, everything is washed, clean, and fresh.

You can almost see things growing before your eyes. Truly, you can notice the difference in the size of the plants from one day to the next. There are innumerable shades of green everywhere

and vivid colors in the trees and plants. The rainy season months, from May to December, are the most beautiful of the year.
One just feels so good to be alive.

## A Closing Comment and My Ideal Country

Probably much of what I've written in this letter seems rather negative to some of you. But it's really not much different from most emerging countries and even from many highly developed countries. Yes, back in the United States, you can walk into a store and have a programmed cell phone with a number in a matter of minutes. Then in a month or two, there's a billing error, and you spend weeks on the phone, mostly listening to endless voicemail menus and messages before ever reaching a person. And who knows then how long it will take you to resolve the problem?

But the thing is that Costa Rica is so far beyond any other Central American country that you just live with the inconveniences—found everywhere—and focus not only on the natural beauty with which you are surrounded and which contributes so much to the wonderful quality of life you enjoy, but you focus on a truly free society as well, a democracy with liberty for all, the lowest poverty rate in the region, a strong commitment to education, no military, virtually no possibility of becoming a totalitarian society, short of a foreign invasion, and a population that is much more often gentle and polite than not. One could do much, much worse than live in this wonderful place.

But I must say that if I could create the perfect country, it would have the climate, ecology, flora and fauna, and geographical location of Costa Rica, the sense of style and design of Mexico, the food of Italy, the telecommunications of the United States, the general efficiency of Germany, and the health insurance of Western Europe.

If anyone knows where that place is, please let us know.

Our warmest personal regards,
Martin and Robin

# Chapter Twenty-One

## January 5, 2003

Hello, all!

Hope you remember Martin and Robin from Costa Rica. It's been a very long time since I last wrote. And yes, tropical indolence is taking a greater and greater toll, which, I suppose, is why I haven't written for so many months. Needless to say, so much has happened since the last letter; there is no way that I can bring you up to date on everything—and no way you would want to read it all, either. So I'll do a brief overview and then just go into detail on a couple of things. There's also a fascinating story of expatriate life here which I call "Greed and Grief in Costa Rica" and which I want to send you. But if I include it with this letter, it would be way too long, so I will send it out first thing tomorrow morning.

### A Major Development

You'll have a hard time believing this, and it will most likely come as a shock to many of you. Robin and I have put our house, Casa Pacífica, on the market. Yes, we're going to sell this little piece of paradise. No, we're not going to leave Costa Rica. Actually, we decided this about three months ago, changed our minds, and now have decided definitely to do it. Here's the story and it's relatively simple.

A few months ago I felt that after two years here I was really feeling cultural deprivation. Remember Goldie Hawn's whining in that movie where she joined the army? "I want to go to luuuuunch! I want to go shooooping! I want to wear my gold lame scuffies!" Well, I don't want to go to lunch or go shopping, and I can wear my gold lame scuffies here anytime I care to. But I do want to go to the symphony and other concerts; I do want to go to museums and art galleries and go to art show openings. I do want to go to lectures at the universities. In a way, I guess I do want to go shopping, too, but I don't want to spend eight hours just to make the round-trip to San José. And I guess I do want to go to lunch after all, but in a really good restaurant from time to time.

And, perhaps most importantly, I really want to be able to do some of these things at the spur of the moment. I also want to have more middle-class Tico friends and be nearer to the friends we do have in San José—though the downside is leaving the friends we have here in Lagunas. Most of these things we can do by planning a trip to San José. But it's a big deal in that you have to plan ahead, make sure we have someone here to take care of the animals (remember, three dogs, two horses, three bats, and four mice), spend a lot of money staying at the hotel, and eating every meal out. So what we're looking for is a place not more than an hour from San José where we can still be way out in the country with lots of land around us as we now have. We also want to be no more than a half hour from a good, decent grocery store (now we're forty minutes to an hour away from a very mediocre one).

In this way we'd easily be able to go to San José for these cultural events on the spur of the moment whenever we wanted to. We wouldn't need to have someone to take care of the animals because we'd not be gone overnight. And whenever we had to do shopping in San José, as we do about once a month, we wouldn't have to make a trip of one or two nights. Also, while we're at it, the place would have to have phone service, too, of course.

For the shopping, it really hasn't been a big deal at all making the trips. As I've described previously, it's truly a beautiful drive. More than anything, it's the cultural things that I miss. Without going into a lot of detail about why we changed our minds a couple of times, basically it had to do with Robin's being worried about whether she'd be able to do her work elsewhere. Finally she decided that she could do everything she wants virtually in any part of Costa Rica. So we've been searching for the right property with a lot of help from our close friend and attorney in San José, Darrylle Stafford.

Thus far we've found one area, Asserí, which is south of San José. It's a very beautiful place, half hour from an excellent grocery store and forty-five minutes to an hour from the greater San José area depending on where you're going. We wouldn't buy any land until we've sold the house. How long that will take is anyone's guess; it could be a couple of months or a couple of years. We have it listed with one realtor now and have a couple of ads on the Internet. We're going to get additional listings. If any of you know someone who is interested in having his or her own private resort in the center of paradise, just let them know you've found it for them. In addition to a full-time residence, it would make an unbelievable vacation home.

## An Anniversary

October 20, 2002, marked our two-year anniversary in paradise.

## Animal Stuff

Batboy, Audrey, and Arthur, their new baby bat, are thriving and all is well with them. Thriving, too, are the horses, Tory and Dorado, given to Robin by her friend, Bea. Also thriving are Jessie and Bug, and Rosie, Pearl, Merry, and Pippen (the white mice babies). Fred and Ethel, the mice parents, have passed on. The boys and girls live separated, and there will be no more incestuous, fruitful multiplication.

We have a new family member, Olive. She's now a nine-month-old puppy. We got her right after she was weaned. We thought that she was about 90 percent Great Dane and 10 percent Mastiff, however, it turns out that she's 100 percent Gray-Spotted Dumb-Dumb. Truly, "just another pretty face." But she's sweet and we love her.

## Yes, We Have Bananas!

All the banana trees we've planted (fifteen of them) have matured and are bearing fruit. What fun! And we have a great need for them. In addition to Batboy, Audrey, and Arthur eating a couple every night, and the horses eating loads of them, and Olive, too, the only banana-loving dog I've ever met, we always keep a stalk hanging outside on one of the terraces, and every night the wild fruit bats come and devour anywhere from five to twenty of them. The gardens are looking quite mature now, and the house looks as though it belongs here. There are several new pictures on the Web site at http://www.homeincostarica.net

## Snakes and a New Car

Robin has a new used car, a 1995 Geo Tracker, two-door, four-by-four convertible, which is really cute. We call it Robbie's Tootlemobile. We really need it, so that when I go to San José with the Jeep, she is not left here without transportation. The importance of this was driven home graphically when poor little Olive was bit by a venomous snake while I was gone a couple of months ago. Fortunately, our neighbor was home and was able to rush Robin and Olive to the vet in time to save her. Had the neighbor not been home, Robin would have had to run all over the community—long distances between houses—trying to find someone to take her to San Isidro to the vet, an hour's drive away. That extra time looking for a ride could have meant life or death for Olive.

## A Birthday

Yesterday was my sixty-fifth birthday! My, my, how time flies. The birthday was great. I had been in San José and arrived home yesterday (birthday) morning about 9:30 AM. Robin said she was sorry she only had a birthday card and no present for me, which was just fine with me. About half past 12, I started to take a little nap. About fifteen minutes later the dogs started to bark, and I heard a car coming up the driveway. So I called to Robin telling her I was undressed and in bed and to please see who was coming—muttering under my breath about not being able to relax. Two minutes later, she called to me and told me I'd better put on my pants and come out.

So I did and there were some of our closest friends and neighbors bearing gifts and booze and swimming suits, etc. It was a surprise party—and really a surprise—I hadn't a clue! Robin had made some great guacamole and enchiladas in *chili verde*. Our friend Liz brought a cheesecake; that's one of her specialties and my favorite, and they all brought various makings for margaritas—our neighbor Bill's specialty—this time mango.

We really had a lovely time, especially because I, who doesn't drink at all anymore, had three and a half of those killer drinks. A great birthday!

## Reading

The Spanish book I'm currently reading is about the history of the United Fruit Company in Costa Rica and the great banana strike of 1934. I'd always known that United Fruit (called *"Mamita Yunai,"* Little Mother Yunai, by the people) was probably the prime example of capitalistic exploitation in the twentieth century, at least in the Western Hemisphere, but I had no idea of just how unbelievably evil they really were. God, what a story!

My reading in Spanish is continuing at a furious pace. I still read the newspaper cover to cover almost every day. I've worked my way through all of Isabel Allende's (Chile) novels and stories, including her latest book for adolescents, *The City of the Beasts,* at least half of Gabriel García Márquez's novels and stories (Colombia), and the same with those of Carlos Fuentes (Mexico) and Mario Vargas Llosa (Peru). While finishing reading the rest of their works, I'm also starting, finally, to turn to the literature of Costa Rica.

## Nice Things about Living Here

And speaking of fun things about living here, such as learning Spanish, between the time I finished the above paragraph, about twenty minutes ago, and began to write this one, Robin called me to take a quick dip in the pool. The sun set about thirty minutes ago, and there was still the faintest pale pink light in the western sky, the direction our pool looks out to. The water was lovely, and it was a wonderful and refreshing end-of-the-day treat. (Even nicer when I think about the fact that it's January.)

## Medical Care Costs

I went through a nasty little bout of kidney stones over the past two weeks (all is well now and I'm feeling just fine). I went to CIMA, a rather new hospital in San José—opened in 1995, I believe—which is affiliated with Baylor Medical Center. It's the most modern hospital I've ever been in and probably has every medical gadget known to humankind. What was involved was a visit to the emergency room with x-rays, ultrasound, intravenous painkillers, and prescriptions; return to meet with the urologist; an operation to remove the big stone from the ureter; a night's hospitalization in a private room with accommodations for Robin to stay there with me; more x-rays and ultrasound; general anesthesia; return visit to remove a catheter. Total cost: $2,800 (with no insurance)!

If you've got to get sick, this is the place to do it! And speaking of health, my blood pressure and blood sugar have been perfect now for two years, and I haven't gained back a pound of what I lost in the first six months after our arrival. I feel just fantastic.

## Robin's Activities

Since we last wrote, Robin has done some interesting things. As I've mentioned, she's closely involved with the Savegre animal rescue center about one and a half hours from here, where she helps the young vet who runs the place in a lot of ways. The most important, perhaps, is her management of their volunteer program. Volunteers come here to work at the center and live with Costa Rican families there. Robin is the main contact for the program.

She's made two trips recently, one to Belize where she participated in a bat watching/trapping/release program and one to California where she attended a class in wildlife rehabilitation and the annual meeting of the International Wildlife Rehabilitation Council. Since she's been back, she's been working hard on a series of bat-identification sheets for fieldwork. She'll also be participating in March with a group traveling around Costa Rica doing the same type of thing that she did in Belize. She's enjoying all of this immensely and is gaining a prodigious amount of knowledge.

## Potty Marty Does Mud

About ten months ago, I took up pottery, something I've always had an interest in but never got around to trying. I've got a wheel and a kiln and have been teaching myself all this time. I'm not very good yet at all—it's a much longer learning curve than I had imagined, especially when you're on your own. But bit by bit my ugly little pots are becoming a trifle less ugly. And I'm having a wonderful time doing it. I've joined an online group called Clayart with a membership of about three thousand people from all over the world. I've received a great deal of help from these generous people and am farther along for it. One of these days if I ever get any good, I can send you all pots as presents. Aren't you the lucky ones?

So, that's it for this installment. Don't forget to look for tomorrow's installment, "Greed and Grief in Costa Rica." We wish every one of you a wonderful 2003. May it bring you everything you want it to

Martin and Robin

# CHAPTER TWENTY-TWO

## January 07, 2003

### Greed and Grief in Costa Rica

If someone told you that you could invest some money here and receive interest payments of 3 percent *per month*—yes, 36 percent per year—you'd probably think that you might as well throw your money into the Pacific, something that would make just as much sense as this investment.

Then, if you learned from many, many people, who had been participating in the investment, that this has been going on for twenty years with never an interest payment missed, you'd probably start feeling a bit puzzled. You'd learn that no one knew how this investment company, called the Brothers because it was owned by the brothers Luis Enrique and Osvaldo Villalobos C., made its money. At the same time you'd most likely feel that this was not a Ponzi scheme as you first thought because from all your reading, you never heard of any scheme like that lasting twenty years.

The next most obvious thought would be that they were laundering money. But with six thousand investors talking about it freely and with high, very high visibility, it would seem impossible that they could be laundering money so openly for so long without getting caught. The way a new investor became part of the scheme was to know someone who was already an investor and have that person introduce you to the brothers. At that point you were a "friend" who was going to lend the Villaloboses money, a minimum of $10,000.

Some loophole in the financial laws of Costa Rica makes it easier to do this kind of thing with loans from "friends" rather than the general public. When you made your loan to the Brothers you had two choices: You could pick up your 3 percent interest during a two-week period every month at their offices in San José, cash in a brown envelope, or you could let it compound at a different rate which came to about 40 percent per year. You could lend them additional money during the rest of the month. Upon lending the money, you filled out a beneficiary form and signed a form stating that the money you were lending came from legal sources. In return, you got an undated check drawn on the Brothers' account at Banco Nacional for the amount of the loan.

Almost everyone understood, however, that all this money couldn't possibly be in the Banco Nacional because it wouldn't be working in any way that could make this kind of interest payment possible. How much is "all this money"? The current estimate is about a billion dollars! It turns out that relatively few people lent the Brothers only $10,000. Some people lent millions; a quarter of a million or half a million was not unusual. And thousands of people put in anywhere from $50,000 to $100,000.

Who are these lender friends? The greatest majority, probably about 90 percent, is from the United States and Canada. Many are from Europe, and some are Ticos. By no means did all of the lenders live here in Costa Rica. Many just lent the money and let it compound and, from time to time, would come here on vacation and pick up a bundle. But the majority does live here and uses the money to live on, in many cases in a style much more luxurious than they were able to afford back home.

People came here to retire because they knew that with the interest payments they could live a retired life here easily, something they could never do at home. For example, if you had a home in the States and sold it for, say, $250,000 and then lent that amount to the Brothers, you'd get a monthly income of $7,500 or $90,000 per year! You'd recoup your entire investment in 2.77 years, and of course, the initial funds would still be there. And, as I'm sure you know from all the letters we've sent, one can truly live a life of astounding comfort here for $90,000 per year. Indeed, you can live a great life here for $36,000 per year.

The most amazing thing from my point of view is that so very many of the investors lent Villalobos every cent they had. They put their lives completely in the hands of a man with a business about which no one knew anything. However, it wasn't only that Villalobos had been doing this successfully for twenty years that gave many people confidence. It was also that Luis Enrique was a man of God, a true pillar of the religious community. He founded and supported charities, built a church, dispensed Bibles in his offices, lived modestly. A man like this, it would seem, is a man who can indeed be entrusted with one's life's savings.

July 4, 2002. The police at the request of the Canadian Royal Mounted Police raided the offices of the Brothers in Mall San Pedro. It seems that there was evidence that a Canadian drug trafficker had lent the brothers $300,000. All Brothers accounts were frozen. However, in Costa Rica the accounts contained only some six million dollars out of an estimated billion.

From July, Luis Enrique Villalobos continued to pay interest but informed his "friends" that, of course, given that his accounts were frozen, he couldn't pay back any of the original money lent until everything was back to normal. He requested his friends and God to continue supporting him in his troubles and to continue lending him money, so that he could keep things going. And his friends responded. One Costa Rican sold his car and mortgaged his house and lent the money to Villalobos. Others added to the money they had lent him.

Then one day in October, people who went to Mall San Pedro to visit the offices to pick up interest or to lend more money found them closed. Luis Enrique had departed for points unknown. His brother, Osvaldo, was arrested and placed in investigative custody for a six-month period. At the same time, another similar operation, the Cubans, who did essentially the same thing as the Villalobos brothers did but who had only been doing it for four years, closed their doors as well. The head person there, a man named Milanés, has also departed for places unknown with an estimated $250,000,000, much of it from the same friends of the Villalobos brothers.

From October until now, much has happened but I'm not going to write about all these details. The bottom line is that Villalobos is gone; the money is gone, and thousands of people still trust him blindly to come back and resume making payments again. People are selling their houses or trying to rent them. Others, still young enough to work, are leaving Costa Rica to try to find jobs back home. Others who can't do that are living in penury and suffering greatly. Others who were being treated for severe medical problems no longer have the money for treatment. Many are in states of great depression. Business that depended on the patronage of these well-off friends of the Brothers are starting to go under. Domestic employees are losing their jobs. A sad, sad story. And, to make it even worse, it seems as though virtually no one ever paid any U.S. income tax on all of those millions and millions of dollars paid in interest over twenty years. Needless to say, the "friends" are totally panicked that the investor list will come to the attention of the IRS.

What about Robin and Martin? I guess many of you are wondering whether we, too, were "friends" of the Villalobos brothers, and whether we "lent" them any money. The answer is an embarrassing "yes," but it's a kind of interesting story.

When we moved here, there was no way that we were going to give the Villaloboses any money. We didn't care whether he had been doing this for fifty years; something had to be rotten. As far as I know, there was only one other North American family in Lagunas in addition to us, who had not lent the good Don Luis Enrique money. Then in May 2002, I decided to make a little loan after all.

As you know, we have no telephones here in Lagunas and our satellite connection to the Internet costs us an obscene $500 per month. We were beginning to feel that this expense was becoming more and more onerous. At the same time, we just didn't want to be without a connection to the rest of the world and our family and friends. Well, $20,000 at 3 percent per month would throw off $600 per month, $500 to pay the satellite bill and $100 to cover the trip to San José to pick up the money every month.

We decided to take a gamble. We knew that this couldn't be legitimate but thought that if Villalobos could hang on for one or two more years in addition to the twenty years he already had, we'd probably have phones here in Lagunas by that time. The odds were, of course, with us in these terms. So on May 7, 2002, we lent our dear friend Luis Enrique Villalobos $20,000. July was the raid. Serves us right, we think. A gamble is a gamble, and even if the odds seem to be in your favor, you never know.

When we did decide to do this, we were fully aware that if we lost the money, there was no one to blame but ourselves. But we also knew that even though we'd never consider going down to the beach and throwing $20,000 into the Pacific, if we did lose the money, it would not affect our lifestyle. Basically we followed that old admonition, "Never invest more than you can afford to lose

I must say that the irony of it makes me blush a bit. Unfortunately, good friends of ours who gave us the introduction to old Luis Enrique were among those people who lent him virtually everything they owned. They're now back in the United States, working.

(Now, in June 2004, a year and eight months since Don Luis Enrique's departure, he is still on the loose and hasn't even been sighted.)

An interesting addendum is that it is quite easy here to earn from 12 percent to 24 percent per year on your money with investments that are fully collateralized, regulated, and legal. Unfortunately we didn't know that when we lent our friend Don Luis Enrique the money. But we do now. Watch those investments, folks.

Our best wishes,
Martin and Robin

# CHAPTER TWENTY-THREE

## January 27, 2003

Hello, all:

Sending that last letter out a few weeks ago has got me in the groove again to share some more of our life in Costa Rica with you.

### More Spanish Bloopers—Not Ours

I was reading a review in the paper the other day of a book just published in Spain, which is a compendium of published errata in Spanish books. Some of them were very funny. For example the one that talked about everyone in society being so familiar with [the hostess's] outstanding bust (instead of taste—*busto* rather than *gusto*). Then there was the one about investigating groins (instead of English—*ingles* rather than *inglés*). Ah, what's in a stress mark! There was a reference to the Lady of the Stretchers (instead of Camellias—*camilla* rather than *camelia*)

I'm so glad to see that the native speakers do it, too.

### An Interesting Comparative Culture Insight

Today I went to pay the garbage bill. Our Lagunas community has an arrangement with a garbage collection company. We have a place to which we bring the garbage, and the company collects it twice a week. For the service, each family pays three thousand *colones* per month ($7.87). We pay the bill by going to the local *pulpería* (little convenience store) in Barú. Somehow, our name got on the company's list three times: Martin, Martin

Rice, Martin Robin. Every month I tell the proprietor of the *pulpería* or his daughter about the error when I find the three bills.

I pay only one, of course, and the folks at the *pulpería* always write a note to the company explaining the problem. Today was the same thing. The proprietor, his daughter, and I were joking about how thick the company seemed to be not to get this. Finally I said that there was really no problem as far as I was concerned, at least until the point of their coming to kill me for not paying my bills.

At this point the proprietor, Arturo, said, shocked, "*No! This is Costa Rica!*" I laughed and told him I didn't mean it; it was just a joke. Afterward, however, thinking about this and talking with Robin, we realized that he probably thought I was serious, based on U.S. TV and movies where most disagreements seem to be solved by violence, including murder. No wonder he thought I might have been seriously worried.

On the other hand, I just read in this morning's paper that thus far this year, twenty-seven days, there have been five murders of passion in the country. Let's hope the garbage collectors don't feel passionate about this.

## Bye-Bye Satellite

We finally did it! We cancelled the budget-breaking satellite service two days ago. What made it possible was the new GSM cellular system that went into service about the middle of December. Most of these GSM capable phones have internal modems, which means that you can communicate with them through your computer's serial port. In turn, this means that you don't have to have a portable computer with a PCMCIA cellular modem card installed. And this, in turn yet again, means that Robin and I can have access to our e-mail and the Internet from our desktops at an almost infinitesimal fraction of the cost of the satellite.

At present, the connection speeds are antediluvian; however, in March, they'll be turning on the next part of the service, something called GPRS, that will give us regular hard-line dial-up speeds of fifty-six Kbs. Not bad!

What eventually happened is rather typical. They turned on the GPRS service in March 2003. The idea was that it would free until July so that they could shake the system down. At the end of July they announced that the free usage would continue until charges for the service were established. Now it's June 2004, almost a year later and the service is still free because rates have still not been set.

## ICE Woes

In political parlance in Costa Rica, ICE is an autonomous institution, as is INS, the nation's insurance monopoly. During the two years since the Combo fiasco, ICE has grown more and more arrogant and autonomous. They are extremely uncooperative with the government's efforts to fight its huge deficit with draconian budget cuts. ICE's salaries and spending rise exponentially. The service they offer has not improved in the least. They are inefficient and extremely expensive. Very ugly, as we say here.

Now that the government has mandated this year's salary increases because of lack of cooperation from the public sector's unions, the ICE unions—very powerful—made their first response, "We'll take it to the streets!" And now plans are made to begin protests next week. Some of the unions' leaders are saying that they are doing this to protest the unacceptably small wage increase, to protest neo-liberalism (globalization) and the fear that ICE might be sold or the market opened to competition— something that will never happen with the current government— and the government's impinging on ICE's autonomy.

And while all this righteous indignation on the part of ICE is going on, the papers are reporting—almost daily— scandals involving the institute. Their business development office was caught approving millions and millions of *colones* of unauthorized costs, approved by unauthorized people. The next day it was reported that ICE had been conned out of 450 million *colones* by three or four companies who had contracted with ICE for doing high-volume international calls and were bypassing ICE's switches. Using today's exchange rate, that's more than 118 million dollars!

The government, in its bid to increase revenues, asked ICE to require that people signing up for cell service and having their phones programmed show the receipts for the phone's purchase and give ICE a copy of the receipt, so that the tax people could make sure that tax was paid on the purchase. (A favorite tax dodge here is for stores to give people discounts if they pay in cash and don't require a receipt. That discount, of course, is the government's tax money.)

ICE refused to do it saying, basically, "It's not our job." Evidently the president put a lot of pressure on them because they are doing it now. And finally, cell service has become so bad with the installation of the new GSM service that there are hundreds and hundreds of complaints flooding into government agencies monthly. Not a promising situation for the country, especially when it's been demonstrated that one of the most important keys to the future development of the Costa Rican economy is world-class telecommunications.

I just can't see how that will happen as long as ICE is a monopoly. And finally, this from this morning's paper. In a certain neighborhood, where there are houses very nearby with landline phone connections; the homeowners were told six years ago that phones were coming to their houses, too. They filled out the papers, paid their twenty-five-thousand-*colon* deposit, and have been waiting ever since—six years.

Every year ICE tells them, "Next year, for sure." Finally, after six years, the homeowners filed a complaint with the Office of the Ombudsman. That's what probably got it into the paper. So the paper contacted the local ICE manager and he said, "Yes, it's really bad. And it's not just this neighborhood either. There are several more. But we're working on it."

## Food Prices

Quite a while ago, I sent you some sample food prices. Here are some more current ones, in U.S. dollars.

Agricultural Products:

| | |
|---|---|
| Broccoli | .50 per pound |
| Sweet Peppers | .11 each |
| Corn on the Cob | .11 each |
| Papaya | .30 per pound |
| Cucumbers | .45 per pound |
| Tomatoes | .35 per pound |
| Lettuce | .21 per head |
| Potatoes | .20 per pound |
| Pineapple | 1.12 each |
| Watermelon | .20 per pound |
| Bananas | .03 each |
| Cauliflower | .53 each |
| Oranges | .04 each |
| Carrots | .12 per pound |

Eggs—Eggs are sold here by the kilo rather than by the dozen. Medium-sized eggs are packed in units of fifteen and run about nine hundred grams in weight. Fifteen eggs currently cost about $1.10.

## Car Inspection Update

You might remember that I wrote about the new car inspection law and the strong resistance to it. There were many street blockages and demonstrations and a bit of violence. However, the government stood firm and brought out the police and tear gas. The instigators were arrested and tried. Eventually the program started and has been going on since last summer.

I have had my first inspection, and tomorrow, I'm going again after making the required repairs. But there has been lots of trouble in terms of inefficiency on the part of the inspection contract holders. For example, here's a letter to the editor that appeared in yesterday's newspaper:

"Loss of Time: After two months of trying to get in touch with Riteve [the Spanish/Costa Rican firm which has the contract for the inspections] they finally answered and gave me an appointment for January 20 at 6:15 PM. I arrived at 6:12 PM at a dark and chaotic parking lot. There were sixty people ahead of me, which meant three or four hours of waiting. This is a totally chaotic, mediocre organization, which is insulting and which rides roughshod over the country's citizens. How many working hours are lost in this scheme? And the nightmare will recur annually. I imagine, as in so many other cases, the people who created this are not going to have to wait in line themselves."

I must say, though, that I haven't had this kind of trouble. I got through on the phone to make my appointment the first time I called. When I got there, there were only two people ahead of me. Because I had to go back after making a small repair, I had to call for an appointment again. This time, I also got through the first time I called.

Because my appointment is quite early (7:45 AM), I don't expect there to be a lot of people ahead of me. And speaking of these inspections, a few days ago the newspaper reported that over 40 percent of the government vehicles inspected failed the test.

Update to the update. A day has passed since I wrote the above, and this morning, I went to get the car re-inspected. I had a 7:45 AM appointment but arrived at 7:10 to be on the safe side. Not a soul there in line. Hurray! So I go into the office, all my papers in hand, totally prepared for any bureaucratic curve ball that might come my way. However, surprise, surprise, I didn't have to get the car inspected until January 2004! Why? Because last year they started in the middle of the year, July, and everyone got inspected between July and December. Beginning this year, the inspection date is the month corresponding to the last number in your license plate. Mine is a 1 so that's why I made the appointment. It turns out, however, that if your car was a 2000 or 2001 model, you didn't have to get it inspected until 2004. So I was happy, but as I drove away, I was thinking, "Why didn't I know that?"

Most likely because I missed it in the newspaper. I don't read the paper every day just to improve my Spanish. The paper is the best source of information here about what's going on in the country.

### *Programa Ciudadano de Oro*

The Golden Citizen Program. I just love this. There aren't too many benefits to reap from turning sixty-five. Social Security is one, and another here in Costa Rica is the Golden Citizen Program, something I qualified for because I'm a resident.

You apply to the Social Security Administration here, and you get a Gold Card. This card entitles you to a great many benefits, including discounts in literally hundreds of businesses, anywhere from 5 percent to 50 percent. That's great, of course, but the very best thing is that in most public offices and banks, with your Gold Card you can go to the head of the line!

Some offices have special windows that just serve us golden citizens. This is going to make life a lot easier.

### Costa Rican Addresses

In Costa Rica you can't use a Costa Rican driver's license or resident's ID card for address verification. You can only use an ICE or AyA bill. You might wonder why. The reason is because your address is only on the latter documents.

Addresses are very strange in Costa Rica. For example, ours is "from the *pulpería* in Barú, 2.4 kilometers north, 900 meters west, 300 meters north." And it's not just in the boondocks where you have this kind of address.

My friend and attorney, Darrylle Stafford, who lives right in San José has this address: "from Matuti Gómez [a landmark house in the city] three hundred meters south, one hundred east, one hundred south, apartment building Indiana, number 12."

## Becoming More and More Tico

So having my Gold Card is another step in my "Ticoization," which is progressing rapidly. Not too long ago, I told some friends who live here and who were going to the States that I'd take care of getting their *marchamo,* that is, renewing their car registration. I had to do mine so doing theirs was no big deal at all. I found a small bank in San Isidro where you can do the renewal and which never has a line to wait in. So I went there, went straight up to the window—no wait—got my registration renewed, and then passed the teller the papers for my friends.

Nope, can't do theirs here. They had a temporary registration from last year, so it's not really a renewal. So I had to go to the office of INS, the insurance monopoly. Rather a long wait, about an hour. Then the young lady tells me that I need to go to the *Registro,* the National Registry, and get some document with the necessary stamps. In addition, I needed photocopies of several documents. By this time it was late, so I decided to finish up on my next trip to San Isidro in a few days.

I returned, did my wait at the *Registro,* then got all my photocopies. Then I returned to INS. Waited about forty-five minutes, surprised that the lines were moving more slowly than usual. Then I heard the announcement that the computer system had crashed, and it'd be half an hour until it was up again. OK, no problem, I needed to go get some lunch anyway. Returned in about twenty minutes to learn that it was probably going to be a couple of more hours until the system was up again. OK, no problem. I'll finish up on my next trip.

And I did a few days later with only about half hour in line. (It also turned out that I only needed one document photocopied rather than the several that had been indicated initially.) Mission accomplished. At that point I realized that not once through all those visits and offices and waits did I get upset. I was amazed. Two years ago I would have had a stroke.

The next week I was riding around San José with our friend José running some errands and I told him the story, especially about how I didn't get angry in the least. And he said that I was really becoming more and more Tico. "However," he added, "you still have one great hurdle to jump." "What's that?" "The next time you have an appointment, you must arrive a half hour late!" If I can ever pull that off, I'll know that my life has changed completely.

## Is This Negative?

When Robin read this installment before I sent it off, she expressed some concern that it would come across as being quite negative, and that you would think that it's horrible here when in fact, we think it's wonderful. Well, certainly much of what I've written here sounds terrible, but what one has to remember is that this is not the United States. Things are just different here, as they're different almost everywhere. It's a way of life that is not the way of life in the United States.

And, just as in the United States, people here express their dissatisfactions with the way a lot of things are, too. But it's their country, and they love it, and they're happy here to the same degree that this is true in the United States with most of the people who live there. We, ourselves, are extremely happy here, and we're learning more and more how to adapt to our new home. And we're being quite successful.

Certainly I feel a bit of frustration from time to time, but I don't get angry and, in fact, smiled to myself a bit on the way home while thinking, "How typical. Robin will get a kick out of it, and it'll make yet another good story to write home about."

Moreover, as I write this at about 5 in the afternoon, I'm listening to "our" toucans' beautiful, plaintive calls from a Cecropia tree not more than fifty meters from where I sit. They call for us every morning and every evening. And I don't know why, but listening to them just goes right to my heart. I feel some sort of acute, pleasurable, happy sadness as they call for fifteen or twenty minutes at a time, for what, I don't know. But I do know that I wish they find what they're seeking, and that I will never have to stop listening to them.

Warmest personal regards to all.
Martin and Robin

# Chapter Twenty-Four

## March 22, 2003

Hi, friends and family:

### Golden Citizen's Card Rules!

In the last letter, I told you I was getting my *Tarjeta Ciudadano de Oro*, or the Golden Citizen's Card. I have it, and what a boon it's been already. The very best thing was when my friend José and I had to go to the *Registro Nacional* to pick up the license plates for Robin's Tootlemobile. The line was so long I could barely see the front. Given my newly found expertise in judging lines, I saw this was a two-hour wait.

There was a young man, an employee of the *Registro*, walking up and down the line helping people with their paperwork. When he got near us, José, in a stroke of genius, asked him if Golden Citizens could go to the front of the line. (I'm not used to asking yet.) Not only was the answer yes, but he walked me there and told the people at the front of the line that I was a *Ciudadano de Oro*. I got a few dirty looks, but who cares?

On that same trip I had to buy some medicine. My card got me a 15 percent discount at one place and a 10 percent discount at another. Wow, do I love my *Tarjeta*!

### Do Not Get a Traffic Ticket in Costa Rica!

The other day Robin took a couple of friends down to Dominical in her Tootlemobile. She had only planned on visiting someone here in Lagunas where there are no police and, thus, didn't bother to take her driver's license with her. Then she forgot about it when they decided to go to Dominical. There are frequently police on the road to Dominical checking licenses and other papers and looking for contraband because it's a main route to and from Panamá.

Robin saw the cops, and instead of trying to drive past in the hope of not getting stopped—it's usually a spot-check—she made the mistake of turning around and going the way she had come. Whoops! The cops noticed and gave chase. So she explained what the problem was. The cop kept her registration and told her to go home and get her license, which she duly did as an honest resident. When she went back, however, he issued her a ticket for not having had her license with her. Not a very expensive ticket, or so it seemed.

It was only two thousand *colones*, about $5.17. She was told she could pay it at one of several banks in San Isidro. I had to go to San Isidro today and took the ticket with me to pay. Went to the bank, waited in line for about fifteen minutes (really weren't enough people there to justify whipping out my Gold Citizen's Card), and paid. They add another 30 percent of the ticket amount (six hundred *colones* = $1.55) for PANI—a good cause. PANI takes care of abused and homeless kids.

Then the teller says that I have to go to a store and get a twenty-*colón* government stamp and paste it on the back of the ticket. Well, twenty *colones* is just a couple of cents, though going to yet another place was a bit of a pain. Then, she adds, I need to get a photocopy of both sides of the ticket. That means another stop and a few more cents. But I was puzzled. "Why," I naively asked, "do I need a photocopy?" "Because," she politely answered, "you have to turn it into the court."

I thought that this was getting a bit out of hand, but there's not much to do about it, and it was yet another experience in the vagaries of the Costa Rican bureaucracy. So I asked her if the court was the building across from the Texaco station on the Pan-American Highway in San Isidro. She took a look at the ticket and said, "No, this ticket was issued in the Canton of Osa, so you have to go there." Even more naively I said, "There's no courthouse in Dominical." And then it happened. She told me that the courthouse for the Canton of Osa is in Ciudad Cortez. I thought I'd stroke out.

Ciudad Cortez is at least a two-hour drive from here! How fortunate for Robbie that she's out of town for the next ten days and does not have to make that horrible drive that I'll make tomorrow and then have to listen to me bitch and complain about it. Which, of course, I'll do anyway when she comes home.

## Getting Health Insurance

I've frequently mentioned INS, the Costa Rican insurance institute, which is a monopoly. Not too long ago, Robin and I applied for insurance through our INS agent. It's really pretty good insurance, not horribly expensive, and you can use it at all the outstanding private hospitals in Costa Rica. Well, I got denied because of my various heath difficulties, even though they're all under control, although the reason they gave for denying me was just my diabetes. So we requested a review, and it was denied again. I told my doctor, and he suggested that I get a lawyer and pay INS a visit.

His reasoning was that INS was a monopoly, and it wasn't as though I could go to the competition. He also said that he knew several people who had done this successfully. So I spoke to my lawyers, and they did some investigation and found out that, first, INS can deny people because there is, in fact, an option. That is, getting insurance through the *Caja*, the Social Security Institute, which accepts everyone. In addition, I was told that if INS did insure me on appeal, they would put a surcharge on the premium that would be so high that I'd probably save money by being self-insured.

The problem with the *Caja* insurance is that you can only use *Caja* hospitals, which are—I'm sorry to say—generally quite poor. In fact, the only reason people I know would go to the hospital in San Isidro or Quepos—the two closest, for example— would be for an emergency such as being bit by a rabid dog or a snake. In addition, you can wait months for an appointment, and lines are so long you're usually waiting in the next county when you join them. And the Gold Card doesn't do much good here because so many patients are elderly and have their own cards.

However, they do pay most of the cost of your medicine bills, and that's my biggest expense. And the premiums are extremely low, about $30 per month. My medicine expenses are hundreds of dollars per month, so it made sense for me to sign up. The downside is that all prescriptions, which are issued by a *Caja* doctor, are only good for a month's supply at a time. This, of course, means that every month I'll have to go to the hospital in San Isidro to get my prescriptions renewed.

Oh well, that's life in Costa Rica. The bright side is that I get to speak a lot of Spanish while waiting in those lines. So today, because while in San Isidro I had to go to the *Caja* offices anyway, as I do every month to pay the social security medical taxes for our employee, I decided that if the lines weren't too long, I'd take the challenge and try to sign up.

I inquired about voluntary insurance for myself. The young man checked the computer, filled out a very short form—which, I learned, said that I was not already signed up—and then told me to go to another place in the office. When I got there, the desk was empty, and no one was in line. One of the employees told me that the woman I had to see was away from her desk and having a *cafecito* (cup of coffee—diminutive form). She returned quickly, and I explained what I wanted and showed her my resident's ID. I don't think that she had ever seen one of these before.

So she took it to check with someone and, when she returned, told me it was OK. Then came the filling out of forms. That's one of the interesting and inscrutable things about Costa Rica. The country is exceedingly well computerized. But no matter how much they do on the computer for transactions such as this, there's always a great deal done by hand, as well. After typing information into the computer for almost fifteen minutes, she then took out a form and put it into her ancient Royal typewriter and spent another ten minutes on that. Then she took out a sheet of printed ID numbers, cut one out with a scissors, got a bottle of glue from her drawer, pasted it on the form she had typed, punched holes in it, and put it in a loose leaf binder. Then she filled out another form on the typewriter, folded that up, and gave it to me. I then was told to go to the cashier's office and pay the first monthly premium and bring my receipt back to her, which, of course, I dutifully did.

She then unfolded the form she had given me, stamped it, refolded it, and gave it to me again. She then explained that I needed to go to the hospital to get my insurance card. I could do that whenever I wanted to, but I'd have to have it to get any services. At that point, I decided to do that on my next visit to San Isidro. It had been a very long four hours there already—what with running several errands, paying the ticket, paying our employee's medical taxes, and signing up for insurance. I didn't think I wanted to spend a couple of hours getting my ID card. Then, of course, I'll have to see a doctor to get my prescriptions. That'll be another adventure next week.

## And You Think You Have Problems?

Here's another letter to the editor of *La Nación*. This will go down as one of my favorites. "As a frequent customer of McDonald's, I'm bothered by the fact that in the drive-thrus they never give you catsup when you order a combination meal. I see no reason for having to ask for this every time. Nelson Guillén A. Zapote, San José"

Here are a couple of others from the same edition: "There's a public health clinic in Cuajiniquil, La Cruz, Guanacaste. But the person who works there spends more time involved in his own activities than in doing what he's paid for. Madame Minister: It cannot be this way. Alejandro Espinoza L. Cartago"

"When the current mayor of Tibás was campaigning, he stopped at my house in Las Reines (and, I imagine, at the rest of the houses in the entire canton, too). He promised us heaven on earth if he was elected. However, in the brief time that has elapsed since the beginning of his administration, the garbage collection trucks have not come by at the scheduled times (sometimes for as long as four or five days). This has automatically—with the help of dogs, cats, and vagabonds—converted the neighborhood streets into a complete fly festival and public trash dump. I, at least, would be ashamed if I were, God forbid, the mayor of this public dump. Fernando Díaz L. Tibás"

Incidentally, this year was the first year mayors were elected in Costa Rica. Until now they had always been appointed.

## Bat Wrangler

I mentioned earlier that Robin is out of town. She's on a two-week trip all over Costa Rica with an international group on a bat and wildlife study tour under the auspices of Bat Conservation International. You might remember that she went on the same kind of trip last year in Belize. But this year she's working as a staff member. She's a bat wrangler. At night, when they capture bats in mist nets to look at carefully (and then release), she's one of the people who is charged with carefully and safely disentangling the bats from the nets. She's been phoning regularly and tells me she is having the most wonderful time (as she did in Belize).

## Why I Love Costa Rica (Traffic Ticket Continued)

I put off driving to Cortez to turn in the traffic ticket yesterday. Today, Saturday, I couldn't do it, of course, because the court wouldn't be open. But I drove down to Dominical to get a newspaper, and there were a couple of cops checking cars. I pulled over and told them I'd like to ask a question. I explained all about what had happened and asked if it were really true that I had to drive down there to the court. What a wonderful answer I got. They said that I really didn't need to bother. No one would notice whether it was turned in or not. Every great once in a while they might notice, and then when you go to get your annual *marchamo* (vehicle registration), they might tell you that you have to go there before you can renew your registration, but that chances of that happening are really slim, according to the two policemen.

They did say, however, that if I happen to take a trip down south someday, I could turn in it then. There wouldn't be any problem because the fine had been paid within a week. So laid-back. How can you not love it here?

## Where Does Costa Rica Stand in Relation to the War in Iraq?

There's been quite a fuss going on in the press the last couple of days. It seems that Costa Rica appeared on a list that the United States published of countries that supported its efforts in Iraq. Part of the problem is that the foreign ministry has not yet issued a statement about where the country stands. That, in itself, has been the cause for quite a bit of ink from a great number of columnists. But then, President Abel Pacheco said that were he President Bush, he'd do the same thing. That really got a strong backlash.

This is generally a pacifistic country—you'll remember it has no army. A former president, Oscar Arias, won the Nobel Peace Prize for settling the conflicts in Central America. Most columnists seem to be totally appalled that a president of this country could condone a war. In general, however, although the feeling of the country seems to be totally opposed to the war, there have been some columnists who have sympathized with the U.S. position and what it is doing. I would say the columns are running four to one against the war. And here, as elsewhere throughout the world, there have been some large protest demonstrations.

Don Abel is not one to back down too easily, and I doubt he will change what he has said. He made the point that Costa Rica has been on the opposite end of many issues with the United States and, therefore, is in no way their pawn. But he also made the point, anticipating, of course, the reaction to his stance, that pacifism cannot be unconditional and went on to give a list of examples about when Costa Rica went to war in the past to protect itself from invasion and to preserve its sovereignty.

The foreign office has been getting a lot of heat lately, most recently for abstaining in the vote that put a Libyan woman at the head of the UN Human Rights Commission. It was a great example of New Speak when the ministry "explained" that an abstention is not a vote for, therefore it's a vote against. Very cute, I thought.

## More Fun with Spanish

My reading continues fast and furious. Lately I've been reading mostly Costa Rican literature. And, of course, I'm learning a lot both about Costa Rica and about the language. Three books I've recently read were about the poor workers in the countryside. And the author reproduces their language accurately, according to the books' prefaces. Needless to say, there are hundreds of words that I would never understand. But each of the books has a glossary in the back, because many of these words wouldn't be understood by city Ticos either.

In addition, many words, which Ticos would understand but other Spanish readers wouldn't because they are regionalisms, are also in the glossary. I had an interesting example of how city people don't understand things that country people do. In one of the books, a father gets angry at his daughter for doing a dumb thing and calls her *cabeza de tinemaste*—most likely best translated as "stone head" or "rock head." A *tinemaste* is a rock, usually one of three that are used to fashion a base around a cooking fire upon which one rests a cooking pot. In fact, there's a village about a half hour from here named Tinemastes.

I've mentioned that our beautiful Great Dane, Olive, is as dumb as a stump. So when I was in San José, I told a couple of people that she was a real *cabeza de tinemaste*. I got a polite smile, and it seemed obvious to me that they didn't know what I was talking about and figured that I was trying to say something in very poor Spanish. But when I said that to Róger, who is from the country and who cooks on *tinemastes*, he thought it was hysterically funny.

Robin and I were really guilty of some folk etymology recently. When we learned one of the words for toilet, *inodoro,* we immediately assumed that it came from the English "in door," meaning a toilet that was not an outhouse. The other day I found out that it comes from the Latin and means "inodorous," which, when you know, makes much sense. In fact, when I typed the word "*inodoro*" and MS Word marked it with a wavy red line, I checked to see what suggestions the program would give me. Sure enough, inodorous was one of the suggested words. No folk etymology for MS Word.

I'm having a lot of fun seeing root connections between Spanish and English words that seem more and more often to pop into my consciousness when I'm reading. For example, I never connected the word *seguir* (to follow) with anything in English until I came across the word *subsiguente* (subsequent). There the relation becomes clear. The same thing with *pensar* (to think). Then I realized that pensive was related. And one more example, *poner,* to put, didn't make me think of a relation until I saw, *pospuesto* (postponed). There's always a new surprise for me every day when I read.

Our best personal regards,
Martin and Robin

# CHAPTER TWENTY-FIVE

## August 14, 2003

Hello, friends and family:

So much has happened since the last time I wrote. But I'm not going to go over much of it at all. Rather I want to tell you about the major changes in our life here in Costa Rica.

### Our Location

In a previous letter, we told you that we had put Casa Pacífica on the market. It is now sold, and we are currently living in a rented house in Santiago de Puriscal (usually just called Puriscal), which is located about forty-five minutes to the west of Escazú, the high-end western suburb of San José, and an additional fifteen minutes from the center of San José.

We believe we've found the ideal spot for us—close enough to San José for easy access—but far enough from it to be in a truly rural area. And the small town of Puriscal is charming.

In Escazú, there's the huge shopping center, Multiplaza, which I call Stanford Shopping Center South. Right next to it is Pricesmart—much like Price Costco—Hipermas, similar to Wal-Mart, and CIMA hospital, probably the most modern hospital I've ever seen (where they got rid of my kidney stones and relieved me of my gall bladder this year).

Before moving, if we wanted to go there for shopping or to see the doctor it meant a four-hour drive to San José and an overnight stay. Now, we can go there on the spur of the moment, do what we want, and be back with less driving time than the round-trip to San Isidro. What luxury!

Tomorrow, Saturday, we'll go to Bagelman's in Escazú and buy some bagels and lox for Sunday breakfast!

## The Trials of the Move

The move was rough. The plan was that the movers (*Mudanzas Económicas*—the name should have been a tip-off) were to come on Thursday to pack, load the truck on Friday, drive to Puriscal to unload the things we wanted to have at the rental house, and then take the rest of our stuff to storage in San José where it would remain until the house we're building was finished.

Of course Robin and I spent the entire week before that packing a lot of stuff ourselves and, more importantly, putting signs on everything to tell the movers what was to go to Puriscal and what to storage.

They were supposed to arrive between 8 and 9 on Thursday morning. At 8, I got a call from them that they were in Barú and weren't quite sure where the turnoff was. I told them, and we expected them in fifteen minutes. Thirty minutes later, I got in the car to go look for them. I headed down the hill toward Barú and found them heading in the same direction I was. It turns out that their large truck couldn't get past a muddy spot on the road.

I suggested that they get the guy with the backhoe and tractor in Barú to pull them through the muddy spot. I headed back home. Then they called again to say that they were going to rent a pickup truck and come up with all the packing things and pack and then figure out what to do with the truck, which they left parked in Barú and in which they were planning to sleep.

So the four young men came up to the house in the pickup. Robin and I explained to them about all the things we had labeled and the various piles and where they went. We also told them that we were going to be there all the time, so that if there were any questions about what went where, they could simply ask us.

They said they understood and went to work, asking questions as they went along. They were extremely nice, friendly, polite, and phenomenally hard-working. They had left San José at 2 AM in order to be at our place at 8 and were going to work packing all day. They didn't finish until about 8 that evening.

The next morning it turned out that they still couldn't figure out how to get the truck to the house, so they came with the pickup truck to take the stuff to the truck in shifts. I calculated that it would be thirty to forty minutes for each trip, and that they would have to make a minimum of thirty trips, thus, meaning that it would take fifteen hours at the best! They agreed with my assessment, so I suggested they get on the phone and find another bigger truck, what they call a cargo taxi here. And so they did.

The transferring to the truck began, and I noticed that they were coming and going at a much faster rate than should have been possible. When I asked them how they were doing that they said that they had been able that morning to get the truck past the muddy spot after all. So why had they agreed with me about the fifteen hours? I never really found out. Probably wanted to *quedar bien*. They weren't able to bring the truck all the way to the house because there's a very steep hill between our house and the main road, but they were only about one kilometer away rather than the three and a half I thought they'd be.

They got done at about noon. At this point we were all ready to leave. That is, they in the big truck, Robin and I in the car with the bats, our friend José in his van with the dogs and several bags and boxes we wanted to carry ourselves.

The plan was that we would drive to Puriscal following José by the direct route, and the guys in the truck would go by way of San José, not at all direct because the direct route has a suspension bridge, which the truck was too big to cross. The truck was to arrive in Puriscal about 8:30 PM.

The first glitch came when we left the house and got to where they had the truck parked for loading. It seems as though they just couldn't fit everything in! Of course I had asked them three different times if they thought the truck was large enough, and of course they assured me that it was.

So, the truck was parked in front of one of our neighbors' houses, and we gave him a huge computer desk that we really didn't want anymore. That helped. Then everyone decided that there were really only about four medium-sized pieces of furniture that couldn't fit, so they decided to tie those to the top of José's van. Robin and I just couldn't bear to watch anymore, so we told them we'd drive down to Barú and wait for them there. And wait we did, and wait and wait. They didn't get down the hill until 1:30. Seems that it wasn't that easy to get the things on top of the van.

So off we went, the movers to San José, Robin and I and José the direct route to Puriscal, which passes through a place called Orotina. It was a very long, hard drive. We were constantly worried about the well-being of the bats, of course, and they squabbled a lot in their cages in the back of our car. But finally we made it to Puriscal and to the house about 6 PM. Whew!

We started unloading the car and van, getting the bats and dogs settled—oh yes—and our last remaining white mouse Merri, too. We were all exhausted. (José had driven the four hours that morning from San José, too.)

About 8 PM, José went to Puriscal to get something to eat and planned to wait there until the movers called. Robin and I put a blanket and pillows we had with us on the tile floor and just tried to rest.

At 10 PM the movers and José arrived. Why so long? Because the movers went to San José, unloaded the big truck, and then loaded a smaller truck with the stuff for Puriscal. Why? I really have no idea at this point. It sure hadn't been part of the plan.

The disaster wasn't that they got there so late, but that they had everything mixed up. Stuff that should have stayed at storage came to Puriscal, stuff for Puriscal went to storage. But that's only part of it. This was stuff we could see. The next day when Robin and I started unpacking the boxes, we saw that in spite of all our signs, in spite of all our directions, they had time and again mixed things for Puriscal with things for storage in the same box. Agggggghhhhhh! What that meant was that we had to re-sort everything here to send some back to storage. And who knows what necessities we might have been missing?

But now we're really quite comfortable and rested and looking forward to beginning our new adventure.

## The Rented House

The rented house is only about ten minutes from the center of Puriscal. What a change. Now, instead of driving an hour to get to the nearest grocery, hardware store, pet food store, bank, etc., we only drive ten minutes! Which also means we don't have to buy huge stocks of things to try to keep our trips down to once a week.

The neighborhood we're in is a nice, typical, middle-class, rural Tico community. Also, as is typical, almost everyone on our block (including the owner of our house) is related. The street is not paved, but in good shape, also typical for many rural Tico communities. None of the roads in Lagunas were paved either, as you know.

The house is a rather standard Tico house, about one hundred square meters. For comparison, our *casita* was only about sixty square meters. The house has a small living room—dining room combination, a small kitchen, three bedrooms, and one bath. There is also a very large room in the house that is a type of storage/utility/laundry room; however, we are using that as a bat home. I'll say more about the bats later.

## Cold Water and Suicide Showers

Also quite typical is the fact that we have no hot water, except for our suicide shower. A suicide shower is an electric gizmo that goes on the end of the shower nozzle and has switches to turn it off or to either one of two degrees of temperature. The water heats almost instantly. You can, in a matter of speaking, mix hot and cold water by adjusting the flow of the shower; the stronger the flow, the cooler the water because the gizmo can't quite heat that much water that quickly. The fact is that the showers are very comfortable.

Research has (supposedly) shown that no one can actually document anybody's having been electrocuted in a suicide shower, so we feel safe. In fact, as far as I can tell, it's only the foreigners who refer to it as a suicide shower.

As far as washing dishes in cold water—something that sounds like a North American's worst dream—it's really quite easy. Because so many people do not have hot water here, the soaps—body, dishwashing, and laundry—are formulated to work just fine with cold water. Thus our dishes are not at all greasy nor does it feel yucky when we wash them. (Besides, there isn't much grease in our diet anymore anyway.)

The thing that was scary for me was shaving in cold water. I still remember with horror what it was like to do that from time to time in the army. But I just rigged up a mirror in the shower and shave there. Works fine.

The house is a bright hot pink, inside and out, which is why we call it Pepto Bismol Manor—but it really doesn't make any difference. Lots of houses here are hot pink. Now that everything is organized, we're truly quite comfortable and are enjoying our stay here.

## The Batties

The first thing to tell you about the batties is that they are now five! Batboy and Audrey and three children: Andy, Arthur, and Blossom, the only girl so far. There was, of course, Spencer, the firstborn, but he seems to have made it safely away during our rather non-successful release attempt. Once we realized that Batboy and Audrey would need to spend their lives in captivity, we decided to allow them to have a family for company. These are colonial bats who thrive on interaction with others of their own kind.

Although Audrey has been an excellent mother, she rejected Blossom. We think it was because of Arthur who kept driving

Blossom out of the roost. It seems Arthur had hit puberty and wanted to take over Batboy's harem of one. Finally, Robin had to take Blossom into the house to feed and hand-raise her. Blossom thrived under Robin's care and is now a healthy, flying bat child.

Audrey is pregnant once again. We hope it will be a girl, so that there will be three boys and three girls. It has become time to separate the genders now that Arthur is sexually mature. We don't want any little battie babies with close-set eyes.

Currently, we have them separated in the house: the boys in a big tent in the utility room and the girls in a large cage in one of the bedrooms. We'll put a tent in there soon, so they have more room.

When we build a new flight cage at the farm, it will be divided into two sections, His and Hers.

## The Weather and Flora

The weather in this area is radically different from that in the Lagunas-Dominical area, which was very warm and tropical. Even though we always had a breeze at Casa Pacífica, it was a warm breeze. And down in Barú and Dominical, at sea level, it was what one would expect at sea level in the tropics.

Lagunas was at 300 meters, but Puriscal is at 1100, quite a difference. And we simply love the weather here; quite cool mornings, evenings, and nights; and beautiful, warm, sunny days. It reminds us a lot of Northern California at its most beautiful times of the year.

This change in weather has also resulted in a major change in the way we dress. For example, for the entire two and a half years in the Dominical area, I don't think I ever wore long pants. Now, I put them on in the morning, change to shorts in the late morning, and then long pants again in the evening. I even wear sweatshirts in the morning before changing later to a short-sleeved shirt. It's really a quite-pleasant change, which both Robin and I are enjoying.

One big surprise was the tropical vegetation here. The area is not jungle, but of course, it is tropical. Consequently, even though they don't grow naturally in the area, it seems as though all the plants that we knew in Lagunas are growing here, too. All types of palms, monstera, crotons, heliconias, etc. And all the fruit trees as well: papaya, orange, lemon, water apple, tangerine, mango, guava, guanábana, everything. So it seems the best of both worlds—that is, not just the much less humid weather, but all the tropical vegetation, too.

## Puriscal and the Farm

We bought a beautiful farm of eight and a half hectares (about twenty acres) where we will build our new home, which we expect to name ¡Aquí me quedo! (Here I stay!).

The farm is mostly gently rolling hills, several lovely forested areas, lots of clean springs and a river. It is fantastically peaceful, and it's only ten minutes from the town of Puriscal.

Puriscal itself is an attractive little town. There is virtually no crime and not much severe poverty at all. Our Tico friends tell us it is prototypically Tico. The area is mostly agricultural; it's famous for its horse breeding and is a cattle center as well. There are very few foreigners, one of the things Robin and I were seeking. All our neighbors at the farm will be Ticos.

We're going to build a home radically different from Casa Pacífica. First, it will be smaller. Casa Pacífica was much too large for us. We'll only have one storey, and the house will be built almost entirely of wood and stone instead of concrete block. Because the area here is so much more "country" than jungle, a log house, farm style, seems much more fitting here than a Mexican or Santa Fe style *hacienda*.

Robin has drawn up a terrific floor plan, and we're working with a firm in San José to complete the design and build it. We will also build a barn for the horses (who are still in Lagunas), a bat flight cage, and a small studio for me to continue working with my pottery.

We are bringing Róger and his wife, Vera, with us. We'll build them a small house. We invited Seidy to join us, but it's just too far from her family. So Vera will help with cleaning.

This week we will cut the long driveway from the road to the building site and construct a shelter for the horses, so we can bring them here as soon as possible. We are also having a topographical study done to decide the best way to construct our water system. At that point we will begin building. The building of a log house with stone foundations will go much faster than block and concrete, and we're hoping to be able to move in within five or six months.

So that's life currently in Costa Rica. We'll keep you updated as we continue along in the new adventure.

Warmest regards,
Martin and Robin

# CHAPTER TWENTY-SIX

## October 31, 2003

Hi, friends and family:

Lots new are going on in our lives. Hope you find it interesting.

### Who and What Are *Maiceros* and *Maiceras*?

Who is a *maicero* or *maicera?* Well, literally it's a person who eats corn—that is—someone who likes to eat corn on the cob. The word is used mostly as a term of derision. People refer to folks around here, Santiago de Puriscal, and other very rural areas as *maiceros*, something like "hick" or "hayseed." But I much prefer the definition given in the following quotation:

> "*Concho* [dregs] as defined by [the philologist, Carlos] Gagini, means a simple person from the country. *Maicero*, according to the [Spanish] Academy [Dictionary], is said of people whose principal food is corn or who, in general, prefer this food. Occasionally, however, according to Miguel Ángel Quesada in his *New Dictionary of Costaricanisms*, it is said to a Costa Rican *campesino* in a deprecatory manner, as though calling him ignorant, uncultivated.
>
> "If Aquileo Echeverría could use the term dregs to refer to his valuable collection of poems, I've taken corn as a symbol for me. Because for me,

the best title life has given me, one with much
honor and pride, is that of *maicera.*

"Being a *maicera,* for me, is not to be ignorant
or uneducated; it's to possess the goodness, the
innocence, the purity, the simplicity, and the
strength of the Costa Rican *campesino.*"
Quoted in Alf A. Giebler Simonet, *"A Lo Tico:
Costarriqueñismos y otras vainas,"* from "María
Mayela Padilla who is from San Ignacio de Acosta,
[and who] dedicated [the words above] to the
maicero and the *maicera* in her *Cantos de Elote
Tierno [Cantos of Tender Corn on the Cob]."*

## Living in Puriscal

Living in Puriscal is a total change for us in the sense that we
feel for the first time as though we're truly living in a foreign
country, one we enjoy tremendously. Or, to put it another way,
we feel for the first time that we're immersed in a foreign culture,
much more than we've felt in the three years we've been here.
(October 20 was our third anniversary here.)

For one thing, there are almost no foreigners here. There is a
handful of other North Americans in the area, but we've only
met three and don't see them at all. What this means, of course,
is that we speak Spanish almost exclusively. We speak English to
one another and to our close friends Darrylle and Ulises, whom
we see about once every two weeks for a Sunday lunch in San
José. But otherwise, it's exclusively Spanish with the very rare
exception of someone who knows some English and really wants
to use it.

In general, living in a Costa Rican neighborhood is a lot of
fun. For one thing, there are vendors who come along the street
almost every day, selling things such as tamales, sugar candy with
coconut, *lomos* (salami-shaped loaves of cornmeal with meat and
vegetables inside and wrapped in banana leaves), freshly baked
rolls, fruits, etc. They come up to the gate and call, *"Upe, upe,"*
which is what you call when you approach someone's home.

Then we go out, see what they have, and almost always buy something, whether we want it or not, mainly because these folks really need the money, and the prices are so very inexpensive.

Everyone is selling or trying to sell something here to get a little extra income. Ana, the woman who cleans for us three times a week, has a sister who lives next door to her, and who has a cow. And Ana sells milk and sour cream to people in the neighborhood. We haven't had any of the milk yet, but we did buy some sour cream, and it was really good. Of course it had to have been the freshest sour cream we've ever had.

This morning, Don Juan Salas, the motorcycle traffic officer, who lives across the street from us, sold me two pairs of blue jeans (at the great price of $7.50 each), which he's selling while on vacation. He said he'd have some woman's jeans for Robin to look at tomorrow.

Because it's a relatively small town, it's easy to get to know the people you deal with and for them to get to know and recognize you, especially when you're a foreigner in a place where there is almost none.

Another big plus about a small town is that the lines are so much shorter here than in San Isidro, not to mention San José. Right after we moved into our rental house, I had to go to ICE several times to arrange for electricity and phone service to the farm. First, there are almost never more than about two or three people ahead of you. The office staff is quite small with only about six people. So you get to know their names and greet them, and they get to know yours and greet you. They'll bend the rules when they can for the customers. If you need to talk to someone who works in the back, you just walk past the desks into the back office.

The same is true of the bank, almost never any lines. (Though even if there were, it doesn't faze me anymore—I have my Golden Citizen card.)

We still get our mail delivered on the bus from San José (forwarded from our Miami address). In San Isidro, the bus terminal was always packed, and there were frequently long lines to pick up packages. The attendants were cordial, but far from friendly. Here, Gerardo, who receives and gives out the packages, recognized me and greeted me by name the second time I went there. Now he knows Robin and her name too. There's very little traffic there, and I imagine he knows everyone who comes in. This morning, we parked across the street from the station, and he came out of the office and called over to tell me there were a couple of packages for us. He has even phoned us a couple of times to tell us we had mail.

Every Saturday morning, there's a farmer's market in town (called a *feria*). We always go. All the vendors we patronize know us and always greet us. We ride down the roads, and everyone waves and shouts a greeting, even if we don't know one another. The elderly farmers all seem to dress the same way when they're in town. They would look at home in small towns in Texas or Tennessee, or almost any rural farming area in the United States. Ten gallon hats, often plaid shirts, wide leather belts with large rodeo-style buckles, polyester pants, and boots. They stand on the sidewalk talking to one another and greeting passersby.

And everyone is related to everyone. This morning for example, I was at the little school here in Mercedes Norte—the community where our rental house is—delivering a computer that Robin and I donated to the school. (Many of the people in the community are poor, and the school is desperate for things that they can't acquire with their small budget.) Anyway, as I was leaving I reminded them to give me a call if they had any problems. One of the teachers there said, "If there's a problem, I'll just come up to your gate and call '*upe*.' Your neighbor across the street, Doña Flora, is my mother-in-law, and I'm over there a lot."

Doña Flora is the mother of Don Juan who lives next door to her. And Don Juan is the nephew of Don Jorge who is the owner of our house, and who is the brother of Don Alberto, Doña Flora's husband or brother; I haven't figured it out yet.

And it's that way everywhere. Fabio, the man who's building our stable and the house for Róger and Vera (more about that below), always has a relative who can do what we need to have done or who can get what we need. It's always an uncle, a cousin, a brother-in-law, a sister-in-law, whatever. In one of the visits to ICE, Fabio and I were in the back office with Don Carlos getting some paperwork done. I was telling Fabio that we needed to find a vet to take care of the dogs and horses. At which point Don Carlos popped up and said that his—I can't remember now, uncle, brother, cousin, something—was a great vet, and that he worked on both small and large animals, and he'd be glad to give me his phone number whenever we needed him.

Which also reminds me that this same Don Carlos, just yesterday, spent about twenty minutes telling me about this fantastic house that his father (maybe) has for rent. He made me promise that I'd come into the office one day next week, and we'd go look at it because perhaps I might run into someone who was looking for a great house to rent. (Of course the fact that an ICE employee can leave the office at anytime with no notice for an hour or so is just another aspect of life with ICE.)

Speaking of Don and Doña, until we moved here, the only person who ever called me Don Martín was a secretary in an office in San Isidro. Here, to the contrary, everyone calls us Don Martín and Doña Robin. And we address most of the people we interact with as Don and Doña as well. It's just another aspect of life here, a place where people are still extremely polite and respectful. It makes one feel very comfortable.

## Breakdown Country Style

Here's a typical experience that one can easily have in *maicero* country. After writing the above paragraphs, I needed to go to the farm to pick up a worker and take him home. On the way there, I had to stop and wait while three men were fixing an ox cart, loaded with sugarcane. The yoked oxen were quietly grazing on grass at the side of the road. After the men fixed whatever was wrong with the cart, they had to re-hitch the oxen, which took a bit of doing because the animals were really enjoying the grass. Eventually they got the oxen hooked up and led them and the cart to the side of the road, so that I could easily pass. We all waved, shouted hello, and I was on my way again.

## Hacienda Arroz

Our farm, *Hacienda Arroz*, is growing on us more and more as we go there for one thing or another every day. It's really big, at least to us. About twenty-one acres (about 8.5 hectares) seems to be a lot of land, which, in turn, allows for a great many topographical features. There are hills, valleys, springs, a river, large pastures, many lovely trees, and beautiful views in every direction. There's lots of sun, shade, and breezes. It's extremely quiet and peaceful, and the road is in quite-decent shape. It's only ten minutes from town and forty-five minutes from the western suburbs of San José, where we do a lot of shopping. We had a topographical map made that shows all the elevations in two-meter increments. This is extremely valuable for us to figure out things such as where to put in our water system and for planting trees, bushes, vegetables, and flowers.

Yesterday, Saturday, we had a young couple, Manuel Víquez and his wife Yamileth, out to the farm for a consultation. They both have degrees in forestry and have several reforestation programs going. They are working hard to save the native trees of Costa Rica and to increase their propagation. They have an interesting Web site (in Spanish) at http://www.elmundoforestal.com. We spent about two hours with them. They explained a great deal about caring for the trees on the property and what type of trees we might want to plant as well as answering many of our questions such as how to attract more birds and wildlife. As Robin pointed out, they're natural teachers who respond enthusiastically to people like us, who are very interested in preserving the environment.

On Wednesday, they'll provide us with a written report of recommendations in order to accomplish the things we want to on the farm. Oh, as an aside, the cost of this is simply amazing. The two-hour visit yesterday (actually four hours for them because they live an hour away) plus the written report all for $100. We also want them to map all the trees on the property and identify them for us. In the report they'll include a proposal for doing all of this.

We have several projects going on. We're building a stable for Dorado, Tory, and another horse we intend to get. We're building the house for Róger and Vera. We're building a gate at the property's entrance. And we're starting to construct our water system. One thing we particularly like about the water system is that we're not going to use an electric pump but rather a hydraulic ram pump. We only have to raise the water sixteen meters to our home site, so the ram pump is more than sufficient to do that.

Because the farm has been a working farm in the past, we have a crop of sugarcane and a couple hundred coffee bushes. This is a big sugarcane—and coffee-growing area. Here's a description of the sugarcane industry, written by a long-time resident:

> "The main product is raw cane sugar (brown sugar), poured into wooden molds to form round blocks of raw sugar. These are called 'tapa dulce.' This is the kind of sugar used before we began refining it. Today it's used to make sweet drinks. There is a great deal of overproduction of 'tapas' so many of the sugar cooperatives are experimenting with other forms. They are making little blocks with peanuts as candy. There's a common rural drink called 'aqua dulce' which is made by adding milk to the 'tapa dulce.' They're trying to premix it and sell it that way. They're also making a product from ground 'tapa' with lemon added to make another traditional drink, 'aqua sapo' (toad water!)." (This was edited from a posting to the Yahoo! group, CostaRicaLiving.)

The cane sugar is ground in a *trapiche*, usually not much more than a little lean-to or shelter with a grinder found in lots of places in the country. Most of the grinders are electric driven, but some of the *trapiches* still use oxen to power the grinders.

Right across the road from us, set back a little ways in the trees, is a small electric-driven *trapiche* worked by an elderly man who lives nearby. He uses an ox cart, however, to haul the cane to the *trapiche*. We'll probably try to work out some arrangement with him to grind some of our cane.

We would love to be able to drink our own coffee, too. Right now is harvest season, and all over the neighborhood, people are collecting the berries. Ours are not being harvested this year. We do know that there are coffee cooperatives where small growers can bring their coffee to be processed. We will look into becoming part of the cooperative. We also don't know how old our coffee bushes are. They have a relatively limited production life.

Robin has recently become greatly enamored with the idea of keeping a small herd of dairy goats. We'd only need two to four of them to provide us with milk and cheese throughout the year. She's particularly interested in two varieties of dwarf goats. She's been doing a lot of research into this and has already learned a great deal. There's quite a bit of goat farming in the area, so that we'll be able to get lots of help with questions. We visited such a farm just the other day and enjoyed it greatly.

### ¡Aquí Me Quedo!

We haven't broken ground yet for the main house, *¡Aquí me quedo!* We still don't have the final design, however, we do know that it will be a log, board, and stone house, most likely made of cypress and river rock. We just love the idea of a natural house like that which will fit in so perfectly with our surroundings. It will be less than 1,800 square feet, quite a bit smaller than Casa Pacífica.

We had been thinking about a wood house from the beginning and had been working with one firm for a while when we saw Architect Antonio Flores's full page ad in *Estilos y Casas,* the Latin *Architectural Digest.* The ad featured a large photograph of a log and stone house that just thrilled us. We were worried that something like that would be way out of our price range. Nevertheless, we decided to call him and meet with him. During that meeting, when we discussed the house in his ad and found out the price, we were sure that we'd be able to work with him. We don't know when we'll start or how long it will take, but we're hoping that we can move in by next June or July. One fortunate thing is that the rainy season is just about to end, so we'll be able to start construction at the beginning of the dry season.

As things move along, we'll take pictures and put them up on our Web site.

## Róger and Vera

Back in Lagunas, Róger and Vera lived several kilometers from our house, much higher up the mountain, in a little community without electricity, called Punta Mira. In the beginning Róger used to walk an hour from his house to ours (and to the houses of others of our neighbors where he also worked) and then, after a long hard day, would walk an hour and a half back home—it took a half hour longer because the return route was up the mountain. Eventually I lent him the money to buy a motorcycle, which, of course, made his life a lot easier.

Róger does not have much education. He left school very early to help his father with their coffee plantation and has been working hard ever since. For many years he was a bus driver and then drove a large truck for a coffee cooperative to collect the harvested beans from the small producers. However, he developed some eye trouble and couldn't be a professional driver anymore. So they decided to move way out into the country where he would be a "chopper," that is, essentially, a grounds keeper. Both he and Vera loved being back in the country and didn't seem to mind living without electricity and cooking on a wood fire. In fact, they often said that they were quite happy with their life.

Vera herself has more education than Róger, loves to read and do various kinds of craftwork. She's also a great cook.

When we decided to move, we wanted very much to take Róger and Vera with us. They seemed to want to go but had a problem. They had built a small house in Punta Mira. They did not own the land the house was built on. The owner of the land told them that they could build there and that he'd sell them the ground when they could afford it. They own a small house in San Isidro, which they've been trying to sell in order to be able to buy the land their house is on. But the market is very slow, and there didn't seem to be any good prospects in the offing.

They were afraid to leave their little house because it would surely be taken over by squatters. The laws concerning squatters in Costa Rica are quite complex, but there are circumstances where they can eventually gain title to the property.

So that's when Robin and I decided to make them an offer. We told them that we would give them title to one hectare of land (ten thousand square meters or a bit more than two acres) and would build them a house if they wanted to come with us. We then brought them out to see the farm and the land that would be theirs. They were absolutely thrilled. They loved the tranquility of the area and its beauty.

So we're building them a nice little prefab house with appliances and electricity, of course, on a lovely site surrounded by lots of trees, with good water, and plenty of land for them to plant the things they want to grow, to keep their chickens and dogs and the pig they usually raise each year. We expect the house (a bit over fifty square meters compared to the thirty-two square meters they now have) to be finished in about two or three more weeks. They're chaffing at the bit to get here. They spent a week with us a little while ago and fell ever more in love with the place.

Róger and Vera are simply lovely, lovely people. They're honest, extremely good-hearted, hard workers, and so knowledgeable about the things one needs to know for living in the country and farming successfully here in Costa Rica. For Robin and me, this is an extremely rewarding experience. To be able to help two wonderful people have a more comfortable and happier life fills us with happiness. If only we could do this for more people.

## The Mudmobile

About six months ago, we traded in the jeep for a Mitsubishi Montero Sport, a powerful four-by-four and quite attractive. But after living here for two months, the car was a disaster. It was so unbelievably muddy and stained that it just looked a total wreck. But what could we expect? It's the rainy season and there's mud everywhere. We have to haul water out to the farm for the horses until the water system is finished. The dogs, of course, ride in the car to the farm, and when they come back, they're covered with mud as well. And we had to haul everything in it. So we decided that before the car became a wreck, we'd get a vehicle for the farm, a real mudmobile that we wouldn't have to worry about.

And it would be Robin's mudmobile because she's the one that hauls the dogs and the water and the horse things most often. So we bought a Chevy S10, a double-cab, diesel turbo cooler, stick-shift, four-by-four pickup truck. And that's now the work truck.

We got the Montero detailed so that it is now our Sunday-Go-to-Meeting car, and we don't have to feel guilty every time we get in it.

## A New Baby

A few weeks ago Audrey had her last baby. His name is Charlie. It's her last because we now have the girls and boys separated. Audrey is continuing to be a good mother and takes wonderful care of Charlie. As soon as he's weaned and flying well, we'll move him over to live with his brothers and father. At least we hope that Batboy is the father rather than one of his brothers. It seems as though Audrey got pregnant just before we separated the sexes, but after her son, Arthur, was sexually mature. We were hoping for another girl, so that it could be three and three, but it looks as though Blossom will be the only girl, and it will stay at four and two.

So those are the latest developments. We hope you're all well.

Love,
Martin and Robin

# Chapter Twenty-Seven

## January 25, 2004

Hi, family and friends:

A lot has happened since the last time I wrote in October, and we'd like to bring you up to date.

### Sad News

After more than three years here, we've had our first really negative experience. Last week, someone poisoned our little dog, Bug. Unfortunately, one hears a great deal about dog poisoning here. I wouldn't be surprised if this isn't a more common phenomenon in developing countries than elsewhere. Attitudes toward animals, both work and pets, is so much different from those we, in the States, are generally used to.

Bug, you might remember, was an abandoned puppy on the streets of San Isidro. A neighbor brought her back to Lagunas to find a home for her, and we took her in. That was in December 2000. She was a smart, very loving little dog, and we miss her a great deal. Needless to say, we will not let the same thing happen to Jessie and are keeping her in our sight at all times. When we move to the farm, she'll be safe.

### The Hidden Face of Poverty

Here, too, is something which I haven't had cause to write about, but it's another important part of our growing understanding of our adopted country. It's the sobering contrast between the middle-class life that people like Robin and me lead here—as do many Ticos—and that of what I believe is rather typical country-dweller life here in Puriscal and, I imagine, all over Costa Rica as well as in all developing countries.

We employ a woman, Ana, who lives nearby and cleans our house three times a week. She previously worked for some other North Americans who used to rent this same house and who recommended her to us. I don't know how old she is, but I assume in her mid-thirties. She's a single mother—her husband left the family some time ago, though he still comes around once in a while to see their eleven-year-old son, Danielito.

I pick her up and take her home most of the time. Like almost all Ticos I know, Ana and Danielito are scrupulously clean. They live in a little prefab house with a little garden and, yep, a little dog. And, as I mentioned recently, again typically, family surrounds them. Her parents live a short walk away with one of her brothers, the only one of the siblings who never married, José Luis. She has a sister and a couple of nephews who live next door. I don't know whether Ana owns her house outright or whether she is paying off a mortgage or just renting.

When we hired her, she told us that she hadn't worked for five months. I don't know how she was surviving other than with the help of her family. There is another brother who seems to be much better off and who lives not too far away. He has a large farm and grows many crops, though he told me when I met him recently that due to current low prices for his crops, he wants to sell the farm. I do know that she gets no support from her husband. She told us that José Luis, her brother, also had not been able to find any work for several months.

Her father, who looks quite old, is still working when he can as a chopper. Her mother can't work because she's quite ill. I've been able to give José Luis work. First, I had him working on the farm until Róger and Vera got here, and now I got him a job on the building crew of our new house.

I think I mentioned in one of my letters that Ana sells milk and sour cream in the neighborhood from her sister's one cow as another way of earning a little more money. She also takes in washing. She has a small washing machine. Because Robin and I have no washer here, we give her the washing to do instead of taking it to a laundromat, so that she can earn yet a little more. So, on the surface and to all appearances, here is a woman and her son who don't have much at all and who really have to scramble to make ends meet. But also, by all appearances, they're getting by. But appearances, as we all know, rarely tell the whole truth, especially here, because we were absolutely shocked to learn—not too long after Ana came to work for us—that before taking out the garbage, she would go through it to find things she could use.

Even as I write this my stomach knots up. The biggest shame Robin and I felt was when we threw away almost an entire loaf of bread. We had run out of decent bread and bought a loaf of sliced, whole-wheat wonder bread at the local *pulpería*. It tasted just horrible and we didn't eat it. We kept it around until it finally became stale, at which time we threw it into the trash.

A couple of days later, Ana told Robin she had found it and had taken it home for her and Danielito to eat. Robin was just appalled. She told Ana that the bread was old and stale, to which Ana replied that it was fine and asked that before we throw out any food we don't want to please give it to her first. Then, just the other day, Robin threw the leaves of some celery into the trash. Ana found those, too, and asked Robin to please give her any celery leaves or similar things before throwing them away.

I said above that writing this makes my stomach knot, but as I continue writing, it becomes even worse. All of us who live in developed, industrialized societies know full well how much we waste. There's certainly no need to go into that here. But I realize now that this is an intellectual knowing. It takes something like this experience with Ana to turn that knowledge into a visceral knowing, at least for us. What we are hoping now is that the visceral knowing will help Robin and me to be less wasteful. We now will throw no food away without thinking about it and thinking about whether it's something that Ana and Danielito would want to have. So this is a cultural lesson for us far different from all the other cultural lessons we've learned here and far different from the type of lessons we expected to learn. I'm so sorry that it's a family's difficulties that provided the lesson, but I'm glad that it was a lesson we could understand with our hearts rather than only with our minds.

## José Luis and a More Upbeat Note

On more of an upbeat note is the story of what we might be able to do with José Luis, Ana's brother. There's no doubt that the farm requires more than one worker. But there's also no doubt that we cannot afford to pay three workers full time (that is, Róger, Vera, who will work for us full time when our house is built, and then José Luis, whom we would like to hire). Thinking about this as the time draws so close to having to let José Luis go at the end of May when our house is completed, I came up with the idea that perhaps we could earn enough from the farm just to pay his salary and benefits.

In other words, would it be possible to plant and sell just enough crops to provide his pay? Even if it meant that he would work half his time on the crops and the other half of his time working with Róger on the grounds; this would at least result in his having continuing full-time work. So I discussed it with him and he was at first very excited. But the more we talked about the same old crops—coffee, beans, corn, bananas, plantains, etc.— the more it became apparent that it would be extremely difficult to justify the investment to get started given the dark outlook in these markets currently.

But then I got the report from the forest expert we've hired, Manuel Víquez, about whom I'll write more later. In the report there are many ideas for productivity specific to this farm and this area. So we're now exploring these ideas that might result, after all, in the opportunity for work for José Luis as well as some new and rather exciting challenges for Robin and me.

272                          MARTIN P. RICE

## Almost Tico

I had a couple of experiences lately that make me think I'm getting more into the swing of life here—about time after more than three years, I guess. First, without going into much detail, those of you who know me well know that I've been a real type A personality all my adult life. I'm a time freak. I can almost always tell you what time it is without even looking at my watch. When I predict times of arrival or the time necessary to get something done, I'm never off by more than fifteen minutes. Add to that the fact that I have not been constitutionally able to be late, ever.

This is not a good match, it would seem, for living in a tropical country. But I've been very open to change and anxious for acculturation. Nevertheless, time has been my big sticking point. But two things have happened recently to make me think that perhaps there is a chance for me after all.

One was a recent Saturday morning, when Robin and I were supposed to pick up Róger and Vera to take them to the farmer's market here in Puriscal. This is a Saturday morning ritual, which we all enjoy greatly. Robin had told them we'd be there at 8 AM. Well, for a variety of reasons, we didn't get there until 8:20, and I was cool as a cucumber. I wasn't uptight; I hadn't called; I barely even thought about being late. I just don't know how that happened; it might be the first time in my life—and that's a long time.

When we got there I did, however, apologize for being late. Of course they had barely noticed and said don't give it a thought. At that I said to them that I was getting to be almost Tico, and they got a huge kick out of that and said they couldn't agree more.

The other side of the coin, of course, is when others are late, which is also something I have always had a very hard time dealing with—again not a desirable trait in Latin America. But about a week ago, I had an appointment at the *municipalidad* (City Hall) for 1 PM to file a property owner's report. I was there at 12:55, of course, and the fellow I was to meet came in at 1:05. I was impressed and pleased. He then proceeded to tell me that he needed to go eat lunch (it was he who selected 1 PM in the first place) and that we could get together in forty-five minutes! Until then I would have been simply livid, at the very least. But to my great, great surprise, I said OK, see you then, walked to the corner, bought a newspaper, went to the nearest little restaurant, had some *arroz con pollo*, and relaxed for forty-five minutes. *Relaxed*?! Over the past forty years, I've had three wives, four children, and countless colleagues and associates telling me I had to relax. I can hardly believe this transformation. Can't tell you how many offices I've walked out of in my life when someone I was supposed to meet was just fifteen minutes late, or how many restaurants I've walked out of before a waiter got to my table? I'm not saying this is in any way admirable; it's just the way I've been.

I must say that I'm enjoying this change and can feel more and more stress evaporating as time passes. Robin even says that there's a good chance I'm going to get a couple of extra years of life out of this if I keep it up. That would be nice, indeed!

## A Fantastic Resource

When we were looking for land in the Puriscal area several months ago, one of the parcels we were considering was quite lovely other than the fact that it was virtually denuded of trees because years ago it had been turned totally into pasture. As it turned out, we didn't buy that piece. However, right about that time, I learned about a Web site run by an arbor culturist named Manuel Víquez and his family. At that time, they were publishing a monthly report about the trees of Costa Rica and sending it by e-mail. I contacted him and said that I'd be interested in consulting with him about reforesting the land. Later, we bought our farm, and it had many more trees than the first one we'd looked at. Nevertheless, I was still interested in getting some input from him. So we contracted with him to make a study of our property and then to prepare a report for us.

A couple of months ago we met him and his wife—also a graduate arbor culturist—on our farm. They spent about two hours with us looking, talking, picture and note taking, and instructing. Then a couple of weeks later, we got the report. We were simply blown away by what he gave us. It's a twenty-one-page, beautifully laid out, illustrated, computer-produced report with an additional five pages of recommendations. A CD that contains the report so that we can print more copies and also a manual on environmental and arboreal management techniques accompany it.

To give you an idea of the depth of the report, here are some of the contents:

1. Macro-environmental considerations: Climate, Geology, Topography and soils, Types of vegetation
2. General diagnosis of the site: Limiting factors, Slopes and unstable soils, Excessive winds, Favorable factors, General objectives for unused areas, Administration, Location and access, Availability of water, A generally healthy environment
3. Actions and strategies: Sectorization, Areas in pasture, Areas for reforestation, Attracting herbivorous mammals, Attracting birds, Attracting bats, Already existing trees, Natural miniforests, Springs and creeks, Healthy trees, Ventoleras. [A ventolera is an area which was once covered with natural vegetation, located precisely where the wind blows with great force and which, when cleared in order to establish pasture or fields for cultivation, the wind began to degrade and negatively transform the location's environmental conditions, converting it in just a few years into this species of micro wasteland in which the soil has lost its fertility, has been compacted, and in which the only thing to grow is pasture grass.]

And finally, a list of trees and other plants mentioned in this document (including Common Name, Scientific Name, Uses, Flower Colors).

That takes up the twenty-one pages. Then come proposals

for technical services, information about obtaining trees to plant, and information about arbor culture courses.

You should also know that very, very little of this report is boilerplate. He speaks specifically to Robin's and my concerns, plans, wishes, etc., all within the context of the specific location of our farm. For example the reason there's a section on attracting bats is because Robin studies and rehabilitates bats and he knows that.

In addition, what you can't see from the contents' listing is how richly informative and deep the material is with fantastic recommendations throughout. I could go on but I'll stop here other than to say that we have contracted with him to do a sector study, which is almost complete.

## Lunch with Fabio

On a Sunday a couple of months ago, we had a great lunch with a few folks who will be our new neighbors when we get our house finished at the farm. Fabio is the builder we hired to build Róger and Vera's house and our stable. He also did some work on our ram-pump-driven water system. We thought he did a very good job and have come to like him.

One day Fabio invited Robin and me to a lunch that he was hosting at Róger and Vera's almost completed house. It was only a week away from being done, and he wanted to have a little celebration for his family, his workers, and for us. So we got there as planned at 11 AM on Sunday. The workers were there, of course, some relatives, and two of his daughters and his wife. This was the first time we met his wife, a short roly-poly woman named Liz, extremely friendly, always smiling, and who talks slowly and clearly, so that Robin and I could understand virtually everything she said.

What a spread! Freshly made pork *chicharrones*, barbequed beef, chopped tomato salsa, refried beans, salsa picante, jalapeños, tortillas, salad of lettuce, tomato, avocado, and hearts of palm, wine, beer, and soft drinks for beverages. There was enough food to feed an army.

The lunch gave us an opportunity to get to know his family, the workers, and some neighbors much better than we had so far. We had a great time chatting, talking about the neighborhood, a bit about the States, and a lot about living in Costa Rica. The guys also joked a lot about Pérez Zeledón, near which we used to live because in Costa Rica it's known as the city of women. That's because so many hundreds of men from there have gone to the States—mostly to New Jersey—to work.

While talking about the neighborhood, the folks consistently talked about how peaceful and safe it is, how the people are friendly and *"humilde."* Funny about language. If you think about the dictionary meaning of *humilde*—humble, poor, base, and lowly among other things—and if you didn't know Spanish and have the experience of hearing native speakers, you would hesitate to use the word, fearing that it sounds condescending. But just as *maicero* can be used in a positive sense, we've learned early on from living in the country, both down south and here, that our Tico friends use *humilde* in a most positive sense when talking about people. We use the word that way, too, now. When we want to praise one of our country acquaintances, there doesn't seem to be anything better to say than he or she is *"muy trabajador(a) y humilde"* (he or she's a very hard worker and just folks).

We all had a great time at the party. Then, about 1 PM, when Robin and I were so stuffed—we had a hard time moving—Fabio shouts to his guys, "OK, time to go back to work." That's right, they work seven days a week! I don't know why, perhaps because the sooner he gets our jobs over, the sooner he can take on a new one. But the man and his workers are simply indefatigable. In general, that has been our experience in Costa Rica. In many of the letters I've written earlier, I've spoken about the workers who built both our houses down near Dominical. They were amazing. Róger is an amazing worker. José Luis never stops. The Costa Rican laborers whom I've come to know are the hardest-working people I've ever met, without qualification.

## Bavaria

No, not the place in Germany. Bavaria is my new horse. She's a four-year-old mare who is exceedingly gentle. We bought her from a neighbor about a month or so ago. She's a beautiful golden color, and we think that was why she was named Bavaria, which here in Costa Rica is the name of a beer. I hope to be riding her regularly when we're living on the farm.

I'll send out another letter in a few days to finish bringing you up to date.

Warmest regards,
Martin and Robin

# CHAPTER TWENTY-EIGHT

## January 28, 2004

Hello, family and friends:
Here's the rest of what I wanted to write about in this current update from Puriscal.

### *Quedar Bien*

Living in the country in Costa Rica, and I imagine in almost any rural area in the world, means that people are very aware of what goes on in your life; there aren't many secrets. I think that this is one of the contributing factors to the concept of "*quedar bien*" or "getting on well with someone." I've written about this previously.

Most Costa Ricans would much prefer to get on well with people than to engage in confrontation. Of course this is a generalization; there is plenty of confrontation and hostility here, but it seems to me to be on a much lesser scale than I've seen elsewhere. In practice, *quedar bien* often translates into quite-friendly relationships. For example: I imagine that between the turnoff from the main road to Puriscal and our farm, a distance of about two kilometers, there are some ten to fifteen houses or families. Interestingly, there are only about two family names: Cerdas and Alpízar. One of our neighbors is named Amable Cerdas—my all-time-favorite Tico name, something like "Nice Pigs." There's also an elderly woman in the neighborhood whose first name is Undésima, which means "eleventh." She says that she's the only Undésima in the country, but that there are many men named Undésimo. Who knows where the name came from?

Perhaps when the eleventh child was born, the parents just ran out of names?

Anyway, everyone knew us and about us from the day we bought the property; in fact, I'm sure they knew about us long before we actually bought it. Now we know most of them, too. *Quedar bien* is something we made up our minds a long time ago that we would do. We waved and still do, of course, to every person and car we see on that road when we go to the farm—about twice a day. There's no bus service along the road, so we almost always see some of our neighbors walking either to town or back home. We always stop and give them a lift, which, of course, is greatly appreciated and allows us all to get to know one another better.

Many of them come up to the building site to see what's going on. We've received a great deal of praise for our new stable—this is big horse country and a well-built stable is highly appreciated. We're often asked to stop by the neighbors' houses and we always do when we can. There's always a *cafecito* ready for us and usually some bread, crackers, or cookies. People understand that it's hard for us to reciprocate right now, living several miles from them in the rental house. We've told everyone that we would invite them when the house is finished.

Once in a while, however, if the folks are coming our way, we invite them to the rental house we're in. So we're able to give them a *cafecito* and some cookies, too, and chat and get to know one another better. You'll remember that in my last letter I wrote about the word "*humilde*." In line with this, I think that we received the greatest compliment since we've been here the other day when we were driving some of our neighbors back to their farm.

As we were driving, the father of the family told us that we were very *humilde*. I was thrilled to hear that, because what it meant to me was that we were not perceived as pretentious. We have so much more than those folks and of course it's obvious. But the fact that we're seen there as "just folks" makes us believe that the relationships we're starting to build in our new neighborhood are getting off to a good start. That bodes well for the future.

## Manuel Víquez

In the previous letter I wrote about Manuel Víquez, the arbor culturist who is doing a detailed study of our farm to help us with ideas for reforestation and preservation. One of the most useful and impressive things Manuel and his family have undertaken is their annual "missions." These are major projects they carry out to help preserve the forests of Costa Rica. The first was called the Trees of Paradise, and the second, Trees of the Heart. If you're interested in a description of these projects (and you can read Spanish) you might want to visit Manuel's Web site at http://www.elmundoforestal.com.

They are now ready to begin the third mission, one that very much impresses me with its importance. What follows is the translation of a letter Manuel sent us about the third mission:

"Hi, Martin and Robin!

"[For the mission] we are going to create the first map with absolutely exact locations of many species of Costa Rican trees, both rare and on the verge of extinction, so that any interested person can find them easily by using the map's geographical coordinates [which will be created by using a GPS device].

"The biggest problem we've had in two years of trying to do the mission has been in finding the trees that interest us.

"For example, this is what always happens when we ask other forestry or biology colleagues about some tree. I repeat, the same thing more or less always happens:

"Manuel:      Do you know where there are any *chirraco* (or other rare species) trees?

"Colleague:   Of course I do!

"Manuel:      Where?

"Colleague:    Well, there's one on the slopes of
               volcano Irazú, and there's another
               quite near to Puriscal.
"Manuel:       But, where, more exactly?
"Colleague:    OK, to look for the first one you
               would have to go to the Pérez farm
               and ask Chepe, but he's almost never
               there. For the other tree, you would
               have to go to a place they called
               Barreal, and it's some twenty
               kilometers in from there.
"Manuel:       And where is the Pérez farm where
               I can find Chepe?
"Colleague:    The problem is that there's almost
               never anyone at the farm. You'd have
               to call the *pulpería* that's about
               twenty kilometers from the farm and
               leave a message for the guy in charge
               who goes by there every 2 weeks.
"Manuel:       OK, to get to the second tree, I have
               to go to Barreal first, and then?
"Colleague:    Look, let's do this. I'll check my
               notes to tell you exactly where the
               tree is. The problem is that
               tomorrow I'm going on vacation, so
               why don't you call me in a month?

"Martin and Robin. This is not a joke. Half of
our trees are becoming extinct, and those who
know them and have access to them, never want
to give any information.

"At this pace, the trees will be gone before
they tell us where they are.

"Using a GPS will once and for all take care of
this problem. Unfortunately, the first time that I
tried to do this map of the location of rare trees or

those almost extinct, the GPS that I had broke down and couldn't be fixed because it was so old."

So that's the background on the next mission. I know that Manuel is looking for patrons to help him, so I've bought him a new GPS for the mission.

## Say Hello to *Cojombro*

And speaking of Manuel, the other morning when we met him at the farm, he had a present for us, two *cojombro* fruits (*sicana odorifera*). They're really interesting looking; they're shaped like papaya (the long kind, not the round). They have a beautiful color, sort of rust colored or maybe orange crimson. The ones we have are over a foot in length.

I did a search on the Internet and found that they can reach a length of two feet. It's a member of the pumpkin family, and Manuel says that you cook it and eat it just like pumpkin or *ayote sazón,* another vegetable in the pumpkin family that's very popular here. You can make pie, jelly, and soup, whatever.

The interesting thing is that it is extremely rare now in Costa Rica, almost extinct. It's a vine that grows supported by trees and can reach great heights, thirty to fifty feet. He found a small piece of a leaf stem and was able to cultivate it, then plant it, and now harvest it.

Robin and I will save the seeds and then plant lots of them. From planting to harvesting takes less than a year. When we get more, we'll share the seeds with our neighbors. The fruit is a bit sweet and is quite fragrant, hence, the *odorifera* in its scientific name. I've read that one use of *cojombro* is to put pieces in drawers or closets to make them smell nice.

I mentioned the plant to a couple of our Tico *campesino* neighbors, both of whom have heard of it, both of whom affirmed that it seems to be quite rare, and also, both of whom said that you can "make honey" from it. One of our neighbors said that there's a saying here: *"Él que tiene cojombro se lo eche al hombro,"* which means something like, "He who has *cojombro* throws it on his shoulder," which in turn means that if you have a family, you have to take care of it.

The good news is that although it's extremely rare here in Costa Rica, it's alive and well in several Latin American countries. It's believed to be native to Brazil. On the Internet, I was able to find places in the United States, England, and Germany that had seeds for sale.

## La Casa de Martín

I have written before about the unusual address system they have here in Costa Rica. There aren't addresses with numbers but rather descriptions of locations. Our address at the rental house we're in is "Mercedes Norte, from the house of Álvaro Guzmán, one hundred meters north, seventy-five meters west, in front of the house of Juan Salas, the traffic officer."

Since we've moved to this house one of the big treats is the fact that we can have pizza delivered! So, frequently, on Friday evenings, we call the pizza joint in Puriscal to have it delivered. And every time, I give them that long address. Well, after a couple of months of this, one evening the young lady taking the order on the phone said, "From now on you just have to say, '*Mercedes Norte, la casa de Martín.*'" Hooray! We're an address landmark! This means that people up the street, for example, can say (if they're ordering pizza), "Mercedes Norte, from Martín's house, seventy-five meters west."

## Ram Pump

We're very pleased with the ram-pump system we've installed at the farm to bring water to Róger and Vera's house, our building site and stable, the house of a neighbor who has used the water on the property for many years, and the old man who has a sugar mill across the road from us.

The reason it's so satisfying is that it uses no electricity to pump the water anywhere. The system is simplicity itself; from the source (which is high up, but lower than our house site), the water drops through pipes to the ram pump. The dropping water generates air pressure, which is used to pump the water back up again, to a point twice as high as the source! There, the water is held in a large tank and distributed to all the users by gravity.

Before we moved here, our neighbor who shares the water source with us had to use an electric pump, which was quite expensive for him. He no longer has that expense.

### Progress in Spanish

Robin and I continue to improve our Spanish. We still make outrageous errors, but the people we talk with are quite gracious about it. Our vocabulary has increased tremendously, and I found out that about 80 percent of the time when I have to speak with someone, I don't have to do any translation in my head; however, that other 20 percent is a bear. I can tell from listening to Robin speak that she's experiencing the same thing.

### *Hacienda Arroz* Again

*Hacienda Arroz* is what we named our farm. People who have a hard time with our last name get a big kick out of it when I tell them that Rice means *arroz* in Spanish. This is because *arroz* would never be used as a family name in Spanish. It sounds as funny to them as "Nice Pigs" does to us. (Though I have a sneaking suspicion that Amable Cerdas might be a little funny in Spanish, too. I need to check.) Finally, one fellow now calls me Señor Paella.

We want to tell you about progress on the house, but so far it's pretty boring. The interesting part should begin in about a week or so when they start working with the logs and boards. We'll bring you up to date on that in the next letter.

Warmest personal regards,
Martin and Robin

# CHAPTER TWENTY-NINE

## April 8, 2004

Hi, family and friends:

It's been about three and a half months since I last wrote, and I thought it was time to bring you up to date on what's going on.

### At Home in Costa Rica: The Book

Robin and I have often thought about gathering all these letters I've sent from Costa Rica into a book. The main audience for the book would be people like us who are either contemplating moving to Costa Rica or who have recently moved. We think that such a book would help them understand what's involved in becoming acculturated here and give them an idea of how wonderful a life they can have. It might even be of value in general to people who are thinking of becoming expatriates anywhere, but especially in a Latin American country. Finally, people who like reading about life in foreign countries might enjoy it as well.

I've decided to self-publish the book using print-on-demand technology because I didn't want to spend two to four years trying to find a publisher and waiting for the book to appear (assuming any publisher would want it in the first place).

We're not expecting to make any money from the book—*A Year in Provence* it ain't. If, however, by any wild stretch of the imagination, we do make a couple of bucks after recouping our costs, then there are lots of worthy causes here in Costa Rica, which we would be able to help.

As far as I understand, once I submit the book in about three weeks, it should take four to six months to appear. I'll let you all know when it's available. By the way, the title will be *At Home in Costa Rica: Adventures in Living the Good Life.*

## Ropa Americana

The other day I wanted to buy some short-sleeved shirts and Robin wanted some shorts. So we decided to go to a store in town that sells *ropa americana,* which is the same thing as saying that we went to someplace like Goodwill, except this is a for-profit store. *Ropa americana* is a synonym, in Costa Rica at least, for used clothing.

Costa Rica is full of stores that sell *ropa americana.* And although it is not usual in Latin America to refer to North America as America, in this case the *americana* does mean the United States and Canada, where all this clothing comes from.

I had heard that *ropa americana* is clothing that is contributed to organizations such as Goodwill, the Salvation Army, St. Vincent de Paul, and others, but I didn't know for sure and I certainly didn't know how it wound up here. So I did some research and found an interesting transcript of a TV show on Channel 7 here in Costa Rica about how it all works.

If Goodwill cannot sell clothing within a few weeks, it is sold to a third party in packs of two thousand pounds for textile recycling at an extremely low price. In this case, what recycling means is selling it elsewhere. So the clothes are bought by a textile-recycling middleman, then sold to used-clothing wholesalers, and then to retailers in Third World countries. Thus, after the charity organizations have made their money, other for-profit organizations will begin to make theirs.

Goodwill sells hundreds of thousands of pounds of these non-salable (in North America) clothes for US$200 per two-thousand-pound package, which nets it about a half a million dollars per year, which is used for Goodwill's charitable activities.

In North America, there are two thousand middleman businesses buying and selling these goods. And there's a lot to buy and sell, some 2.5 billion pounds per year!

The reason there are so many people engaged in this business at the wholesale end is because the profits are enormous, some 300 percent to 400 percent.

The clothes go all over the world, many of them to countries in Africa. As far as the rest of the developing world is concerned, according to one reseller, Costa Rica is quite different. It's much more prosperous and people are looking for more fashionable used clothes. The clothes come here in thousand-pound packages.

The packages of clothes come in by boat to Limón on the Atlantic Coast and then are transported by truck to San José. According to an employee at Combo-Combo, a chain of five *ropa americana* stores in San José, good-quality, name-brand clothes that are suitable for our climate will mostly be sold within five hours of appearing in the store. According to the owner of another store, people will wait in line from early in the morning on days that the stores receive new stock.

So the way the system works is first, the clothes are donated to charity. Then the charity sells the things that don't sell within three or four weeks to a textile recycler for US$0.10 per pound. This person sells the clothes to the people who sell to the retailers for US$0.50 per pound. The retailers in Costa Rica will pay about five hundred *colones* per pound (about US$1.17 today). But there are a great many lightweight shirts and blouses in a single pound of these used clothes. And these shirts and blouses, in turn, sell for about $1.50 each. Of course there are more than shirts and blouses; shorts, dresses, pants, suits, etc., are all available.

For our part, Robin and I found some nice shirts for me and shorts for her. I paid $1.50 each for the shirts—a great deal for me and a good profit for the retailer. The clothes are freshly washed and ironed. They don't have spots or holes and aren't frayed. There are big differences in prices though from one store to the next, so shopping around is worthwhile.

## A Great Blooper

Recently we were at the farm talking to Róger about the next day's *tope* (more about the *tope* later). We told him that Gil, the former owner of my horse, was going to ride her in the *tope*. Robin said, "Yes, tomorrow he'll come over with his shrimp and take her to the *tope*." Róger got hysterical with laughter while Robin looked blank. I told her what she had said. Then she looked really embarrassed. But it was an easy mistake to make: *camarón* means shrimp and *camión* means truck. And now, of course, whenever Robin's around, Róger refers to all trucks as shrimp.

In fact, we contribute greatly to Róger's amusement. The other day I was saying that I wanted the finish on a concrete floor to be very smooth. Unfortunately I said *suave*, soft. Now every time the subject of concrete comes up (often now because of the building), Róger asks me if it's soft enough for me.

## The *Tope*

*Topes* are very big in Costa Rica. What they are, essentially, is a horse rally, like a car or motorcycle rally. The two biggest in Costa Rica are in San José and a place about an hour north of there called Palmares. The third biggest is here in Puriscal. Essentially, several hundred horses and riders get all decked out, assemble somewhere, and then set out on a ride. Usually their initial route after setting out will be past a lot of people waiting to see them. In the case of Puriscal, they all paraded around the central square, a city block in size.

The thing that makes it different from just watching several hundred horses file by (not that this is not impressive in itself) is that almost all the horses are taught to do a high step when they walk. In addition, many owners teach them to "dance" in place. This, too, is quite a sight if you've never seen it before and is a matter of great pride amongst Costa Rican horse owners.

As it turned out, much to our surprise, neither Robin nor I enjoyed the *tope* very much. The fact is that walking and dancing like that can be very uncomfortable, even painful for the horses. Most of them look scared, and after a while, they're hot and exhausted looking. Looking in dictionaries for the meaning of *tope*, I've never been able to find a definition that has anything to do with what I've described other than in an oblique way. The defining words always include buffer, bumper, butt, collision, encounter, limit, and stop. And that's what the ride is actually like. The horses are all jammed together and have little room. They do indeed bump, collide, butt, and stop.

To top it all off, a *tope* is a big social event as well, and consequently, many of the riders and onlookers are really drunk. So, all in all, for us at least, the *tope* is not a very pretty sight.

## CAFTA

I don't know how much coverage CAFTA (Central American Free Trade Agreement) is getting in the United States. Here, however, it has been very big news indeed. Negotiations went on for most of 2003 with the idea that the United States and all the Central American countries would sign the treaty by the end of the year. As it turned out, in December 2003, all Central American countries except Costa Rica had signed.

The big sticking point, as you might guess, was the demand by the United States that Costa Rica open its communications and insurance monopolies. From reading our letters, you can imagine what kind of response was to be expected from ICE and INS. In addition, of course, there were other sectors of the economy opposed to the treaty, just as there are sectors in the United States opposed to free trade agreements as well.

The Costa Rican representatives to the negotiations asked for and received an extension with the idea that there would be a couple of more meetings between them and the U.S. representatives in January.

In the meanwhile, the United States started negotiations with the Dominican Republic, which would serve as a replacement for Costa Rica should things not turn out. As it did turn out, however, Costa Rica signed. (An agreement will most likely be reached, if it hasn't already, with the Dominican Republic as well.)

Now it remains to be seen whether the legislature here will ratify the agreement or not. Most of the deputies are petrified of the unions, and many are coming up with excuses they say will make it difficult for them to ratify the agreement.

On the other hand, *La Nación* has been conducting surveys throughout this whole process, and currently a whopping 65 percent of the Costa Ricans support the agreement. Needless to say we who "suffer" from latest technology withdrawal are keeping our fingers crossed that the agreement does go through. Finally, there's no guarantee at all that the United States will ratify the agreement.

### Button and Paulie Possum

Well, surprise, surprise! Two new baby orphans, Button and Paulie Possum, have temporarily joined the Rice family.

Button, the female, came to us by way of our friend Bea in Dominical. It seems that Button was found in a dog's mouth on March 10. The man who found her took her to Bea. Bea was going to care for her but has so many things to do raising her four (!) kinkajous, numerous dogs, stable full of horses, and a few birds, that it would have been just too much. She called Robin, and Robin suggested that she contact the National Opossum Society in the United States. When Bea did that, they told her that "Our woman in Costa Rica is Robin." So Bea made the long drive to San José to deliver Button.

And so Robin once again swung into action as baby opossum mother (you'll remember that she raised three of them a year or so back and was able to release them into the wild). Because of how very young Button was, Robin had to go into intensive care mode—making extremely complex formulas, feeding her by hand every couple of hours, everything that makes rehabilitation so difficult.

Then, as luck would have it, just a few days later, on March 29, a woman in Escazú, a western suburb of San José, found little Paulie, who had been attacked by dogs. She already knew about Robin through the society and called her to ask if she could take care of it. So on March 30, she delivered little Paulie to Robin.

The big bugaboo is that the two are different species and, consequently, require different care, develop at different rates, and, in general, make for more work than two of the same species would. I'm really happy to say, however, that once again Robin has come through. The little critters seem to be thriving and developing on schedule. It probably won't be too very much longer before they'll be able to be released.

Whoops! Today, June 16, 2004, Robin has decided that she'll only be able to release Paulie. This means that Button will join the Rice menagerie.

## The House in Puriscal

*¡Aquí me quedo!* at *Hacienda Arroz* is really moving along now. All the log walls are up, the roof is half installed, the stone for the facings has been delivered, and we're still on schedule for a May 20 completion date. We still have loads to do, of course. Lots of things to pick out for finishes, working with the kitchen and bath folks, frequent meetings with the architect and head engineer. But it's fun and it's exciting to watch a new dream house take shape.

Yet again: Whoops! Now it looks as though we won't get into the house until June 30, more than a month late.

## Neighbors

As time goes by and Robin and I spend more and more time at the farm, we also have the opportunity to see our new neighbors there much more frequently. I mentioned the Alpízar family who lives about a kilometer away. Their son, Andrés, has become Robin's good riding buddy. They go riding together about twice a week. Andrés's cousin, Iván, who lives next door, often goes along, too. Yesterday the father, Martín, joined them. Martín, like most Costa Rican *campesinos*, rides very well. But he hadn't been riding for a long time and had a grand outing with them.

Andrés's mother, Mary (yep, not María), gave Robin a couple of dishes of food she had just cooked to bring home with her. Often, when they're riding along the road and through the fields, the boys stop under fruit trees and pull down the low-hanging fruit to eat there and to take along. One day, however, the fruit was not so low hanging, and Iván really wanted some. So he simply stood on his horse's back and reached up for the fruit. The horse, however, was getting bored, so she started to walk off. Robin panicked, but Iván simply stepped off the horse's rear end. He came down hard but didn't fall and was absolutely no worse for wear. These young men—as are most young men, I guess—are simply fearless.

Today, while Robin and Andrés were riding, they saw our neighbor Don Guillermo, a real horse lover, working in his fields. He waved them down because he wanted to get a better look at Tory, who he thinks is a very beautiful horse. He suggested that Robin and Andrés ride over to his house and get his daughter, Sandra, an accomplished horsewoman, to go riding with them. So Sandra joined them, and the three of them continued on the ride.

They also recently went on an outing to Amable Cerdas's *trapiche* while it was being worked. I couldn't go but will go soon. They work twice a week. Robin said that it was fascinating to watch the process, and she enjoyed the visit immensely. When I do go, I'll be sure to write and tell you what it's like.

In the meantime, I've been helping Andrés's older brother, Alejandro, with some problems he's been having with his computer. He goes to college in Cartago and lives there all week. He returns home for the weekends and holidays. He's majoring in computer programming.

We're still giving our neighbors lifts to and from town whenever we see them on the road, which is frequently. And, of course, we're getting to be on friendlier and friendlier terms with them. We're looking forward to living on the farm where we'll be able to have them visit us and get to know them even better. An added bonus is that none of them speaks English. So all our contact is completely in Spanish. This is what we wanted from the very beginning.

## Tying Up Some Loose Ends

When I started reviewing these letters with an eye to publishing them, I noticed that there were a few things I wrote about, which I never resolved. That is, I let stories hang or didn't give explanations about why certain things changed. I thought this might be a good place to catch up on those things.

I never told you, for example, what happened with our Great Dane, Olive. She was an absolutely beautiful dog, and we really loved her. Unfortunately, she began attacking little Bug, and eventually, she did this badly enough so that Bug had to have dozens of stitches. It seems as though Olive just didn't like little dogs. In addition, as she matured, she clearly felt her place was no longer at the bottom of the three-dog pack she was part of.

Things worked out well, however, because our vet knew a man who had another Great Dane, which he had to leave alone all day. He was anxious to find company for his dog. So Olive went there to visit and got along excellently with the other Dane. She's now living there in San Isidro.

I also noticed that, very early on, I spoke quite glowingly about a cab driver named Rudy. Then a few letters later I wrote much about José, our friend and driver, and never mentioned Rudy again. The reason for the change was as follows.

Many taxi drivers here seek out associations with hotels. That is, a group of drivers will be vetted by a hotel and then become the authorized drivers for that particular place. This results in the clerks' being able to assure their guests that these drivers are trustworthy. This is especially important for tourists. The drivers, in turn, have a place to acquire fares, which is not overrun by the competition. Frequently, as was the case with us, some of these fares become regular customers.

Rudy was a driver at the first hotel Robin and I used to stay at in San José. But we soon switched hotels and that's where we met José, who was associated with the new hotel.

And, speaking of José, you might be interested to know that he's the proud father of twin boys, who are about three months old now. The mother is not the same girlfriend I mentioned before. I haven't met the twins' mother yet, but José seems to be smitten with her, and he's completely gaga over the twins. I also wrote that someday I'd ask José why he's the only one in the family who never graduated from college or who wasn't a successful businessperson. I never actually asked him, but in the course of the hundreds of hours we've spent together over the years, the answer eventually came out. It's a simple and common story. He was just a very wild kid who didn't want to go on in school and who, therefore, didn't continue on to college after he finished high school, in spite of his parents' and family's attempts to convince him otherwise. And, as happens so often with people who take that route, he's terribly sorry now but can't find a way to go back to school. What a shame. José is really intelligent, and now he's going to have to scramble the rest of his life to keep his head above water. He also told me that years ago he dated a young woman from the family of Oscar Arias, the former Nobel laureate and (perhaps soon to be again) president of Costa Rica. But her family squashed that budding romance given that José's prospects were not very promising.

Relatively early on while writing about health insurance, I told you that I got signed up at the *Caja* but still had to go to the hospital to get my card and that I was going to do that the following week. Well I did go there, but the lines were so horribly long that I just couldn't bring myself to spend all day there. (The Golden Citizens' card is not much good there, too many old folks.)

But here in Puriscal I did go to the local *Caja* hospital, and there was no wait at all at the window where you get your card. It took all of fifteen minutes. In fact, the transaction itself only took five minutes, but as so often happens here, the clerk turned out to be a close relative of some of our neighbors (can't remember if he's a Cerdas or Alpízar). So we chatted on about the neighborhood for a bit. He, too, made me feel very welcome.

So I think we're all up to date now. As new things go on happening, I'll continue to keep you posted. And perhaps, who knows, in a couple of years there might even be a sequel to *At Home in Costa Rica.*

All our best,
Martin and Robin

CPSIA information can be obtained at www.ICGtesting.com
Printed in the USA
LVOW101802261112

308881LV00001B/95/A

9 781413 460285